I0810537

IMAGES
of America

GRAND HOTELS OF WEST VOLUSIA COUNTY

On the Cover: The Grand Hotels of West Volusia County were the major attractions to many visitors to Florida in the 19th century. De Leon Springs and the Ponce De Leon Hotel in 1957 continued to draw visitors, as seen in this gathering of Stetson University students. (Courtesy of Stetson University, duPont-Ball Library, Memorabilia Collection.)

IMAGES
of America

Grand Hotels of West Volusia County

Larry French
Foreword by Dana Ste.Claire

ARCADIA
PUBLISHING

ISBN 978-1-4671-2885-8

Published by Arcadia Publishing
Charleston, South Carolina

Printed in the United States of America

Library of Congress Control Number: 2017958910

For all general information, please contact Arcadia Publishing:
Telephone 843-853-2070
Fax 843-853-0044
E-mail sales@arcadiapublishing.com
For customer service and orders:
Toll-Free 1-888-313-2665

Visit us on the Internet at www.arcadiapublishing.com

To my wife and best friend, Robin, whose faith and encouragement have helped me to fulfill a lifelong dream to bring my passion for history into print form making this book a reality

Contents

Foreword

Some of the best memories of my life are from the time spent in the little historic town of Lake Helen. When I arrived in 1994, I did what most people do when they move to a different place—I learned about my surroundings. I wandered down to the local library to read anything I could find on Lake Helen. Soon after, practically every neighbor offered bits and pieces about the stories of their historic houses and how the town was founded.

But Lake Helen truly came to light for me through the eyes of my longtime friend and colleague Bill Dreggors, who knew about the history of Volusia County. His passion for historical detail was contagious. We walked around town, and Bill explained who lived in what house a century ago and why they came here. Bill knew it all, and it was like getting a private tour from Henry DeLand himself. We walked to the site of the former Harlan Hotel, where I gained an understanding of what the grand hotel looked like from Bill's vivid description. Bill had a knack for reassembling history because he collected thousands of pictures, early postcards, souvenir photos, and family albums. He pieced together the life ways of yesteryear with great precision. It's a real tragedy when we lose an historical record, or worse, when it's never written. This is why books like Larry French's *Grand Hotels of West Volusia County* are so important. Larry has taken the time to meticulously research an important chapter of Volusia County's glorious past, one that was filled with hat-topped gentlemen and parasol-carrying ladies—winter visitors who relished the picturesque Florida landscape with its trademark sunshine. Many of the images in Larry's *Grand Hotels* are from Bill Dreggor's private collection. I'm pretty sure Bill is smiling somewhere right now because he inspired someone to take up the cause to put together a book about these hotels. As he often said, history belongs to all of us and it's up to us to protect and propagate it. He would have been proud of Larry and his endeavor to assemble this compendium of old hotels, one that may not have ever been written or truly understood without Larry's dedicated effort. Bill would be pleased that Larry used his pictures for his publication. I hope this book finds its way to the Lake Helen library.

—Dana Ste.Claire
Citizen Emeritus, Lake Helen

ACKNOWLEDGMENTS

The author wishes to thank the following people and organizations for their generous support. Without their help this book would not have been possible: DeLand resident Judee Boland for her postcard of Hotel Putnam; DeLand historian Jim Cara; the City of Lake Helen; the Bill Dreggors family, for the use of their fathers' collection of historical images; the Lake Helen Historical Society & Museum; Florida Memory; the late steamboat authority Edward A. Mueller; De Leon Springs State Park manager Brian Polk; living historian Lynn Purvis; director of the New Smyrna Museum of History, Robert Redd; DeLand author Tom Roberts; Barb Shepherd, owner/publisher/ CEO of the *West Volusia Beacon*; Amber Stark for photography; lifelong friend Dana Ste.Claire, national director of tourism with Historic Tours of America, Inc.; Stetson University Archives, duPont-Ball Library, and Angela Story, archives specialist at Stetson's duPont-Ball Library and her student archive assistants and intern Meredith Kaffer, Monica Escobar, and Kyla Roush; and Cindy Sullivan of the Enterprise Heritage Center.

The author consulted a number of resources for the writing of the introduction and captions of this book, both past and present. These resources can be found listed in the bibliography.

INTRODUCTION

There are many accounts of Florida history. Most of them tend to focus on the settlement of Florida from the perspective of its coastline. This has come about naturally. The state after all is a peninsula surrounded on three sides by ocean. Florida is also crosscut by several large rivers. Wetlands and lakes comprise a great deal of the surface area. A number of its lakes are linked to rivers. So it should be no surprise that water has played quite a role in just about everything related to Florida's past.

Grand Hotels of West Volusia County approaches the history of Florida from the perspective of how its longest river, the St. Johns River, helped shape the settlement of interior Central Florida. For centuries, the easiest travel into interior Florida was accomplished by conveyances on water. Early European-based settlements were primarily located along coastal areas. Travel into the wild interior of the state was difficult except where inlets or rivers provided access further inland. Only trails existed where there were no rivers or streams big enough to explore by boat, and for a long time, native peoples hostile to foreign intruders where a further deterrent. The St. Johns River is a 310-mile river that flows northward from its origins in East Central Florida and empties into the Atlantic Ocean. Its size and gentle flow has made it an easy means of access into the very heart of Florida. Visitation to Florida has been either by way of its coast or by way of its major rivers. The St. Johns River offered settlers one of the deepest penetrations into the Florida interior. Thus, countless people made their way into Florida via the St. Johns River and in so doing encountered early on what West Volusia County had to offer.

The land they found was teeming with wildlife and natural resources. It had attracted early people and sustained them for centuries with its sources of food and water. European interests made note of its potential early on, and empires rose and fell over attempts to dominate and exploit the resources it bore. The English sent naturalists such as John and William Bartram to explore Florida's flora and fauna and to report on its many assets. During the age of sail, live oak and pine trees were deemed extremely valuable as resources for ship building. Naturalist John James Audubon also traveled here and recorded what he observed through art and collection of specimens. Each of these explorers left accounts of some of the native peoples still inhabiting the land whom they observed and the places where they resided. The stories and recollections of other travelers to Florida painted inviting impressions of a land ripe with plenty and ideal for settlement.

Still, despite what some accounts related of Florida, it was not a paradise. The soil was poor in many dry places because of its sandy content. Where it was richer with nutrients for crops near water insects were a nuisance. The heat and humidity posed challenges for most people's stamina and comfort. Living in Florida was difficult for many except for those who were close to the ocean or near a freshwater source. Thus, the land of flowers initially described by Ponce de Leon for many was far from being an attractive place to be year-round.

For many years, only the hardest and most daring of individuals ventured further inland away from the coasts to settle. After the acquisition of Florida by the United States in 1821, actions were taken to displace the Seminoles from the state. The land made available by the removal of the Seminoles created incentives for settlers to move into the interior. One of them was Cornelius Taylor, a cousin of Gen. Zachary Taylor. Taylor helped establish Enterprise in 1841 on the northern shore of Lake Monroe along the St. Johns River. Travel into the interior by waterways helped establish and sustain ventures like Enterprise.

No major railroads would be built throughout the state until after the Civil War. Prior to that time, a couple of railroad lines were established in panhandle Florida. A line ran from Jacksonville west to Tallahassee. Another had been just completed between Fernandina Beach near the Georgia border and extended southwest to Cedar Key on the Florida Gulf Coast. Travel by water was the primary means of reliable travel for most of the state. Steamboats traversed the length of the St. Johns River, linking people in the various settlements along its length with the outside world.

Early on, certain visionary entrepreneurs realized the commercial value of providing supplies to these settlements along the St. Johns waterways. One of these individuals was Jacob Brock, a steamboat captain. He was one of the first to engage in steamboat traffic on the St. Johns River. Brock started providing shipping service from as far as Jacksonville south to Enterprise and Mellonville (later Sanford). Brock realized the value of providing visitors traveling to see the wilds of Florida with civilized amenities. Brock was also one of the first to introduce comfort and accommodations for those fleeing the cold of winter to vacation in sunny Florida. Some might say Brock helped introduce the art of tourism to Florida. But his refinement of this market had to wait until after the war.

Brock sympathized with the Confederacy during the war. He even went so far as to try and outrun the invasion of Fernandina Beach and Amelia Island by piloting one of his steamships, the *Darlington*. The escape attempt failed, and Brock was captured and imprisoned. His steamships were seized by the federal government and used to transport troops and supplies for the Union armies operating in Florida. During the war, Florida remained virtually in a state of limbo. Commerce was tightly monitored and controlled, and anything deemed a potential resource to the Confederacy was either confiscated or destroyed to prevent it from being used by Confederate forces. As a result, there was little development in the state for over five years. When the war ended, Brock was freed and given back his fleet of steamships. Brock's enterprise in shipping and tourism then resumed.

The post–Civil War era began the real taming of the Florida frontier. During the late 19th century, West Volusia County served as the entry point for countless numbers of pioneers entering Central Florida on the inland waterway of the St. Johns River. The stop points along the river for fuel and cargo became established settlements, and some of these locations flourished and became communities that survived to the present. Several of these waypoints were also home to lavish hotels that sprang up and grew to accommodate the needs and visits of guests who came to Florida for decades to settle and recreate. Many of these hotels sported amenities as plush as those more widely known and associated with the grand hotels along Florida's east coast.

In 1854, Jacob Brock built Brock House on the shore of Lake Monroe to serve as a hotel for the many guests who booked passage on his steamboat line. His steamboat line offers some of the earliest examples of Florida tourism. Brock House served the needs of notables and celebrities from all over the world. Among its guests were Grover Cleveland, Ulysses S. Grant, Jay Gould, the Vanderbilts, James Rockefeller, and Gen. William T. Sherman. This opportunity Brock envisioned for capitalizing upon Florida's natural draw was also noticed by others.

Another person who caught this vision was Frederick de Bary, a successful wine merchant from New York who built a vacation home not far from Enterprise. Unfortunately for Brock, the financial resources of de Bary were greater than those of Brock. Sensing the mounting competition, Brock overextended himself by purchasing an additional steamship. De Bary outspent Brock and built his own steamboat line that eventually won out over Brock for control of the commerce and tourism shipping in the upper St. Johns River.

The race in both tourism and capitalization upon development of Central Florida was on. It would be a boom that would go on for decades fed by another facet of Florida's natural beauty. Like California and Alaska, Florida had its own Gold Rush; only here, the frenzy was over "Orange

Fever," the pursuit of wealth through the growth and production of citrus. High sandy soiled parts of Central Florida and parts of its coast were discovered early on by early inhabitants and the Spanish to be ideal for growing citrus. This understanding became the promise to thousands who came to Florida seeking a new life and the opportunity to gain a fortune. Thus, the citrus industry worked to bring about settlement in parts of Florida in a way that may have taken centuries longer to accomplish.

The St. Johns River served as the highway to bring much of this about. The steamships that plied its waters carried citrus and commerce from the interior to major city ports like Jacksonville for distribution elsewhere. Many of the same steamships brought a steady load of passengers who came to Florida on a seasonable basis to escape northern winters. These same visitors became the tourists that enjoyed the hunting, fishing, springs, and beaches that made Florida a popular destination. Reconstruction and the years following the Civil War brought many war veterans to Florida. Five years of war had devastated farms and industry throughout the South, and many, including Northern veterans, sought a fresh new start. Just as countless numbers of people sought a new and better life traveling westward across the Great Plains, thousands also came south to Florida looking to start over. These people helped establish towns all over undeveloped Florida. Along the course of the St. Johns River, these new settlers started countless towns, including some of the ones mentioned in this book. This new time of growth in Florida was the boom era for the steamboats and lasted some 20 years.

As railroads were built and crossed the state, the steamboat industry found itself with a mighty challenger. Industrial magnates like Henry Flagler and Henry Plant copied the business plan Jacob Brock had pioneered with their railroads. Both Henrys built their railroad lines through the state with magnificent hotels to accommodate their own passengers. In time, the influx of seasonal visitors to Florida began to shift to the much more affordable and faster means of rail travel for their sojourns here. The steamboats saw their day in the sun fade as both passengers and commerce chose rail over river travel. The demise of steamboat travel was hurt further after the great freezes wiped out the citrus in many areas. The final death blows for the steamboats came with the arrival of the internal combustion engine in the form of the automobile. Once this means of affordable travel conveyance became available for both pleasure and commercial use, the entire tourism market changed. By the 1890s, the steamboat commerce and tourism on the St. Johns River was gone. In the end, not only the steamboats but the railroad too lost out to the automobile. Highways and automobiles transformed the landscape of Florida, and tourism marketing literally drove the waves of people visiting Florida to those places with their best appeal and advertising.

The history of Florida has changed drastically since these latest developments in technology came into play. The growth that came with the influence of the automobile brought about changes in how and where people traveled and vacationed in Florida. There were newer flashier attractions. In some areas, large homes transitioned into hotels offering traveling motorists varied choices for accommodations with competitive rates. DeLand, for example, at one time had several of these style hotels in addition to the grand hotels. The grandeur and appeal of the grand hotels that once drew seasonal visits from people outside Florida slowly waned. Economic change from the decline of the citrus industry and the departure of steamship and rail passenger travel in West Volusia County fostered more automotive-based commerce and tourism along the ocean coast. Some of the grand hotels managed to survive. They adapted to the new tourism market and lasted to this day. Most of them, however, did not. Those that still stand are landmarks that people enjoy today, such as remnant Flagler hotels like the Santa Monica Hotel in St. Augustine and the Henry Plant Tampa Bay Hotel, a historic landmark that houses the University of Tampa. In West Volusia County, only the DeLand, Putnam, Cassadaga, and DeYarman Hotels still remain as reminders of the days when West Volusia County served as the gateway to Central Florida.

Grand Hotels of West Volusia County is an attempt to perhaps for the first time identify and relate some information about some of the places that served to furnish comfort and accommodation to the many settlers and visitors who came to Central Florida. It in no way is a complete accounting of all of the establishments that served a similar purpose for the countless visitors and tourists who have frequented this area of Florida, for they are indeed many. *Grand Hotels of West Volusia County* has focused on the popular roles a select number of these early lodging places had in developing the special sense of place parts of Florida convey to visitors even today.

There is a great deal of information about Florida history for those with interest. It is hoped that this work will provide a glimpse of that unique record and encourage others to discover the vast accounting of Florida history that exists in a myriad assortment of museums, archives, and libraries. Those that are accessible to the public offer an excellent opportunity to all who seek to see the relevance of how our past serves as the bridge to our future.

CLYDE ST. JOHN'S RIVER LINE

(DE BARY LINE)

Between
JACKSONVILLE
PALATKA
SANFORD
ENTERPISE
And Intermediate Landings on the St. John's River

THE POPULAR ROUTE BETWEEN NORTH AND SOUTH FLORIDA FOR THE TOURIST, MERCHANT OR INVALID

STEAMERS

"CITY OF JACKSONVILLE"
Capt. W. A. Shaw

"FRED'K DE BARY"
Capt. T. W. Lund, Jr.

These steamers are the finest in Southern waters, and have all modern improvements. Table supplied with the best the markets afford.

Fare between Jacksonville and Sanford, including meals and berth $3.75

CONNECTIONS

At Jacksonville—With "CLYDE LINE" for Charleston, New York, Philadelphia, Boston, and all points North, East and Canada; F. C. & P. R. R.; Florida East Coast Ry.; Plant System; Atlantic Valdosta & Western.
At Palatka—With Florida East Coast Ry.; Plant System; G. S. & F. R. R., and Ocklawaha River Lines.
At Sanford—With F. E. Coast Ry., and Plant System.
At Enterprise—With Florida East Coast Railway.

Tourists returning from Havana, Cuba, South Florida and the Indian River, Lake Worth or Biscayne Bay, will find this a most delightful route to take, as it will give them a Daylight Trip on the interesting portion of the beautiful St. John's River.

Through Tickets on sale covering all points in South Florida and the famous Indian River, Lake Worth and Biscayne Bay.

WM. P. CLYDE & CO., General Agents

Chesebrough Bldg., 15 State St.
Facing Battery Park, NEW YORK
(Broadway Cars pass door)

12 S. Delaware Ave.
PHILADELPHIA, PA.

This 1888 travel advertisement is typical of those used by the Clyde St. Johns River Line (De Bary Line) for regular trips on the St. Johns. The De Bary Line was one of the largest steamboat lines that dominated the tourism traffic on the St. Johns. (Courtesy of Edward A. Mueller, *First Coast Steamboat Days: A History of Travel by Steamboat from Georgia and South Carolina to Northeast Florida.*)

One

De Leon Springs

Ponce De Leon Hotel

For more than a millennium, the crystal-clear water flowing from De Leon Springs into Spring Garden Run has attracted people. Early inhabitants of the area built shell mounds around the spring. The site was originally called Spring Garden and had a plantation that was destroyed during the Second Seminole Indian War.

Following the removal of the Seminoles, interior Florida became available for settlement. Settlers made their way inland from the St. Johns River using Spring Garden Run. By the late 1800s, Spring Garden became a tourist destination with both steamboats and later the railroad providing transportation to the area.

To attract tourists, local residents changed the name from Spring Garden to Ponce de Leon Springs and referred to the spring as the Fountain of Youth. There is no evidence to support that the Spanish explorer was ever at this location. Despite that, tourist advertising for years associated Ponce de Leon with the spring. In 1920, the spring was dammed for use as a power source.

The Ponce de Leon Springs Hotel and Casino ("Casino" referred to a large room for events and dining, not gambling) was built in 1925. The hotel only had 14 rooms and catered mostly to wealthier northern visitors. The dining room was popular for its servings of steak, lobster, and mountain trout. During World War II, the spring and adjacent areas on the water became sites for recreating US Navy personnel. After the war years, the popularity of the hotel and spring diminished. In 1953, Ponce de Leon Springs opened as one of the many attractions in the state that drew tourists. The attraction had tropical gardens, a jungle cruise, a tram tour, and even featured a water skiing elephant. The Ponce de Leon Springs Hotel and Casino operated until the mid-1960s. By then, the hotel was termite-infested and torn down, and the park was operated as a private park. Local support for preservation of the spring prompted the State of Florida and Volusia County to purchase the site and 44 acres around the spring, and in 1982, De Leon Springs State Park opened.

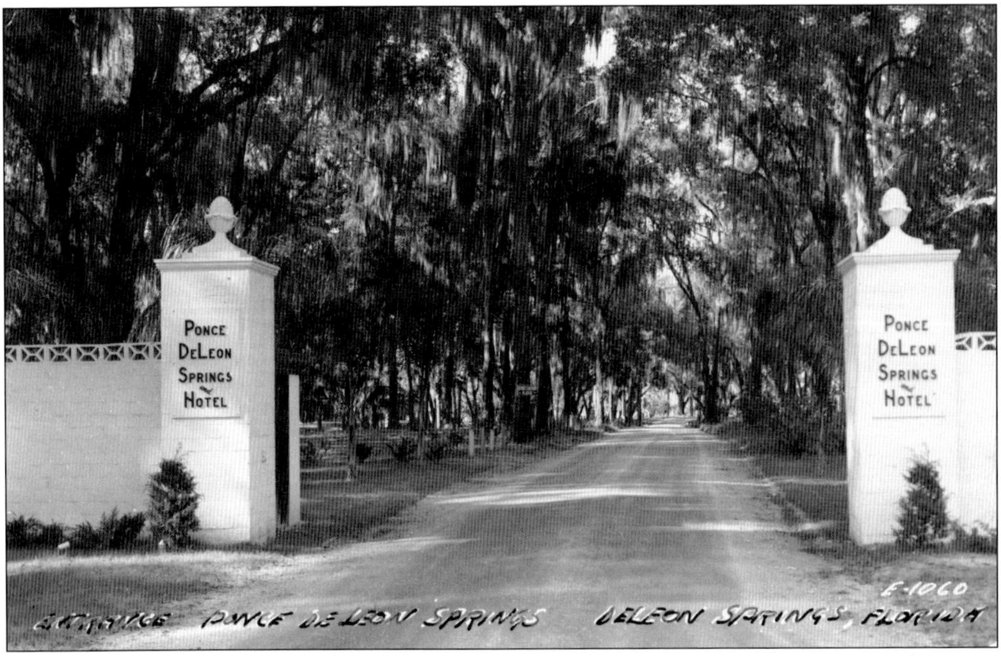

Visitors who arrived as guests of the Ponce De Leon Hotel in De Leon Springs used to pass through these welcoming gates. The entrance is different today, but the Florida Park Service has maintained the natural pristine appearance of the site and its historical assets. (Courtesy of Stetson University, duPont-Ball Library, Memorabilia Collection.)

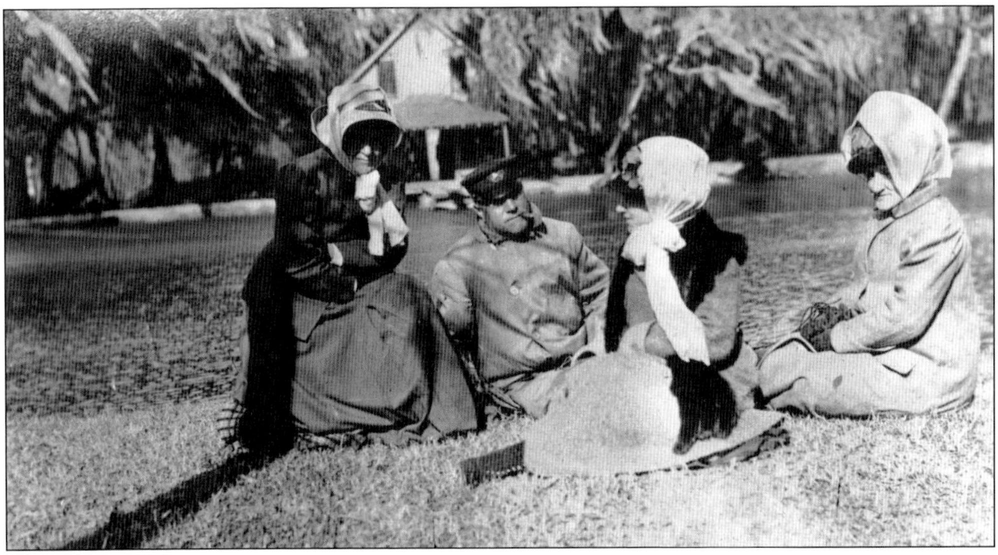

Florida was already an attractive seasonal location for those seeking escape from cold winters. This 1912 photograph shows how winter visitors could enjoy the warming rays of the sun and the beauty of De Leon Spring. (Courtesy of Stetson University, duPont-Ball Library, Memorabilia Collection.)

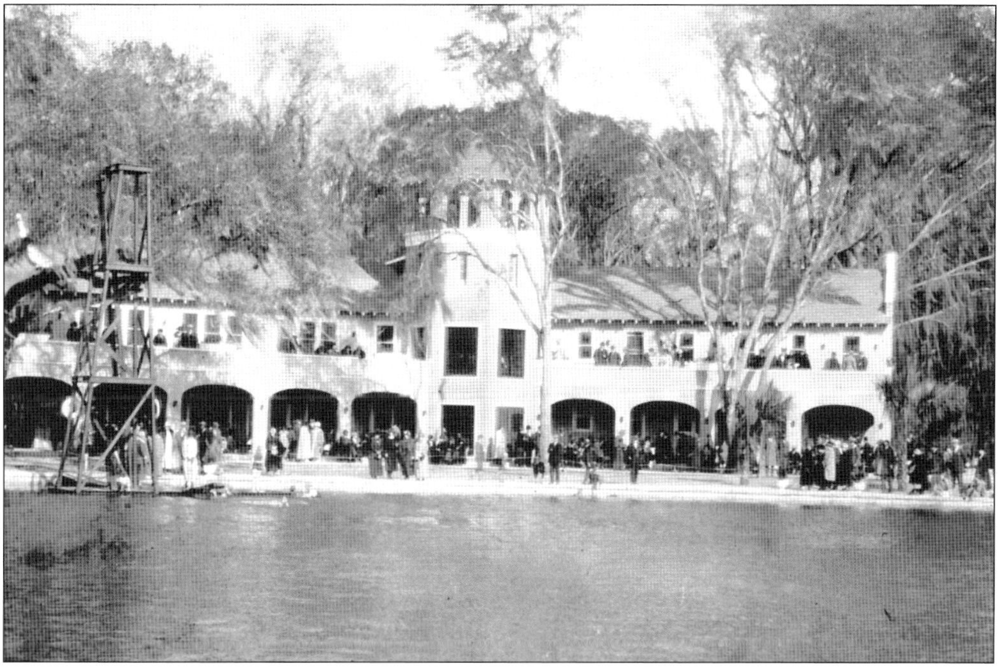

By the 1920s, people visiting the spring enjoyed both swimming and the amenities of the Ponce De Leon Hotel and Casino. The addition of the word "casino" at times was used to refer to the large meeting room the hotel offered guests and not to a gambling casino. (Courtesy of Florida State Parks.)

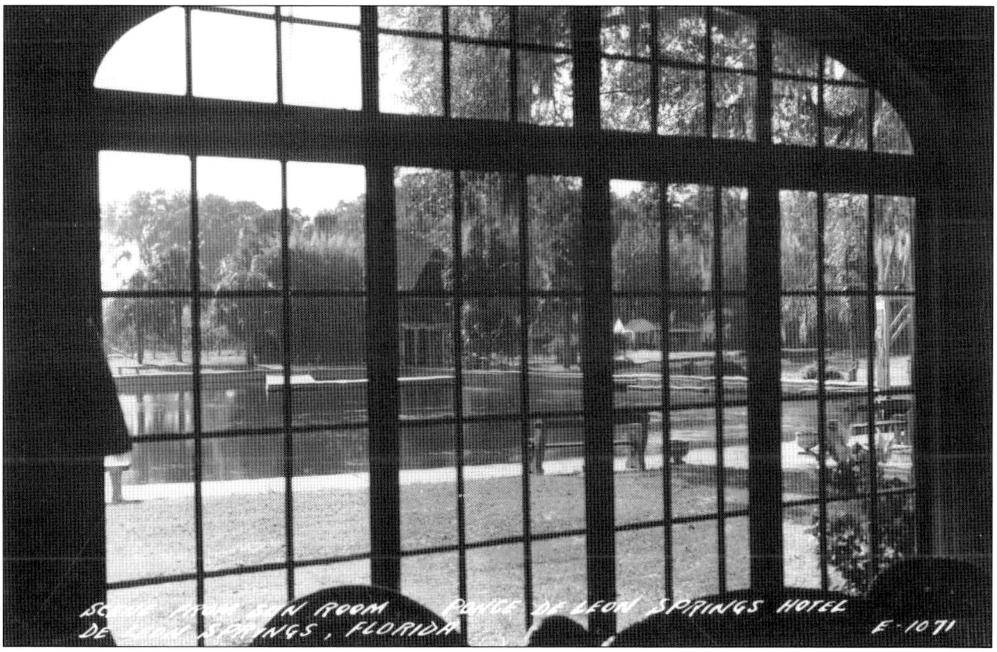

From the hotel, guests had a scenic view of the spring and natural surroundings. The hotel and spring became quite popular in the winter season since the water from the spring stayed a constant 72 degrees year-round. (Courtesy of Stetson University, duPont-Ball Library, Memorabilia Collection.)

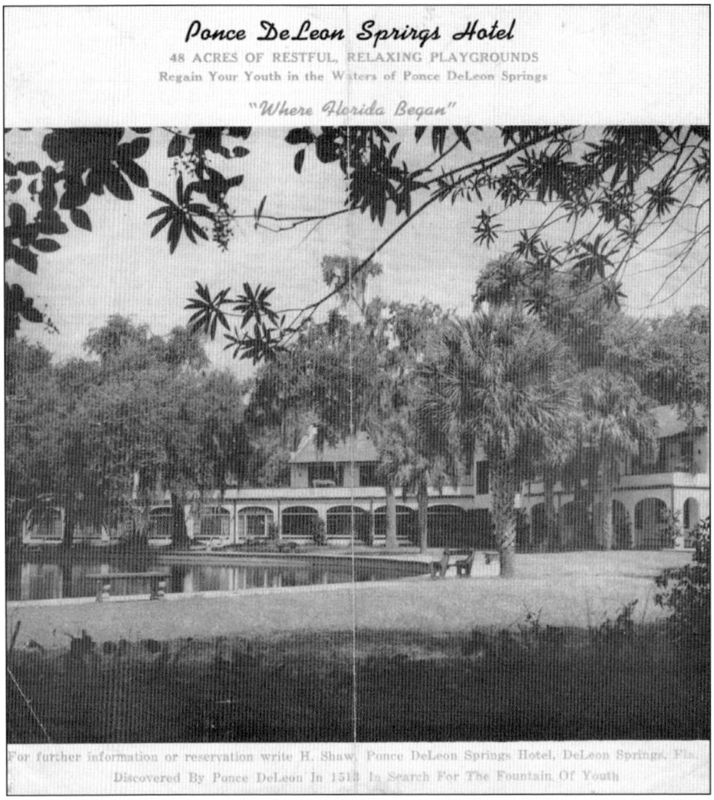

The natural setting of the spring created a relaxing location for the hotel that was widely advertised. Early advertising, as seen here, perpetuated the false information that the spring had been discovered by Ponce de Leon. (Courtesy of Florida State Parks.)

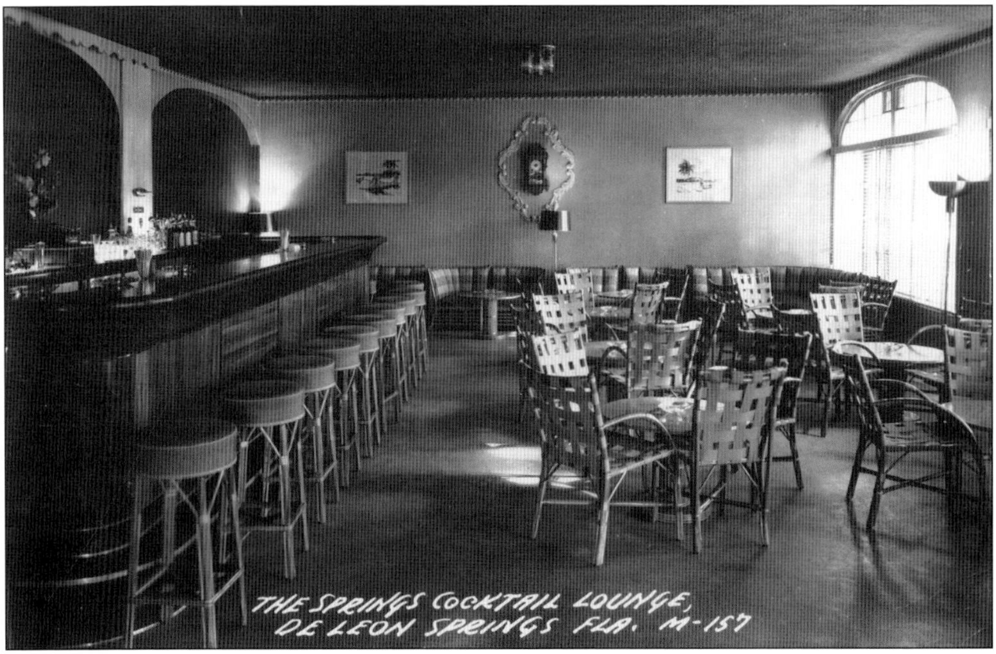

The picturesque room views guests of the Ponce De Leon Hotel enjoyed were not the only attraction. The hotel also had the Springs Cocktail Lounge, which overlooked the spring. (Courtesy of Stetson University, duPont-Ball Library, Memorabilia Collection.)

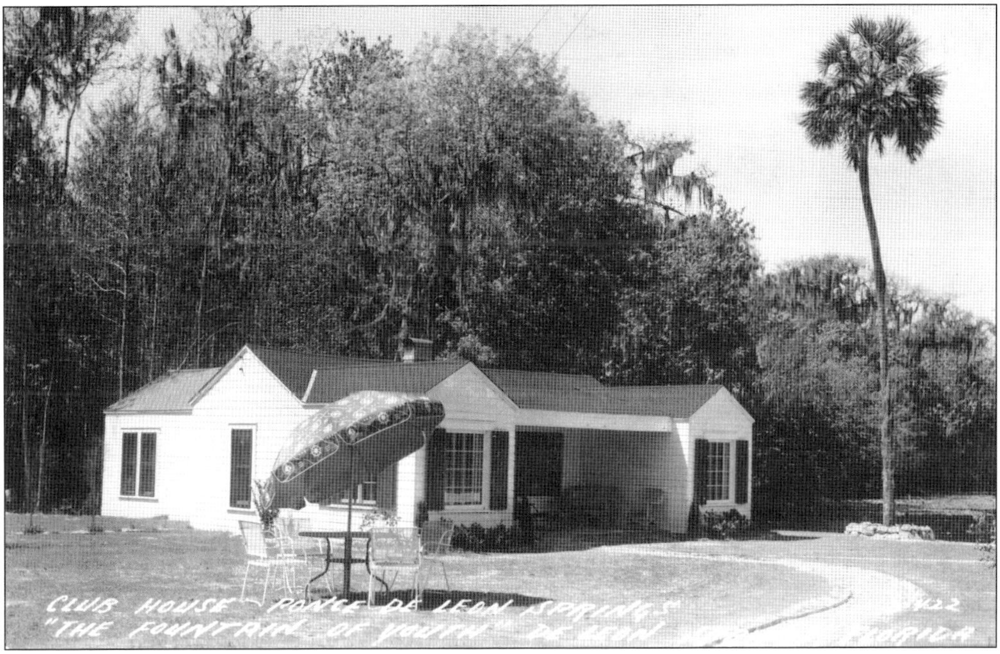

The builders of the Ponce De Leon Hotel considered the natural setting of the spring in their design of the hotel. By the 1950s, there was even a clubhouse for the convenient use of the guests. (Courtesy of Stetson University, duPont-Ball Library, Memorabilia Collection.)

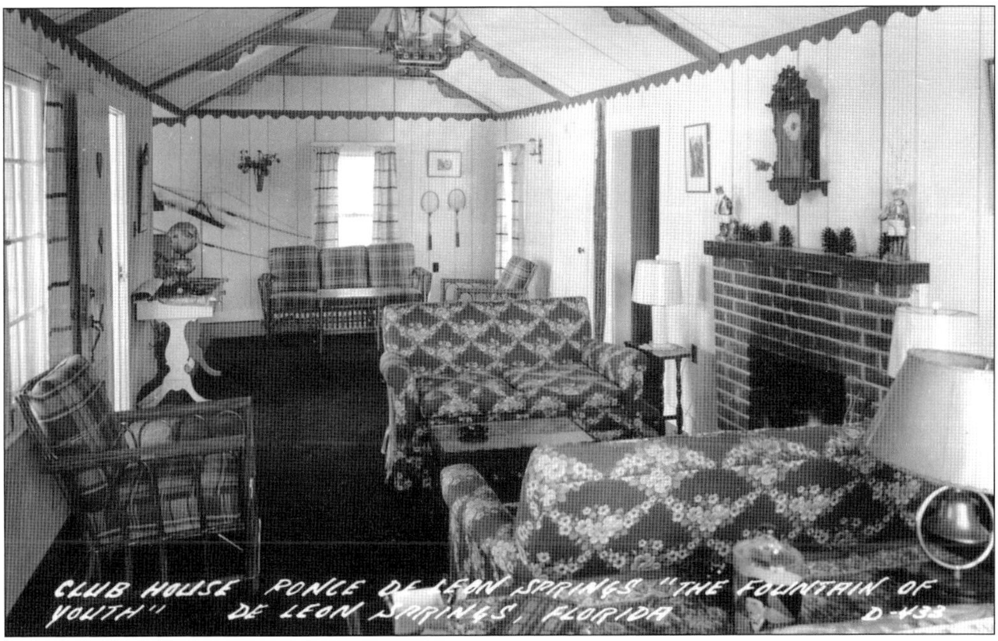

Guests of the Ponce De Leon Hotel had comfortable accommodations. The clubhouse also provided guests with a relaxed atmosphere and pleasant decor. (Courtesy of Stetson University, duPont-Ball Library, Memorabilia Collection.)

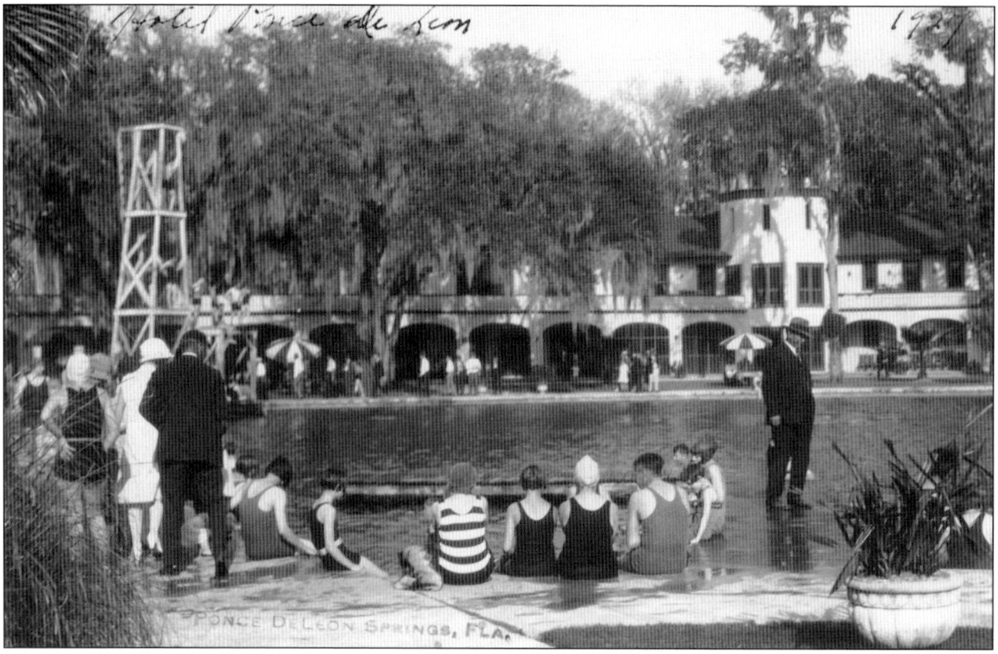

By 1944, the hotel had reached a peak in its popularity as a seasonal destination. Following the Great Depression and World War II, people were no longer coming to West Volusia County by steamboat or train and became more mobile and selective in where they went in their automobiles. (Courtesy of Stetson University, duPont-Ball Library, Memorabilia Collection.)

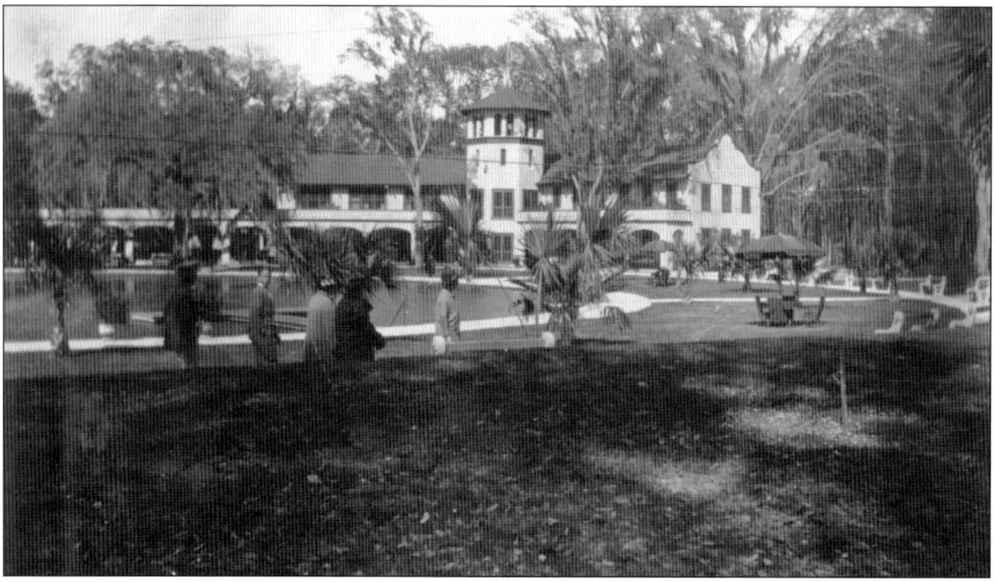

As the tourism industry changed in Florida, West Volusia County experienced a massive shift in its seasonal tourism. Places like the Ponce De Leon Hotel and other attractions that did not fit the trend of Florida marketing transitioned into were left by the wayside and became virtually unknown to the new visitors to Florida. (Courtesy of Robert Redd.)

Places like the Ponce De Leon Hotel attempted to adapt to the changing tourism market and compete with the other attractions of the time. Advertising brochures and images like this jungle cruise ride in the 1950s were used to attract visitors. (Courtesy of the Florida Park Service.)

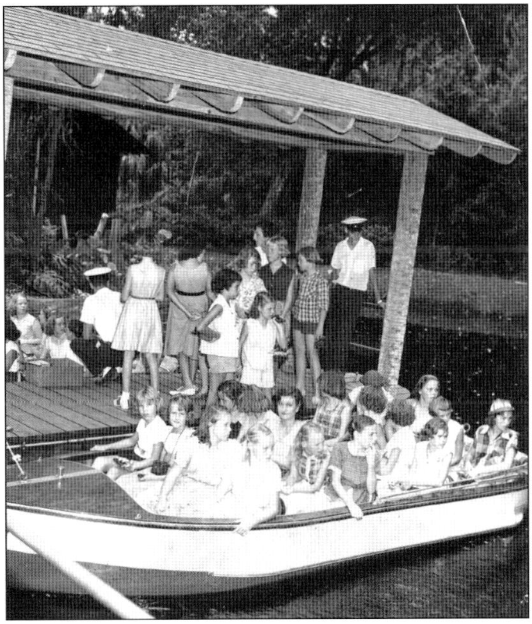

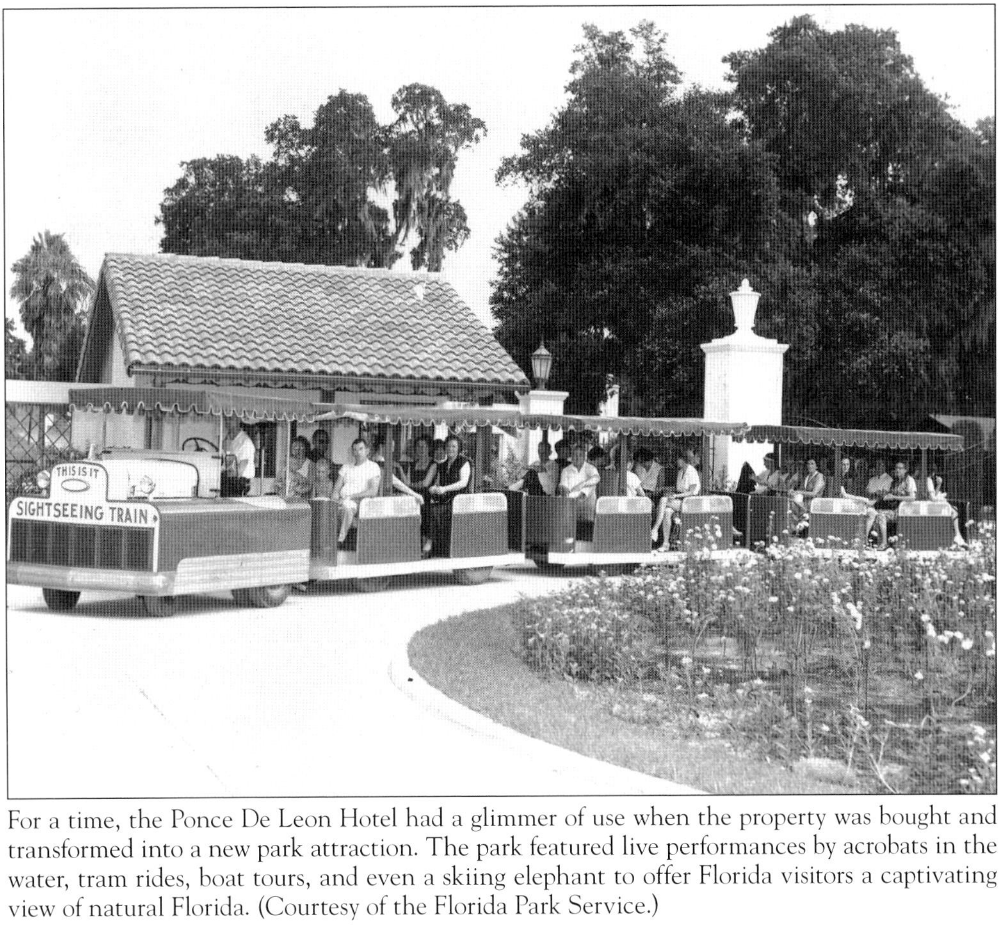

For a time, the Ponce De Leon Hotel had a glimmer of use when the property was bought and transformed into a new park attraction. The park featured live performances by acrobats in the water, tram rides, boat tours, and even a skiing elephant to offer Florida visitors a captivating view of natural Florida. (Courtesy of the Florida Park Service.)

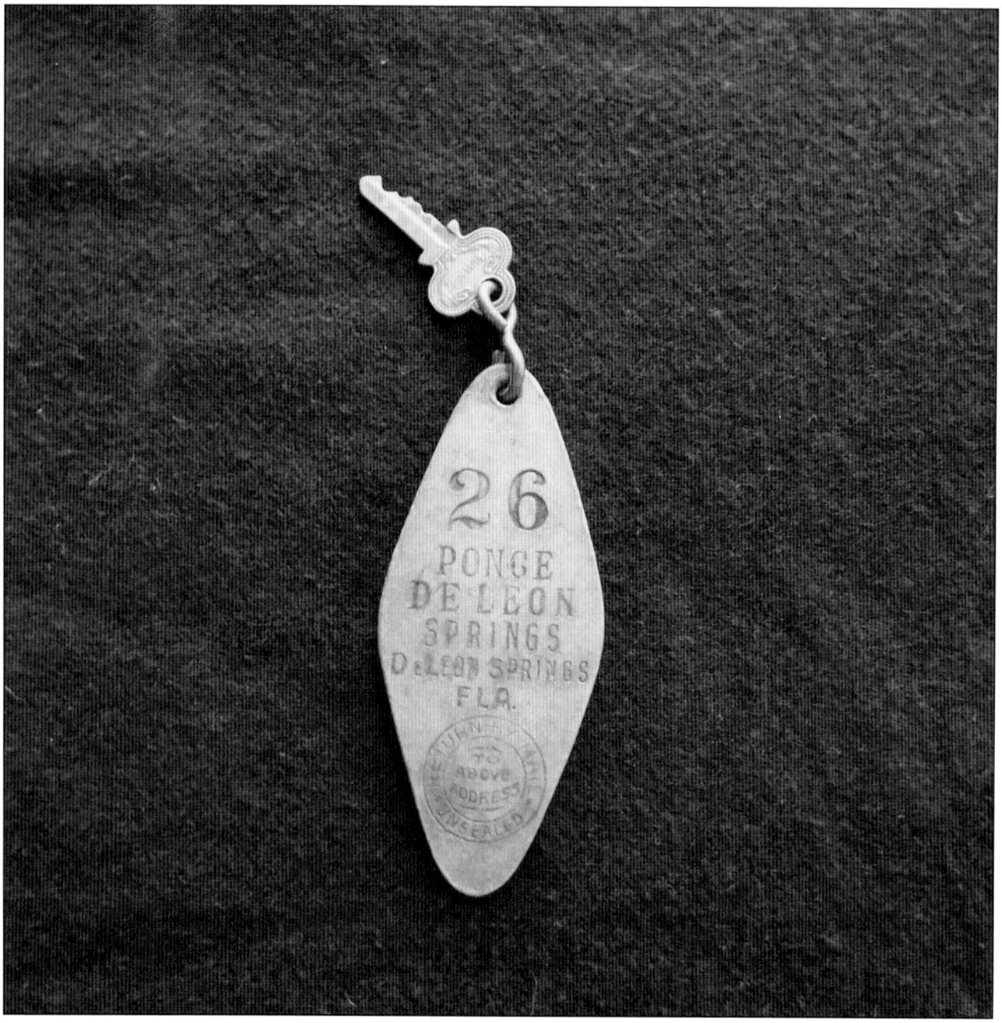

A room key from the Ponce De Leon Hotel is all that remains of the hotel today. In the end, like the steamboats and railroad, the Ponce De Leon Hotel could not compete with the wave of change that took Florida into the 20th century, and it too faded away. The old hotel was torn down, and the De Leon Springs attraction closed after some 16 years in business. Tourist traffic had been diverted away from the area by the widespread use of the interstate highway system and travel by air. The site was operated as a private park until 1982, when the State of Florida and Volusia County purchased the 55 acres around the spring. It then became De Leon Springs State Park, which has expanded to 625 acres in size. (Courtesy of Jim Cara.)

Two

DeLand

Carrollton Hotel

The Carrollton Hotel is but one of several resort lodgings that welcomed visitors to central Florida. It was a landmark feature in the thriving town of DeLand. This community in West Volusia County became quite popular during the boom of the steamboat era. Located a few miles east of the St. Johns, this community steadily grew after its founding by New York State chemical merchant Henry Addison DeLand. DeLand immediately realized the potential of the hilly long leaf pine–forested area after seeing similar land elsewhere being used for growing citrus.

A steamboat landing on the St. Johns River west of town or other such landings to the south served as the major access points for the earliest travelers to DeLand. Well-maintained roads were not established for decades, so the waterway served as the major route for most settlers and visitors. Many of those that stayed to develop the land and the city became involved in the evolving citrus industry. The pine forest steadily gave way to open up land for planting citrus. As the pine trees came down to clear the land, the same wood was used to build the expanding town.

In 1882, George Augustus Dreka built a two-story department store that later expanded to four floors. The Carrollton Hotel was above the store. Dreka's store and hotel barely escaped the virtual destruction of most of the town during a fire in 1886. Everything in the building was kept damp with water from the rooftop water tank, and wet blankets hung from the balconies. Dreka then relocated his store and built one of the first concrete fireproof buildings in town. Dreka later discontinued operation of the hotel and utilized all four floors for the department store. Dreka's Department Store became the largest department store in Central Florida. It operated in the present building on the corner of New York Avenue and Woodland Boulevard until 1949. The building still stands today and bears historic markers indicating the significant role of Dreka's in DeLand's history.

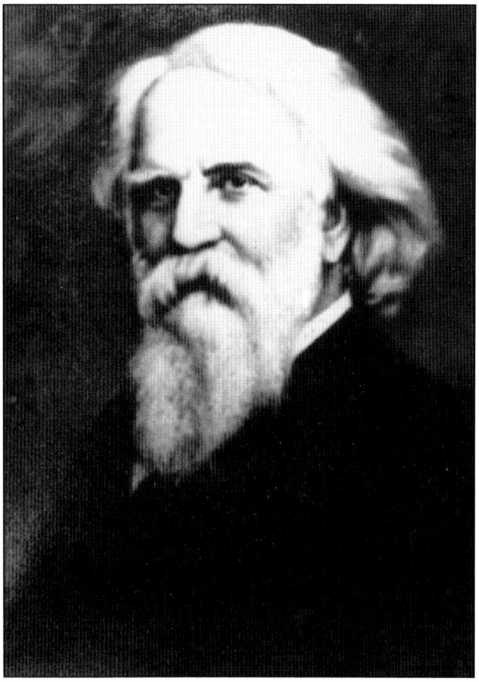

Henry Addison DeLand founder of the city of DeLand visited the area in 1876 after traveling by steamboat down the St. Johns River to Enterprise. Traveling overland by wagon, he saw the citrus potential of the land and envisioned a town that would be a center of culture, education, and enterprise. (Courtesy of Stetson University, duPont-Ball Library, Memorabilia Collection.)

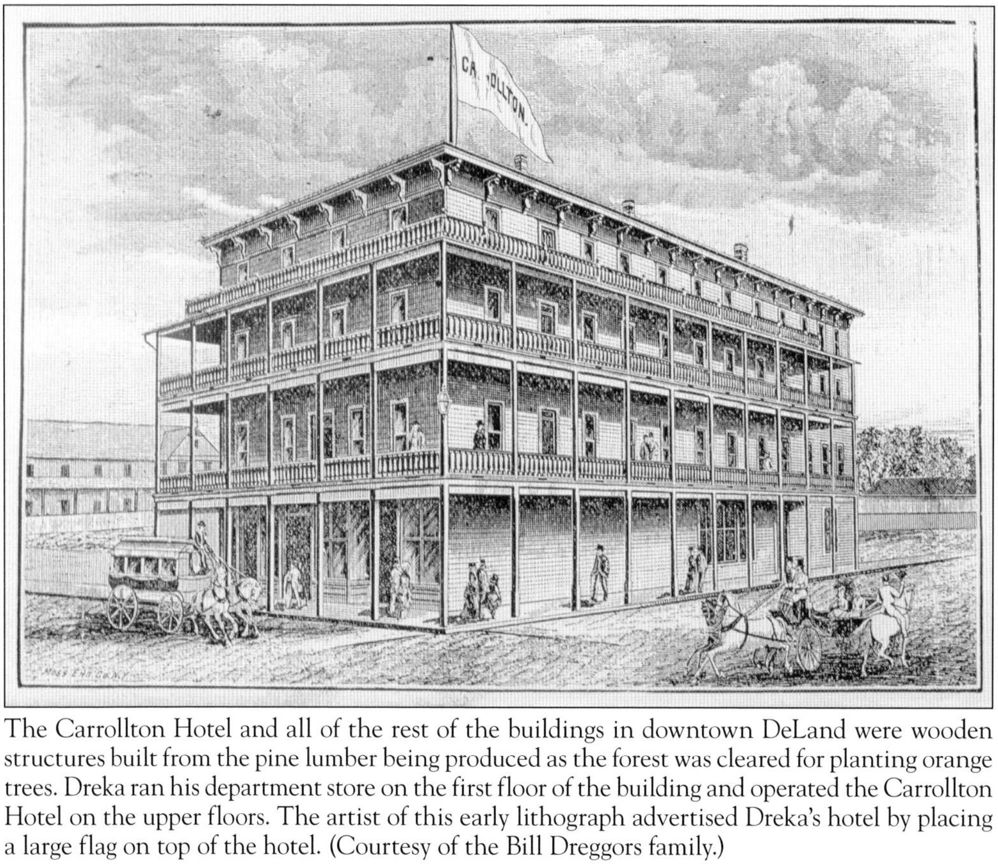

The Carrollton Hotel and all of the rest of the buildings in downtown DeLand were wooden structures built from the pine lumber being produced as the forest was cleared for planting orange trees. Dreka ran his department store on the first floor of the building and operated the Carrollton Hotel on the upper floors. The artist of this early lithograph advertised Dreka's hotel by placing a large flag on top of the hotel. (Courtesy of the Bill Dreggors family.)

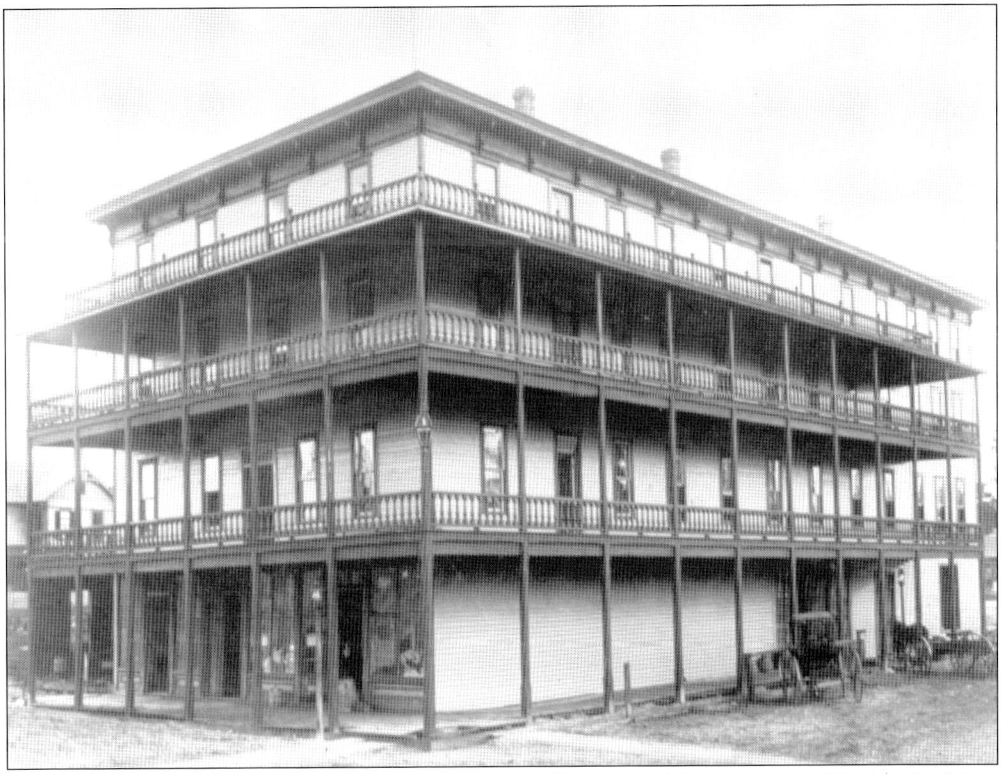

In this photograph predating 1886, the distinctive differences of the two uses of Dreka's building are more evident. The Carrollton Hotel on the upper floors sports an open wraparound porch with large windows for guests to enjoy a breeze, while the front porch of the ground floor shows the display windows of the store and associated businesses. (Courtesy of the Bill Dreggors family.)

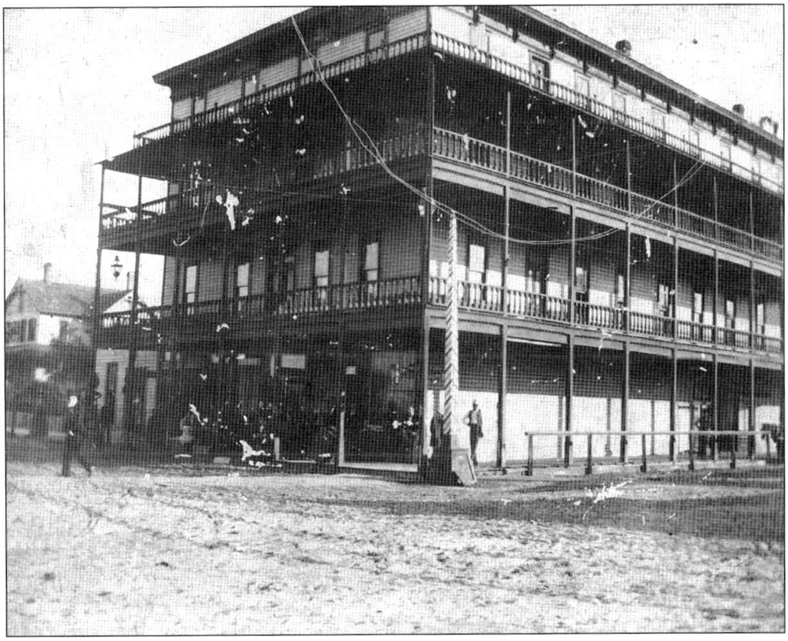

This undated photograph of the Carrollton Hotel shows the front porch of the ground floor where Dreka operated his department store. The upper floors of the building hosting the hotel can again be seen clear and open for easy guest access. (Courtesy of the Bill Dreggors family.)

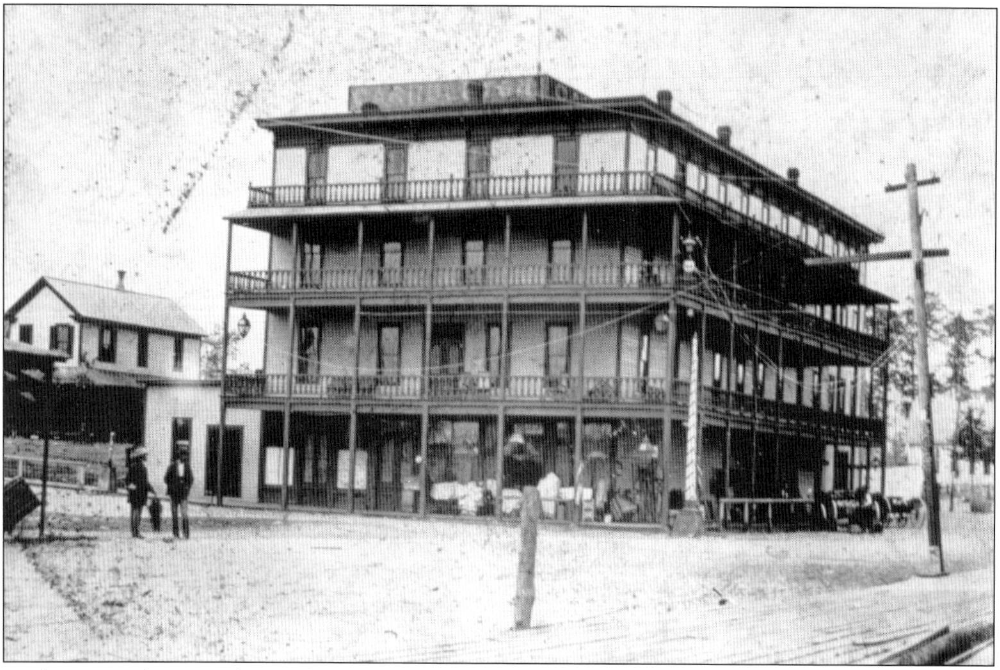

In this 1892 photograph, goods from the store and porch seating are more visible as well as power lines. DeLand received one of Thomas Edison's early power plants in 1886, thanks to winter resident John B. Stetson, who had the plant, which was too small for his hat factory, built instead near his home to produce ice. (Courtesy of the Bill Dreggors family.)

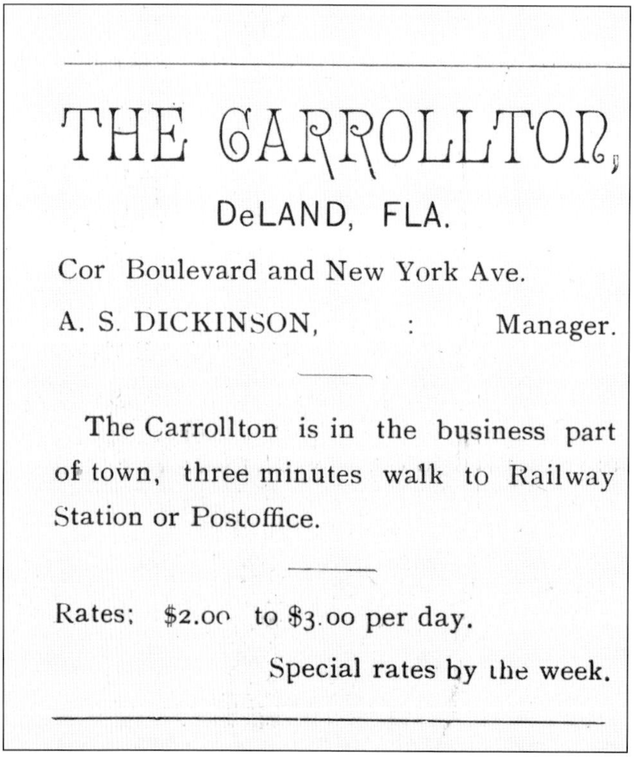

THE CARROLLTON,

DeLAND, FLA.

Cor Boulevard and New York Ave.

A. S. DICKINSON, : Manager.

The Carrollton is in the business part of town, three minutes walk to Railway Station or Postoffice.

Rates; $2.00 to $3.00 per day.

Special rates by the week.

The Carrollton Hotel was located in the business part of town. This 1895 advertisement from the *Stetson Collegiate* newspaper boosts a room rate from $2 to $3 a day with special rates by the week. (Courtesy of Stetson University, duPont-Ball Library, Memorabilia Collection.)

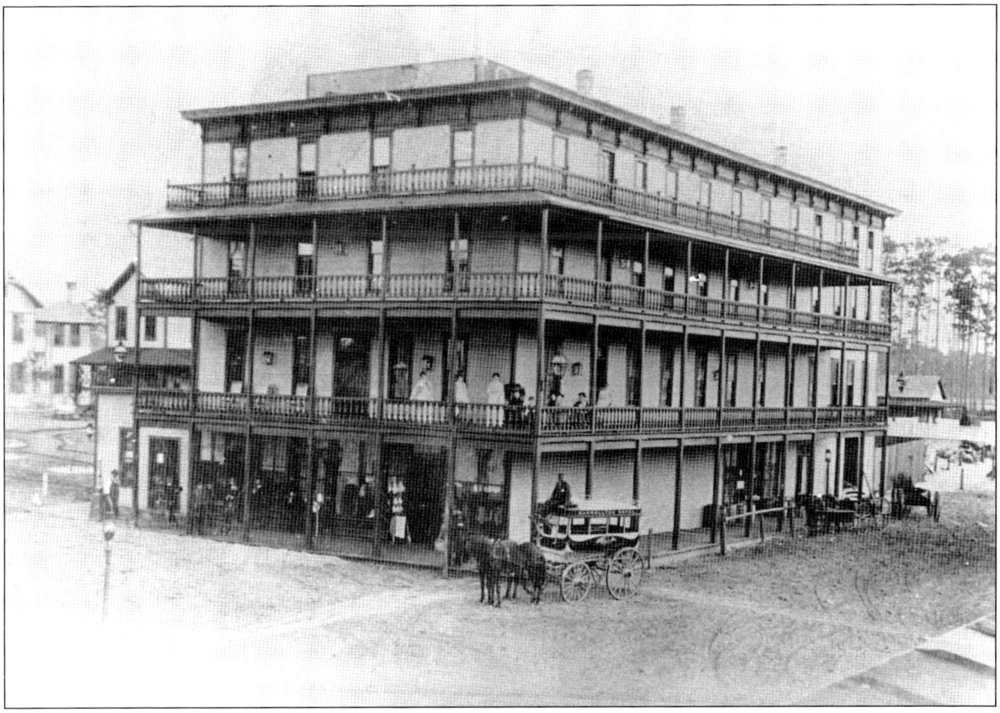

Like other local hotels, the Carrollton Hotel furnished transportation for its guests. This 1895 image shows the courtesy wagon sitting out front waiting to take guests as guests look on from the second-floor porch of the hotel. (Courtesy of the Bill Dreggors family.)

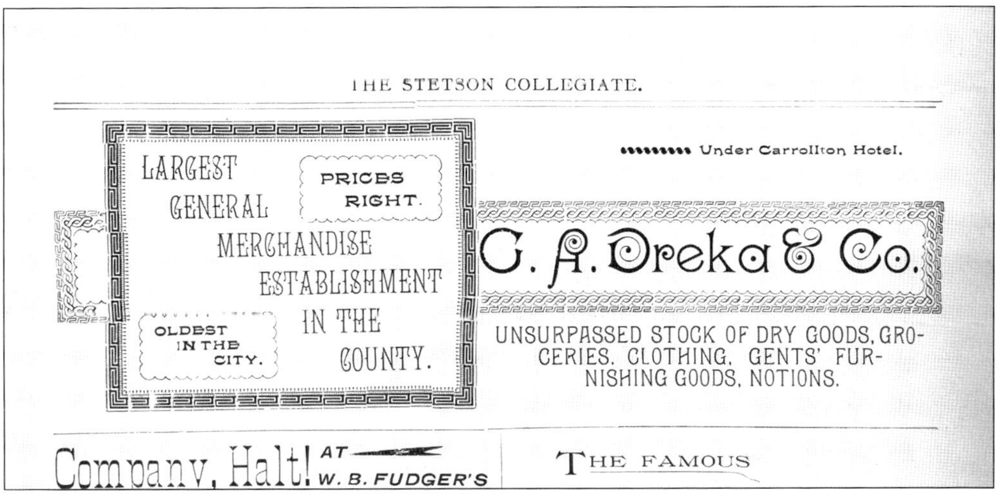

This 1895 advertisement from the *Stetson Collegiate* newspaper is for Dreka's Department Store, located in the same building as the Carrollton Hotel. Dreka gained a popular reputation for his ability to provide many of the goods and products people of the day needed. (Courtesy of Stetson University, duPont-Ball Library, Memorabilia Collection.)

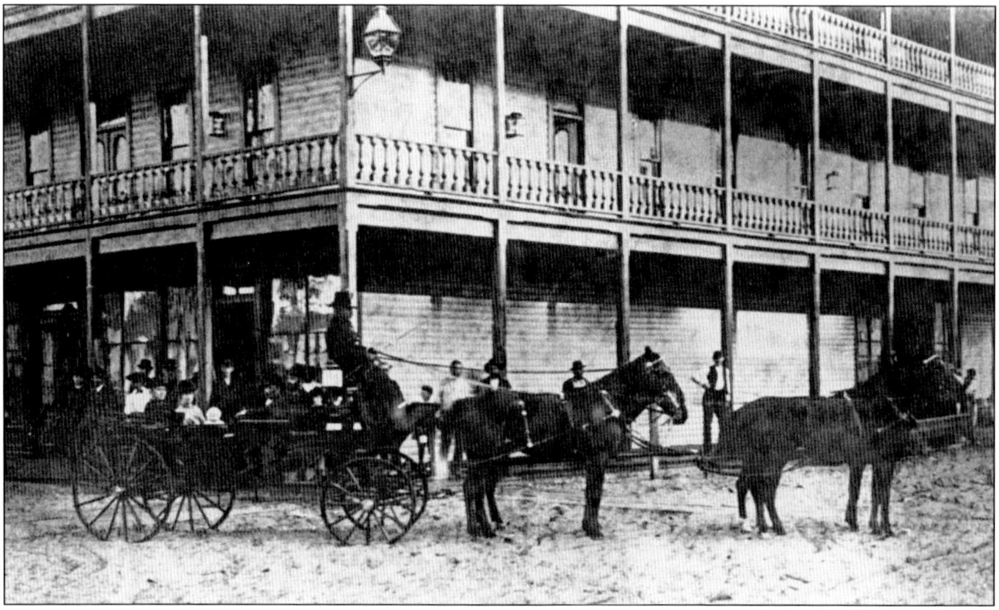

Dreka's store excelled more than his lodging, and he became a major supplier of goods and commodities to residents of the town and surrounding country. The store was the most successful and popular store in Volusia County, and John B. Stetson and his family shopped there as evidenced in this image of the Stetson family carriage parked outside of Dreka's in 1900. (Courtesy of State Archives of Florida, Florida Memory.)

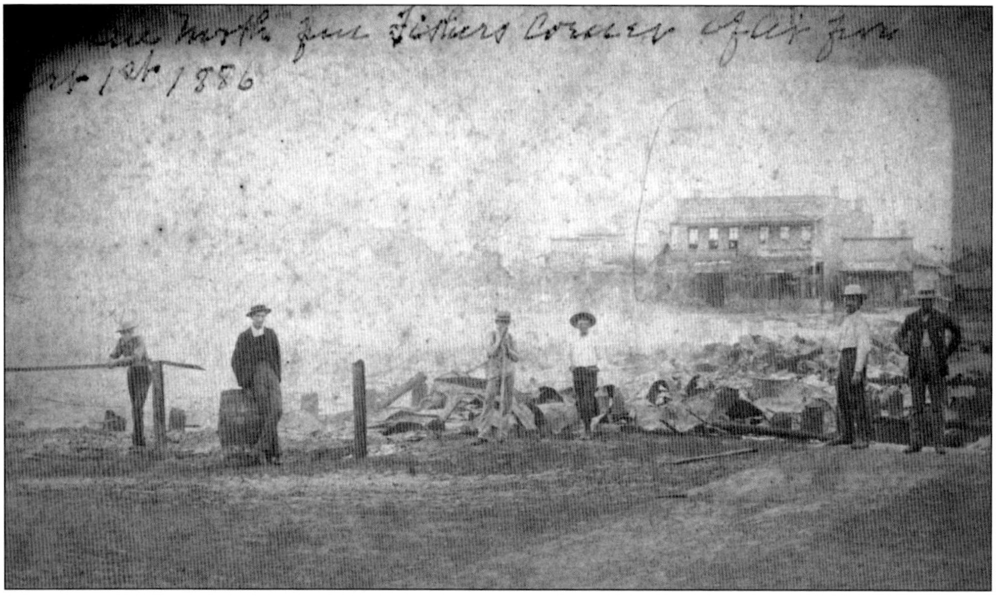

Late one evening in October 1886, a fire started in a local downtown saloon. The fire destroyed 22 buildings that held 33 businesses on Woodland Boulevard between New York and Rich Avenues. City leaders then adopted an ordinance requiring brick or stone construction in rebuilding the town, and that contributed to the survival of many of the buildings and remaining hotels of the downtown main street historic district today. (Courtesy of Stetson University, duPont-Ball Library, Memorabilia Collection.)

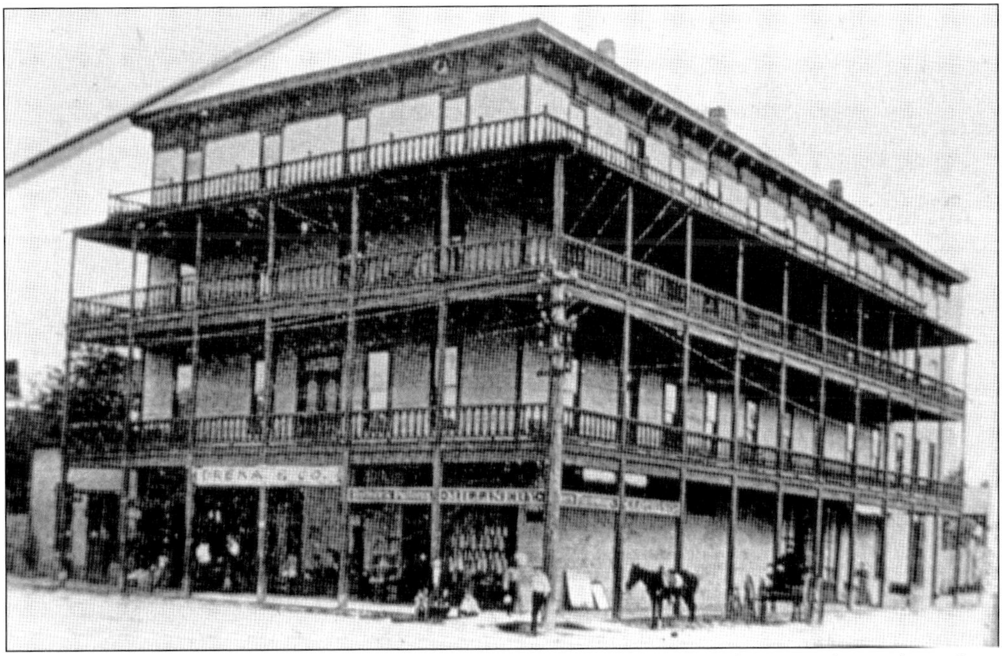

Dreka's building at the time was saved by the heroic effort of people keeping sheets draped on the sides of the building wet from water stored in a water tank on the roof. The action saved the Carrollton Hotel and Dreka's Department Store from the same destruction of other businesses. (Courtesy of the Bill Dreggors family.)

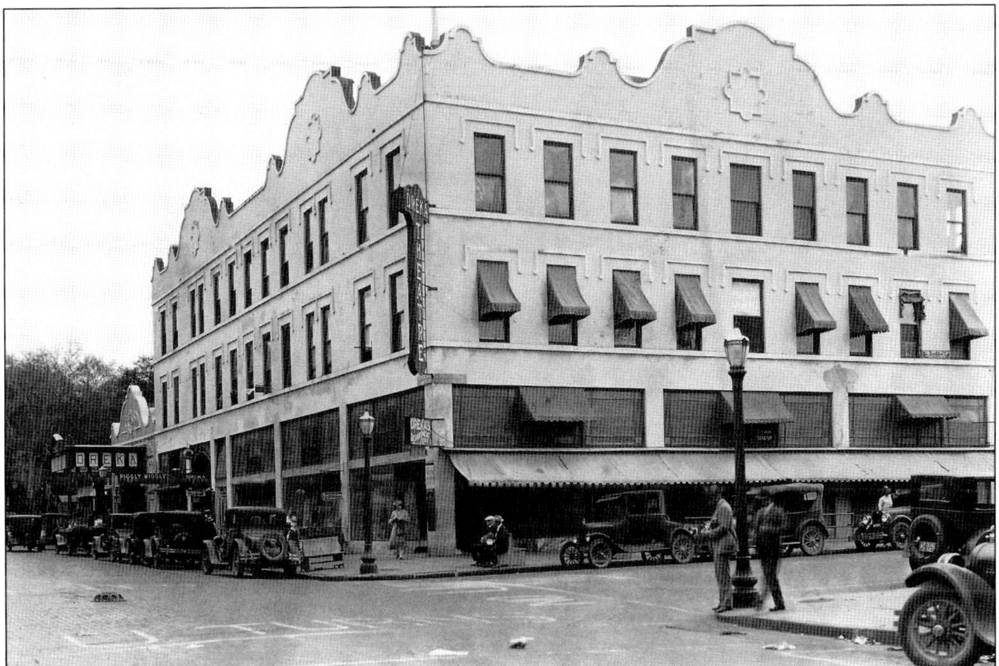

After the fire of 1886, buildings had to be either brick or mortar, so Dreka had his businesses relocated to a new fireproofed building he had built. Dreka dropped out of the hotel business and used all four floors of his new building for Dreka's Department Store. (Courtesy of Jim Cara.)

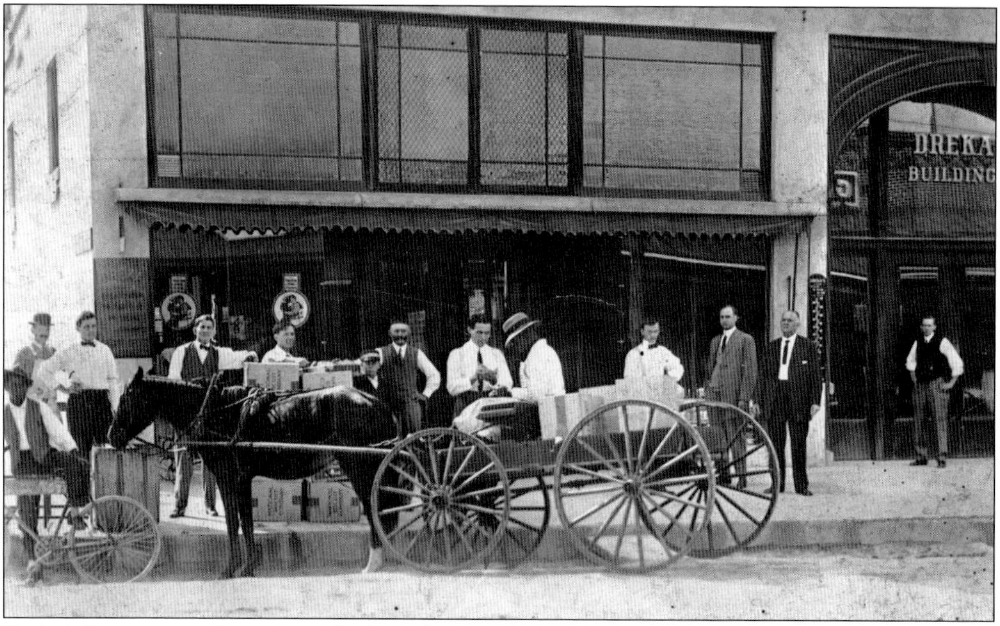

Dreka's Department Store furnished residents with just about every commodity that they needed for over 70 years. In this 1912 photograph, a wagon of goods for the store is being unloaded as Dreka looks on second from the right. (Courtesy of Stetson University, duPont-Ball Library, Memorabilia Collection.)

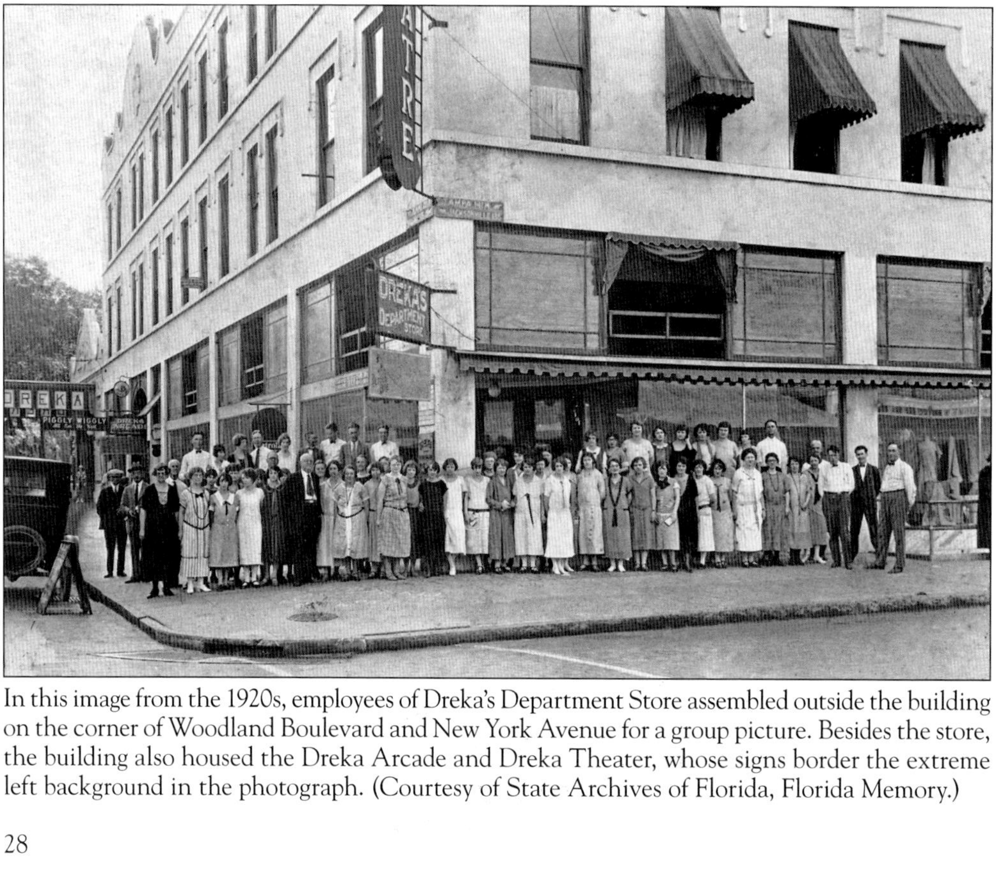

In this image from the 1920s, employees of Dreka's Department Store assembled outside the building on the corner of Woodland Boulevard and New York Avenue for a group picture. Besides the store, the building also housed the Dreka Arcade and Dreka Theater, whose signs border the extreme left background in the photograph. (Courtesy of State Archives of Florida, Florida Memory.)

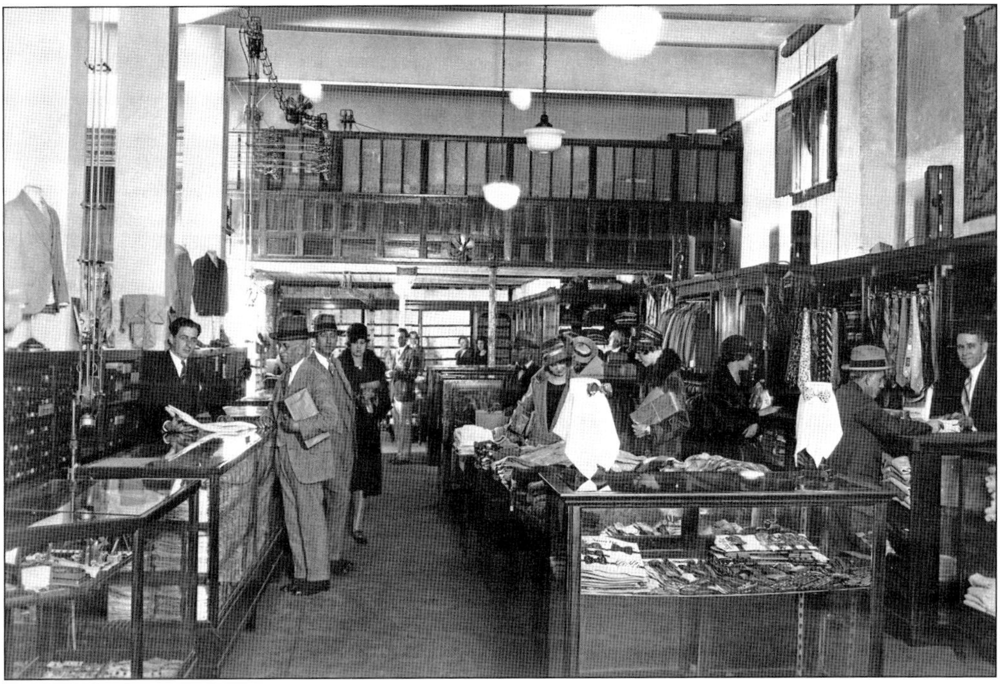

Seen here is the Dreka's Department Store building as it appeared in 1925, with its men's department. The building also had a basement, which many of the other buildings downtown were built with. (Courtesy of State Archives of Florida, Florida Memory.)

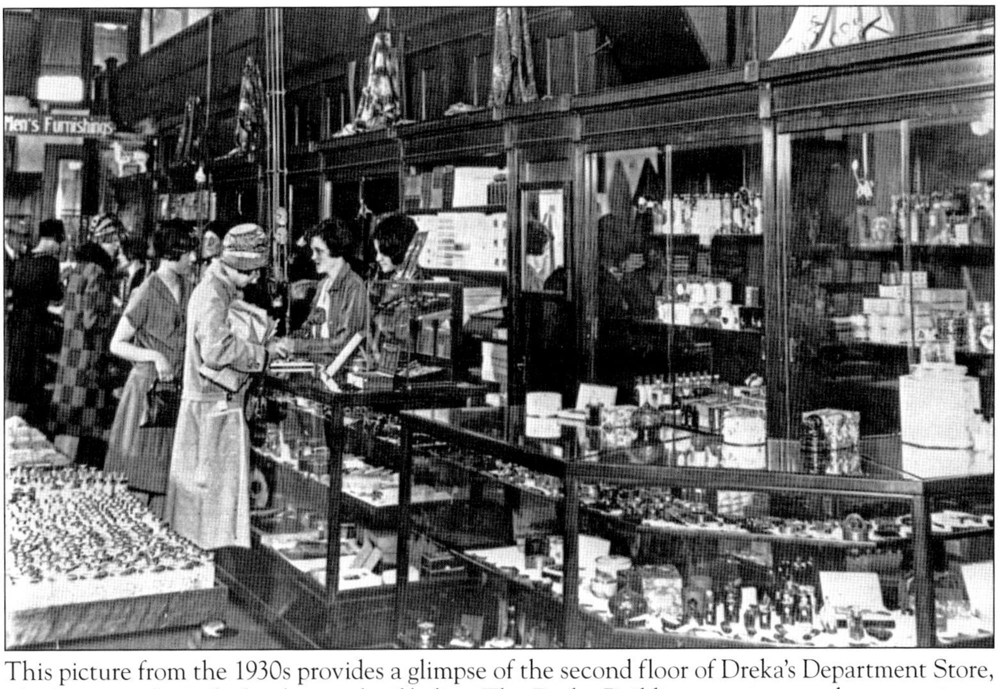

This picture from the 1930s provides a glimpse of the second floor of Dreka's Department Store, which was exclusively for the needs of ladies. The Dreka Building continues to be a prominent landmark in the center of historic downtown DeLand on the corner of Woodland Boulevard and New York Avenue. (Courtesy of State Archives of Florida, Florida Memory.)

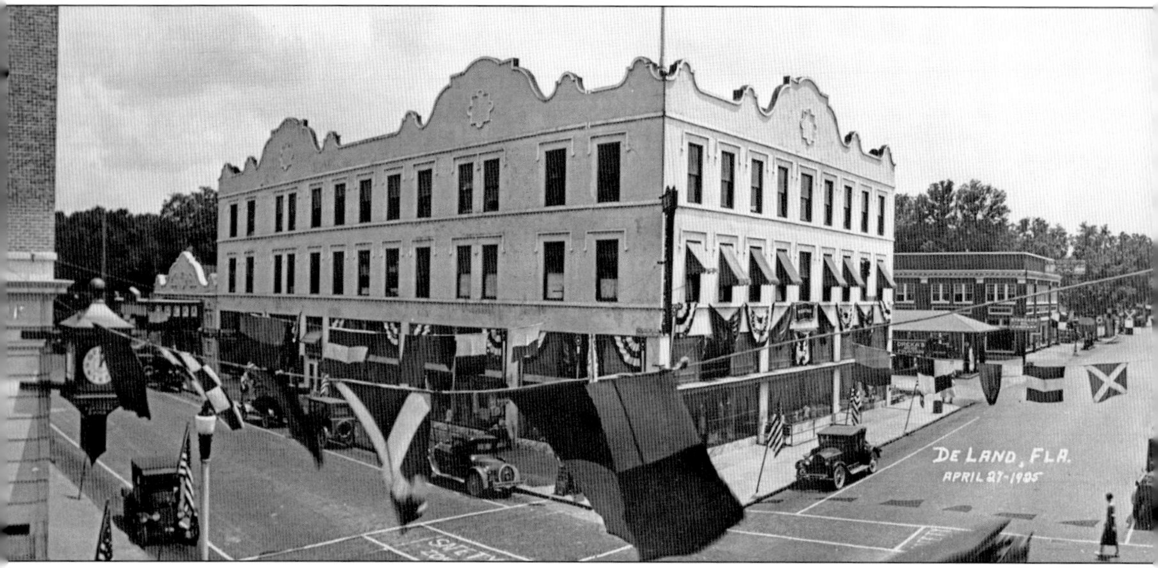

This is a panoramic 1925 image of the Dreka Building on the corner of Woodland Boulevard and New York Avenue in DeLand. The Dreka Building continues today to be a prominent landmark in the center of historic downtown DeLand. (Courtesy of State Archives of Florida, Florida Memory.)

Three

DeLand

College Arms Hotel

The College Arms Hotel began as the Parce Land Hotel. In 1885, the Leete family built a large hotel among the pines on 10 acres they owned fronting Amelia Avenue. Amelia Avenue is named after Amelia DeLand Leete, the sister of Henry A. DeLand. Leete sold the hotel to Joseph Yale Parce. The hotel was quite popular with guests who traveled the St. Johns River by steamboat to winter in Florida. Guests arrived at Alexander Landing on Lake Beresford on the St. Johns River. From there, they journeyed by wagon or rail into DeLand.

When the railroad was built three miles west of town, a spur line was branched off east into town. The line ran to a depot opposite the Parce Land Hotel on Amelia Avenue. From the depot, guests conveniently could reach the hotel a short distance away. The location of the depot, with the hotel in the background, is part of an historical scene captured on early film and was used for one of the murals displayed in present-day DeLand.

The hotel and 10 acres were sold in 1896 to a new seasonal resident of DeLand, John Batterson Stetson. He changed the name to the College Arms and hired an architect named Pearson to enlarge and remodel the hotel. Most of the original pines that graced the grounds immediately around the hotel were left during the expansion. At each end of the hotel, large square towers were added to give guests scenic views and places to enjoy the breeze.

One of the attracting features Stetson added to the College Arms was golf. On acreage adjacent the hotel, a first-class course was created with its own clubhouse. Many of the College Arms seasonal guests include avid golfers, and the site was included in professional golfing tours of the day. The hotel was a popular destination for decades.

During the Great Depression, business waned, but World War II brought a flurry of activity to the town. The US Navy established the DeLand Naval Air Station, a flight training base at the DeLand Airport. Tugboats and gliders used for the Normandy Invasion were built west of town. The US Navy during this time also utilized the College Arms as a naval rest center.

The hotel was torn down in the 1940s, and Fish Memorial Hospital was built on its site. Later, the College Arms Towers residential high-rise was built across the street on the site of the former rail depot. The hospital was eventually replaced by the newer Volusia County Courthouse.

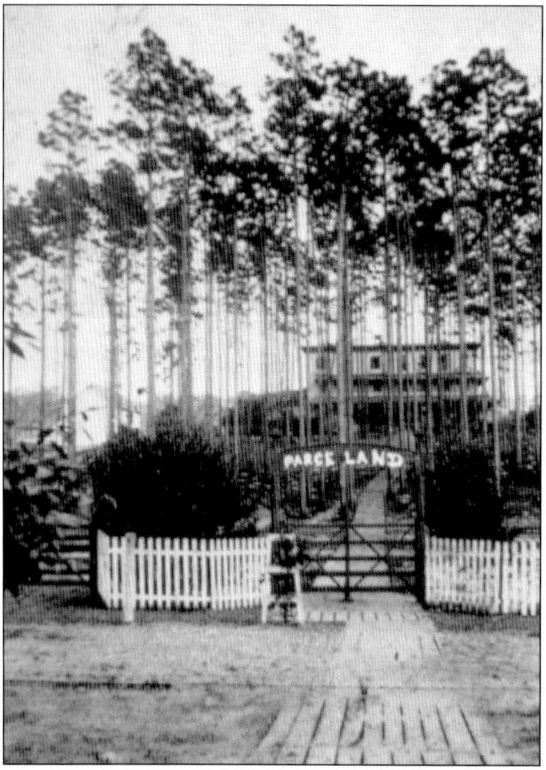

As the town of DeLand grew, the forest of long leaf pines which dominated its sand hill terrain was cut down to plant citrus. The land around the Parce Land Hotel, pictured here, was one area of town where the trees were not cleared. (Courtesy of the Bill Dreggors family.)

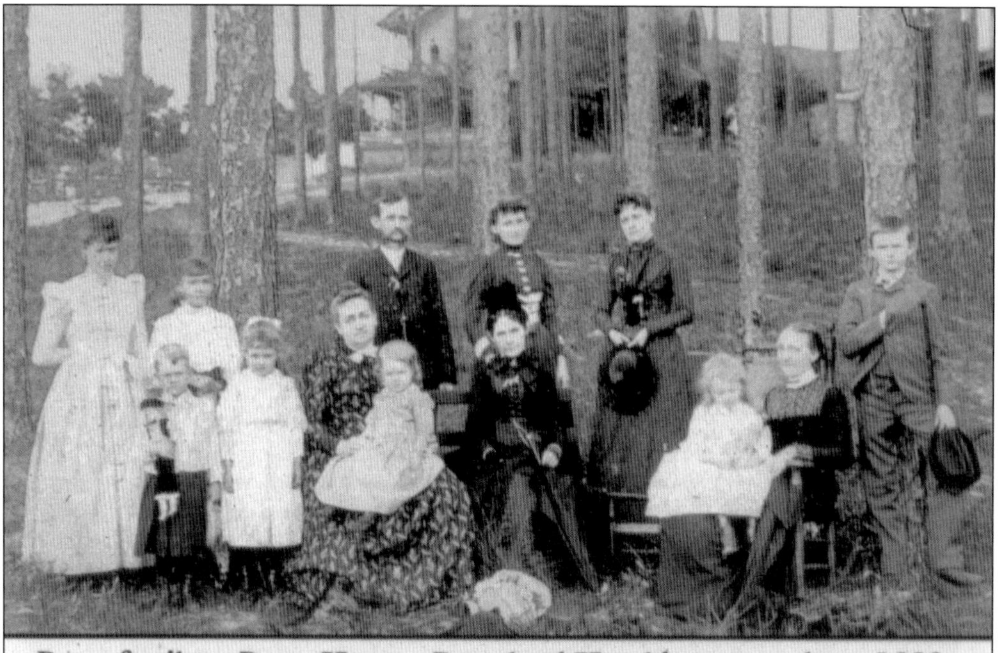

This c. 1882 photograph shows members of the Parce family, for whom the hotel was named, posing with their hotel in the background. The gentlemen standing to the left is Joseph Yale Parce. (Courtesy of the Bill Dreggors family.)

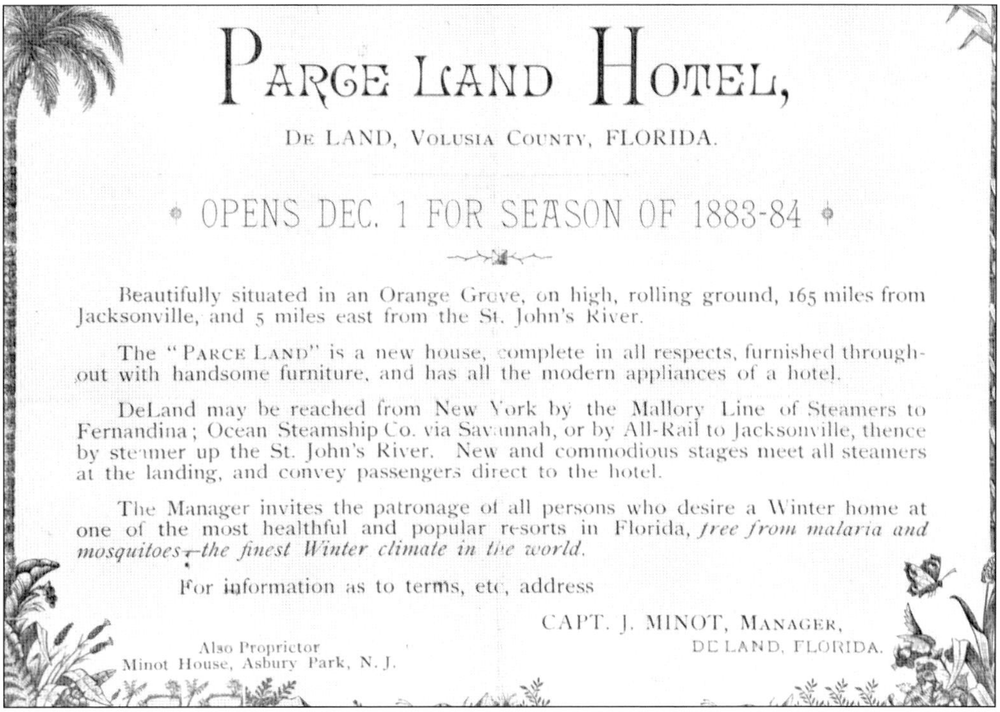

An advertisement from 1883 describes how winter guests can best reach the Parce Land Hotel. The proprietors of many early Florida hotels also assured potential guests that their location was free of malaria and mosquitoes. (Courtesy of the Bill Dreggors family.)

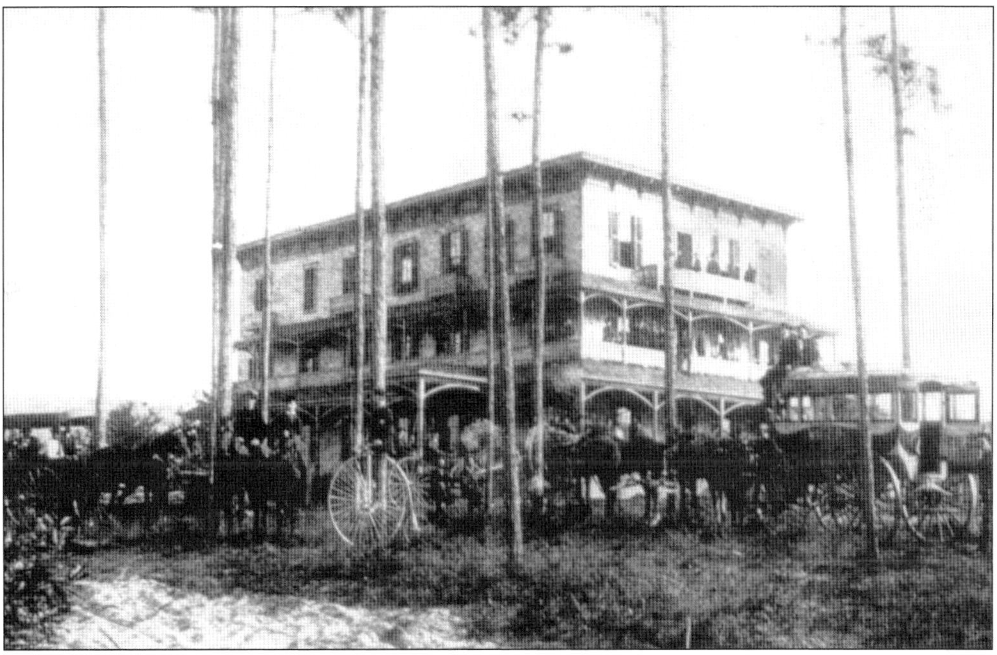

The Parce Land Hotel was a popular accommodation for visitors, as seen in this image. Guests line the balcony and porch of the hotel while horsemen, wagons, and an early bicyclist pose among the Parce Land's pines. (Courtesy of the Bill Dreggors family.)

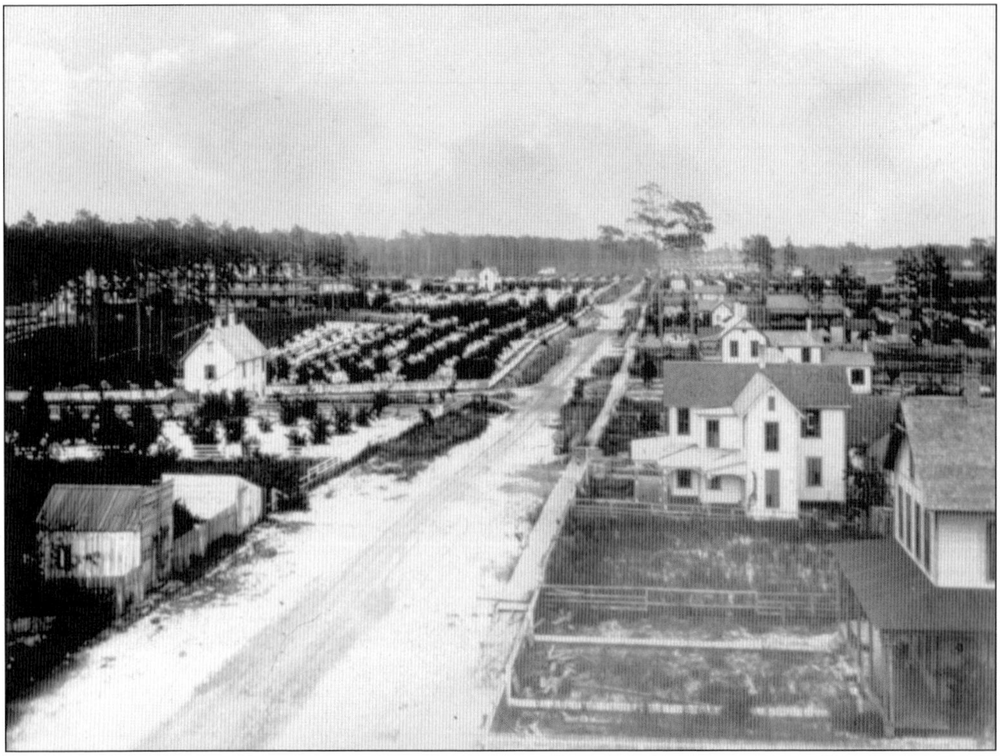

This panoramic view of early DeLand in the 1880s illustrates how the citrus industry was a big part of the local economy. The Parce Land Hotel can be seen to the left of the photograph hidden among pines and surrounded by orange trees. (Courtesy of the Bill Dreggors family.)

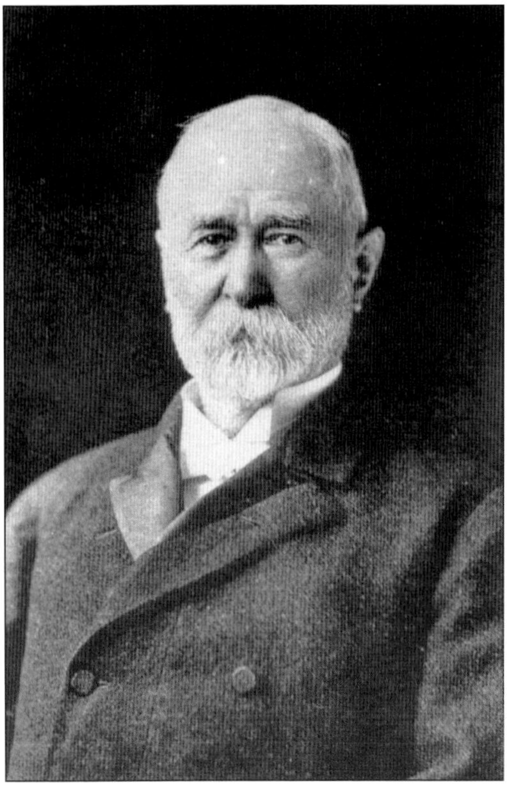

In 1886, hat manufacturer John Batterson Stetson visited DeLand at the invitation of Henry Addison DeLand. Stetson liked the area and built a vacation home and also purchased the Parce Land Hotel. (Courtesy of the Bill Dreggors family.)

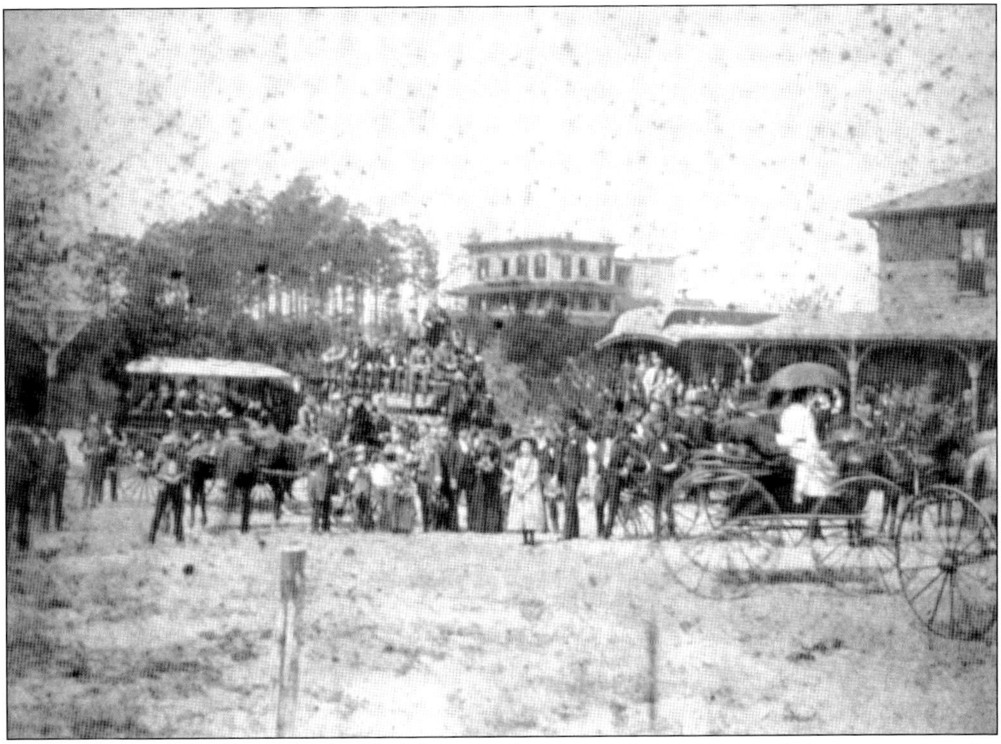

Stetson had a railroad spur built off of the main line west of town that ended at a depot not far from his hotel. This photograph from the depot with the hotel in the background shows a multitude of visitors, with some of them posing with oranges, and is the basis for one of the colorful murals that illustrate the history of DeLand today. (Courtesy of the Bill Dreggors family.)

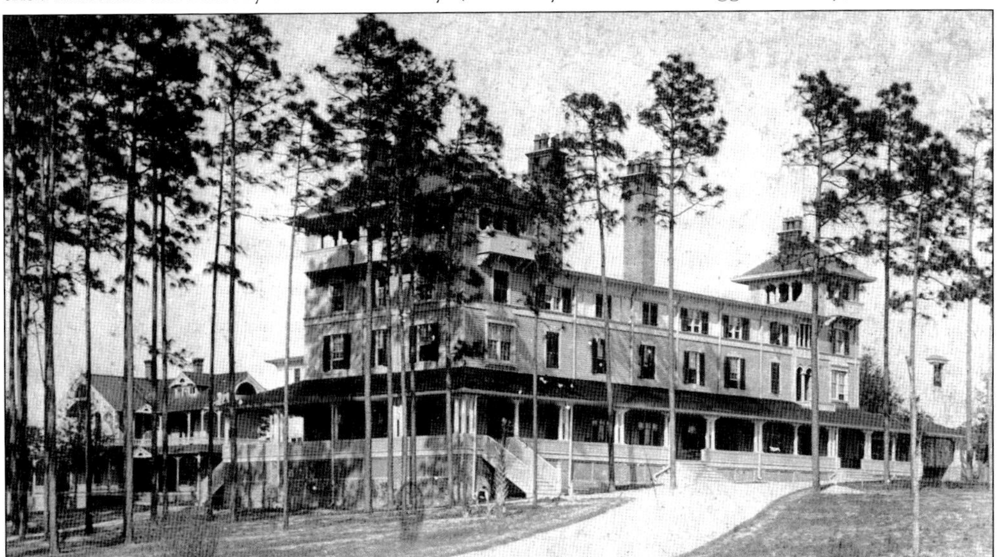

Stetson enlarged the hotel to increase its capacity and changed the name to the College Arms Hotel. This 1905 view of the College Arms Hotel shows the entry drive and the structure of the former hotel can be seen to the left of the newly added wing. (Courtesy of Stetson University, duPont-Ball Library, Memorabilia Collection.)

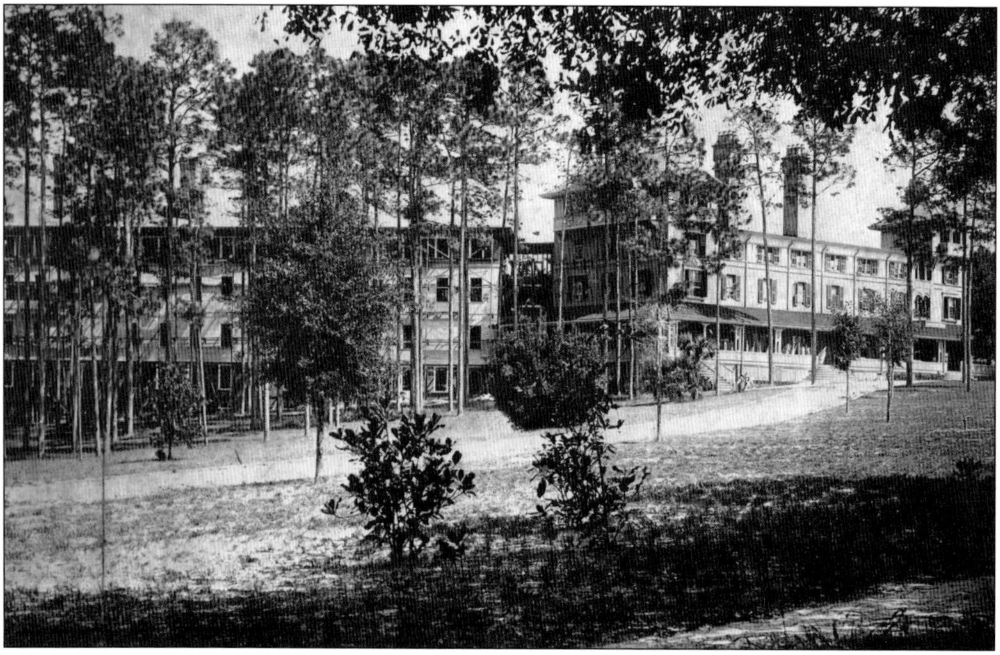

This image of the College Arms Hotel shows the additional wings and scaffolding that were part of the expansion that took place in 1905. Stetson also added an expansive entryway but preserved the majestic pines around the hotel. (Courtesy of Stetson University, duPont-Ball Library, Memorabilia Collection.)

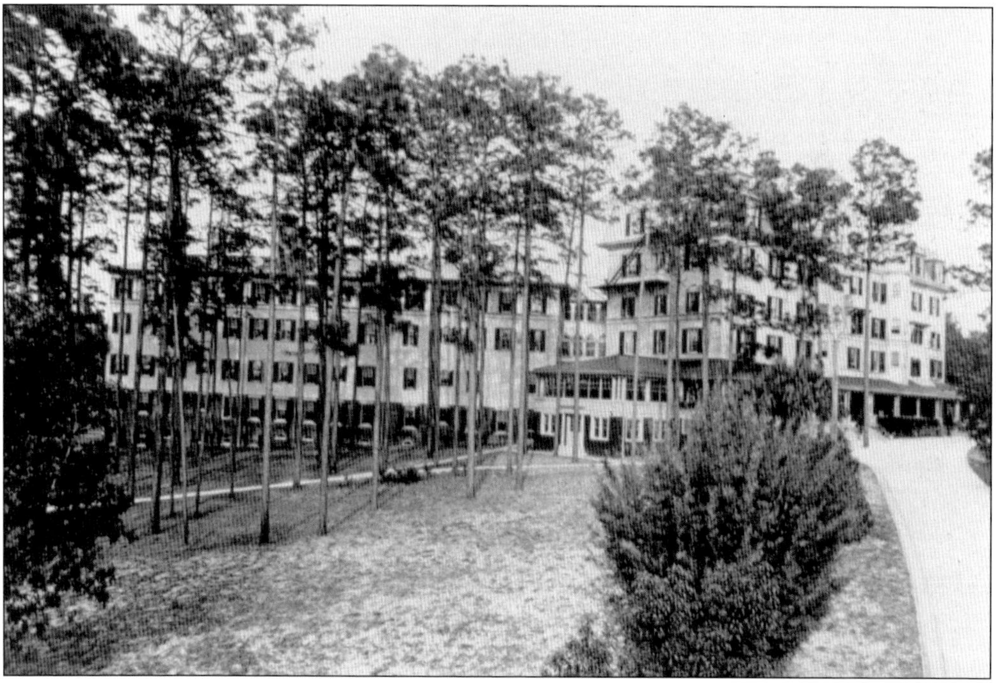

A later image of the College Arms Hotel shows the completed new wings to the hotel. The pines have remained, but the huge additions to the hotel now completely envelop the former hotel structure from view. (Courtesy of the Bill Dreggors family.)

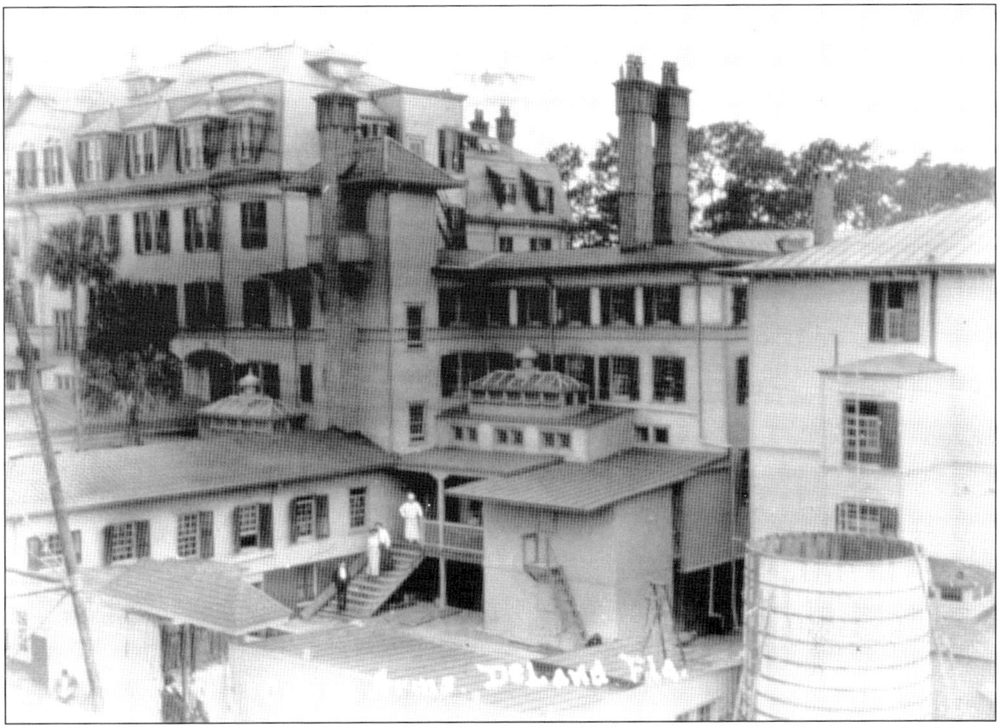

This image taken after the expansion shows the elaborate construction and support buildings behind the hotel (on the west side). A series of stairways and entries gave hotel staff access points from the staff preparation areas to the main guest sections of the hotel. (Courtesy of the Bill Dreggors family.)

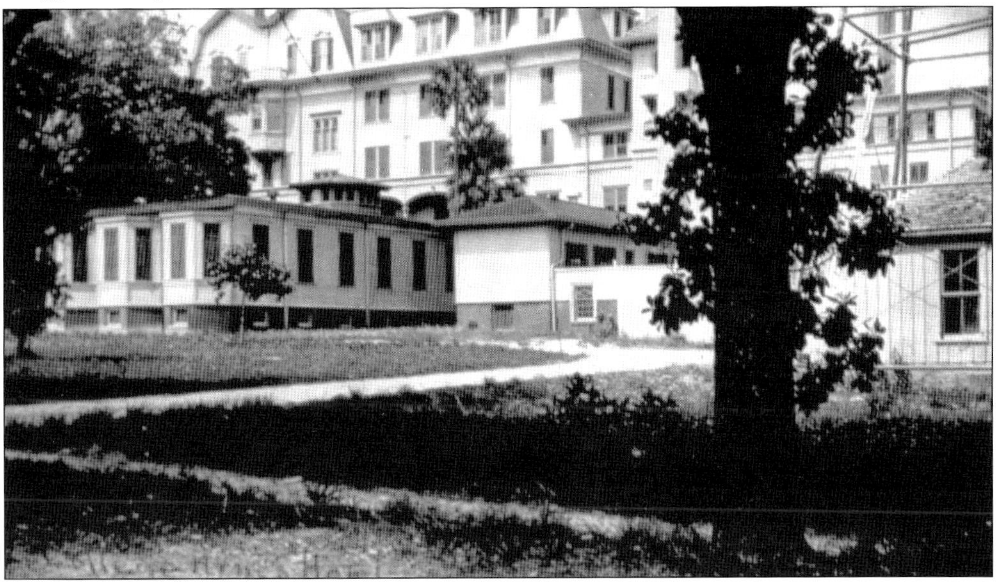

This ground-level view of the same general back area of the College Arms Hotel shows the road access used by service vehicles. These back areas of the hotel were mostly unseen by regular guests and in some large hotels may even have included staff accommodations. (Courtesy of the Bill Dreggors family.)

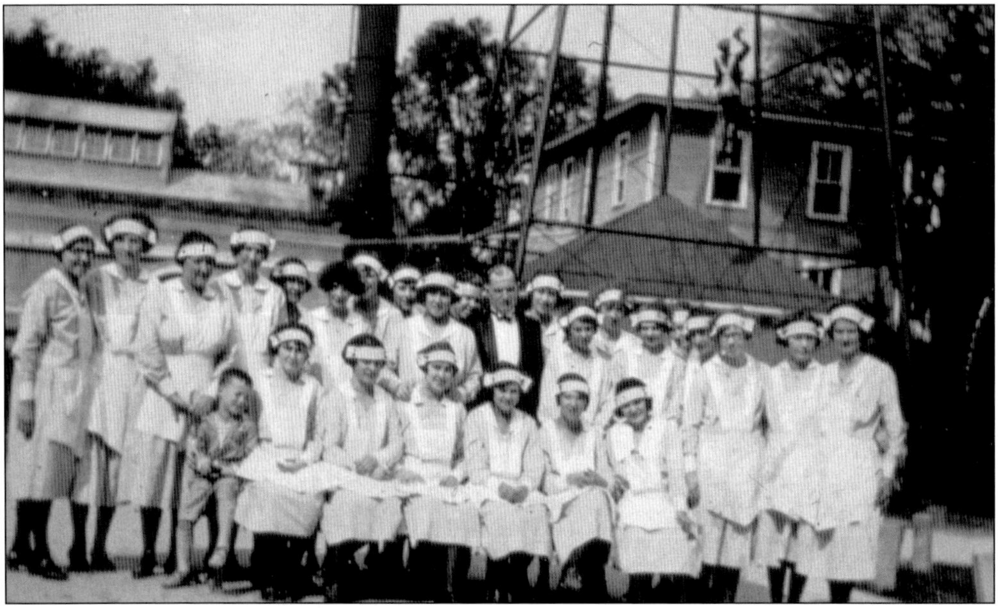

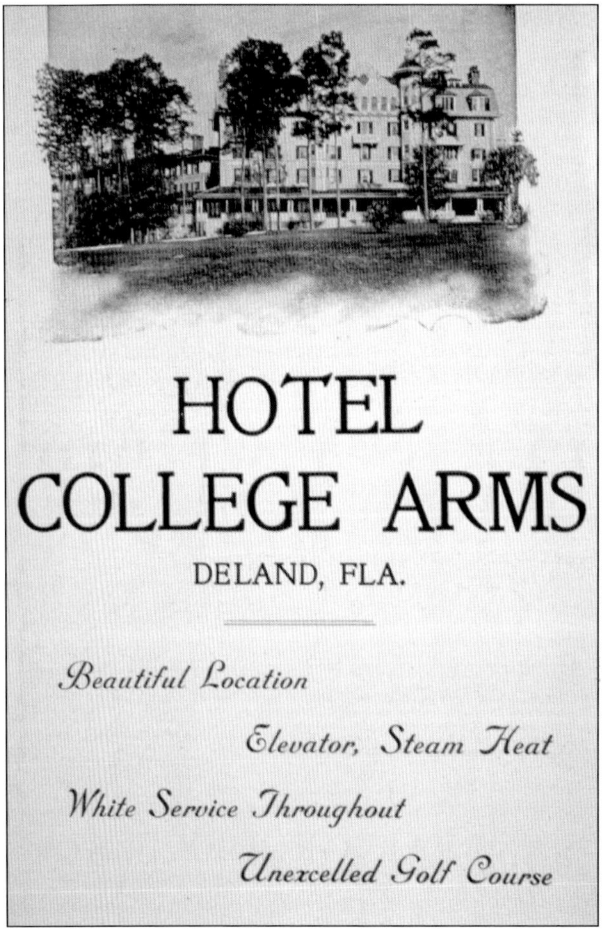

In this 1920s photograph of some of the College Arms Hotel staff, employees of the hotel wore uniforms that identified their positions in the staff. In the upper right-hand corner of the photograph, a maintenance man is seen working on the water tower. (Courtesy of the Bill Dreggors family.)

The College Arms Hotel furnished guests with information booklets on the hotel amenities much like some hotels do today. Note how some of the major features provided at the hotel are displayed on the front cover. (Courtesy of Jim Cara.)

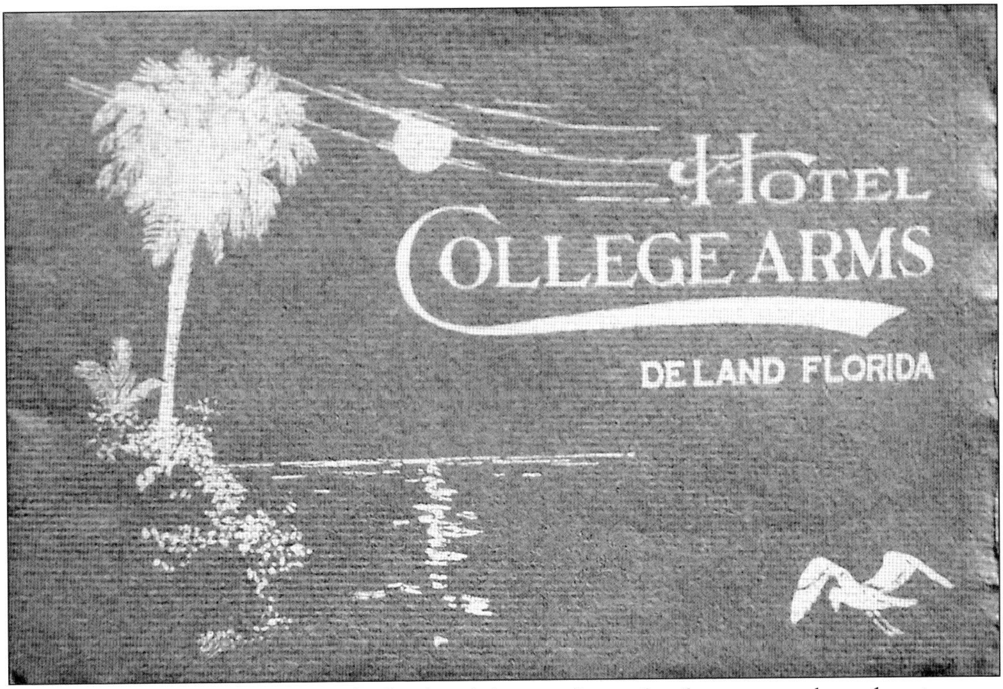

Booklets on the College Arms and other hotels became keepsakes for guests and an advertisement for the hotel. These hotel booklets were sometimes printed up seasonally and mailed out to regular guests each year. (Courtesy of Jim Cara.)

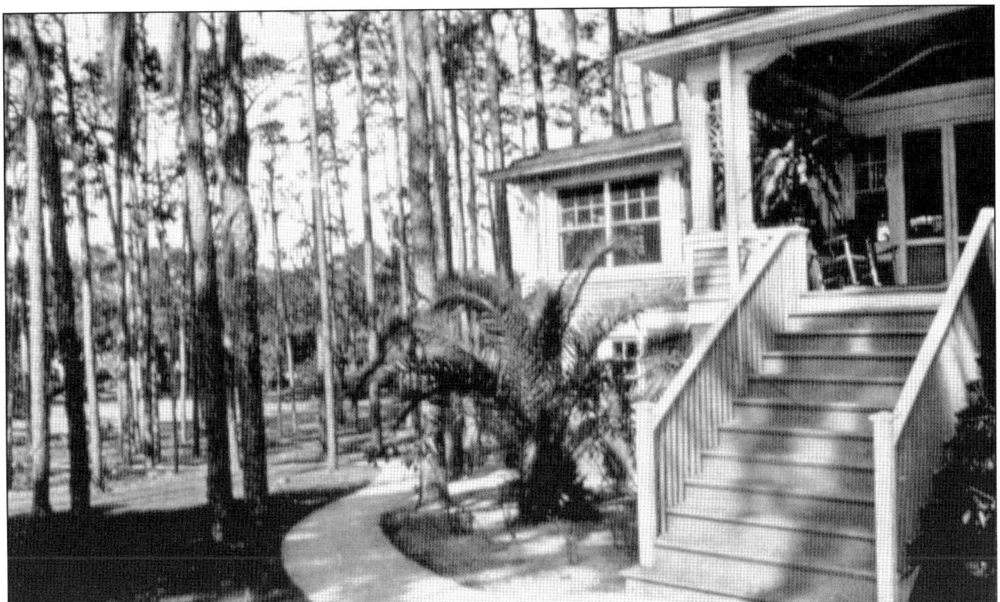

END OF PORCH, SHOWING GROVE OF TALL PINES

This picture shows the stairway onto the end of the long front porch with its trail that wound through the pines. The doors at the head of the stair lead inside to the enclosed porch. (Courtesy of the Bill Dreggors family.)

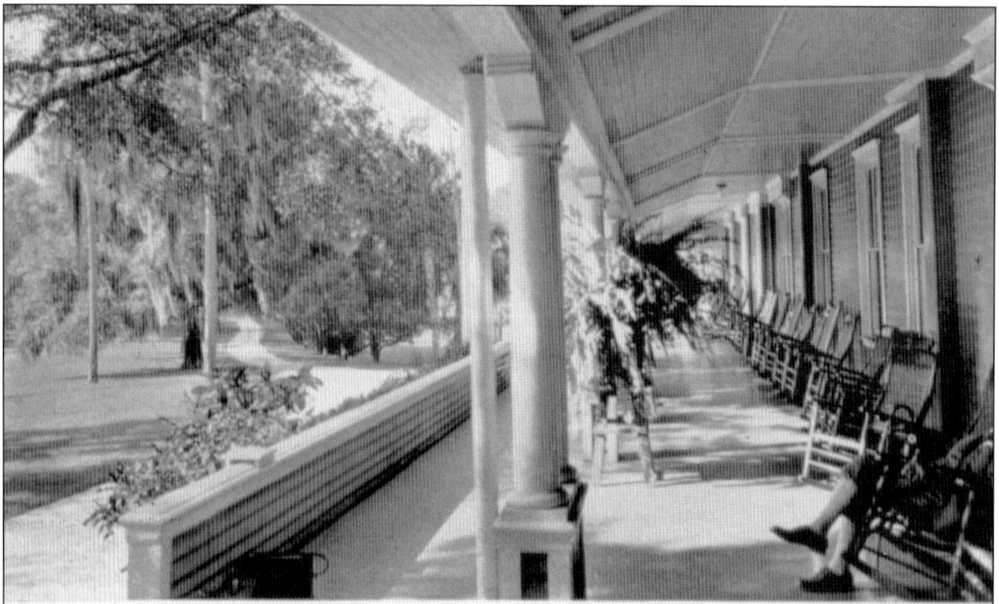

FRONT PORCH AND ENTRANCE PATH

The view in this 1930s photograph is from the far-right end of the front porch opposite the stairway and trail through the pines. The main central stairway into the hotel is directly in the foreground. (Courtesy of the Bill Dreggors family.)

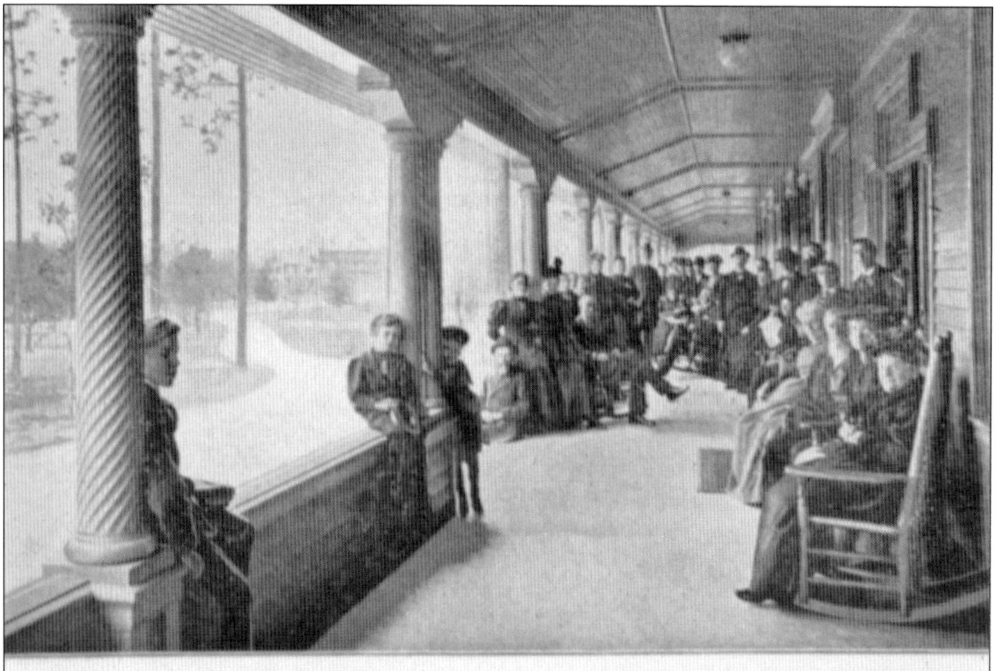

VERANDA OF THE HOTEL.

Another front porch view taken from just beyond the central stairway shows guests of the hotel. Just left of center is the winding entry road into the hotel seen in other images of the hotel. (Courtesy of the Bill Dreggors family.)

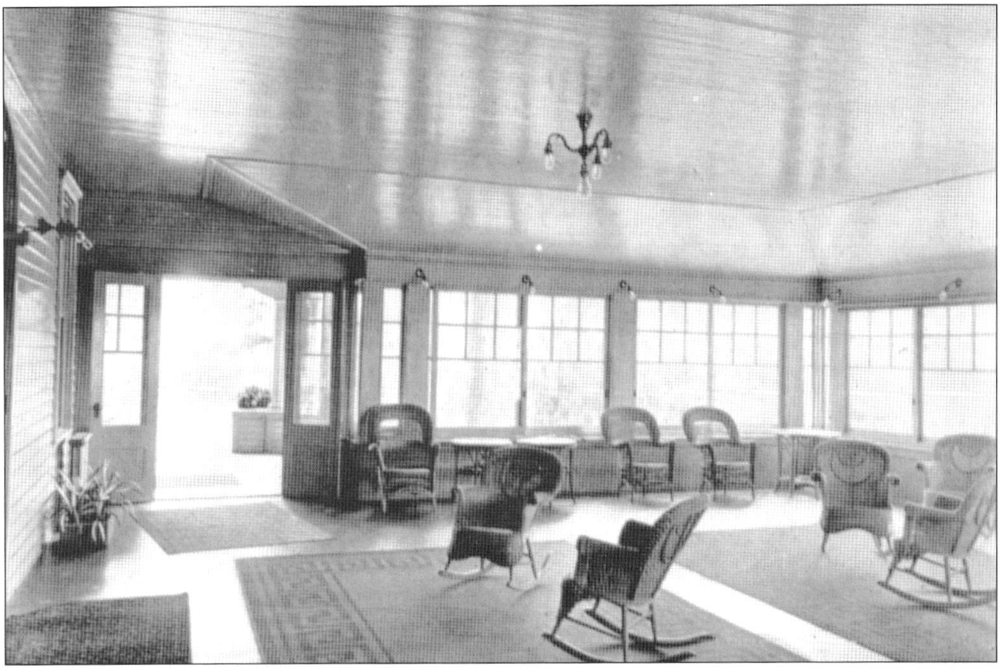

Venturing up the trail through the pines and climbing the stairway at the south end of the front porch, one would find this room. This was the screened in porch of the College Arms Hotel. (Courtesy of the Bill Dreggors family.)

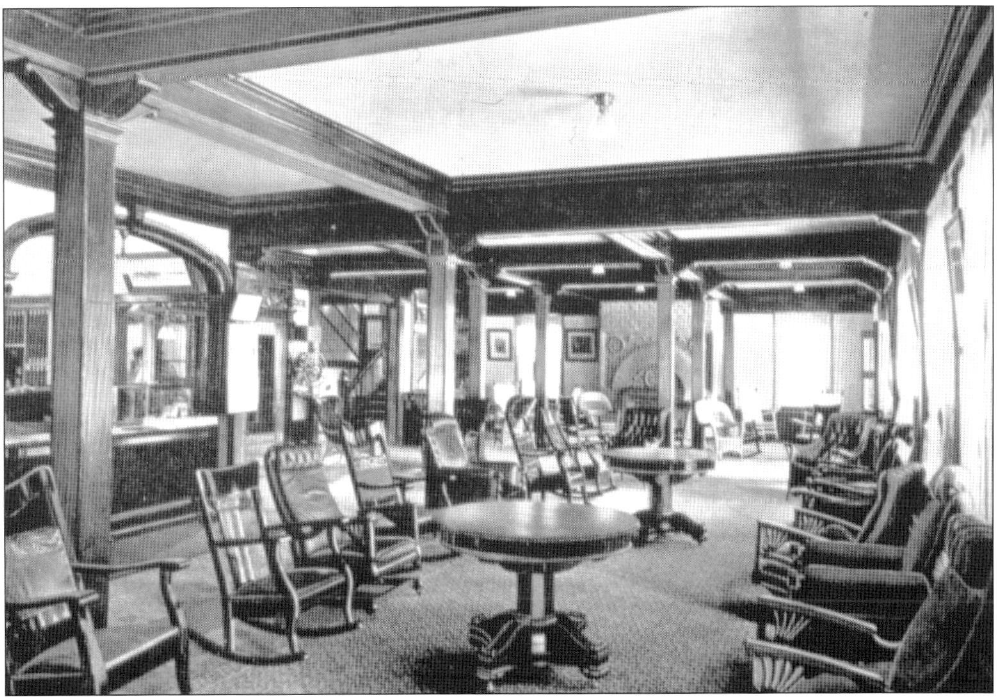

Rockers and easy chairs line this image of the interior lounge. To the left, part of the front desk counter can be seen, and across from it is a partial view of the stair and elevator. (Courtesy of the Bill Dreggors family.)

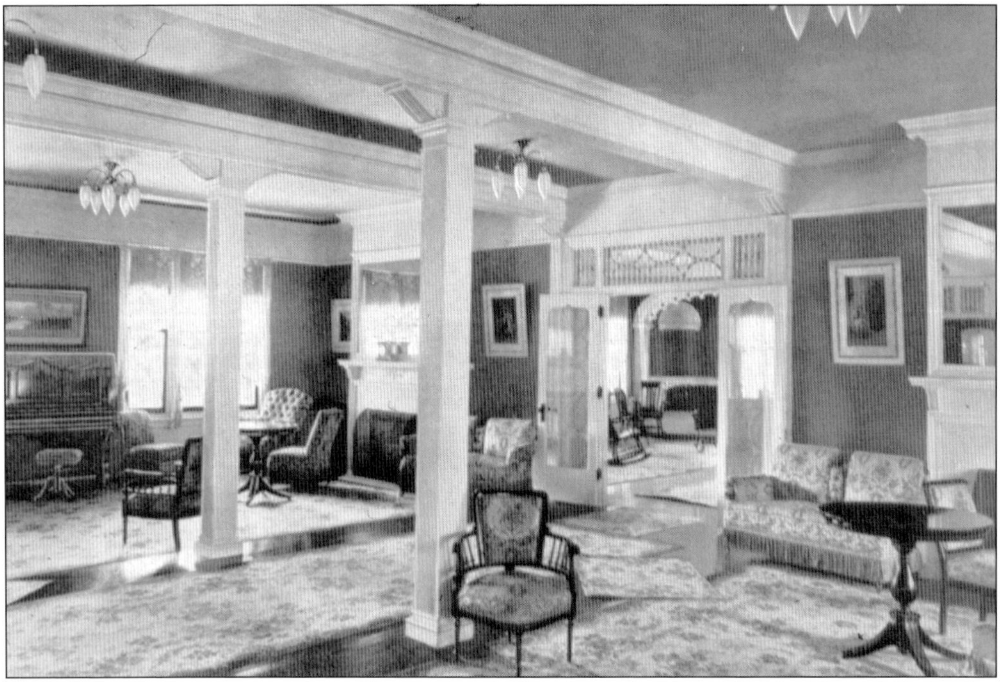

Spacious large rooms with lavish furnishings made up the public areas of the hotel. Stetson wanted to make sure that his visitors and guests were afforded all of the creature comforts available at the time. (Courtesy of the Bill Dreggors family.)

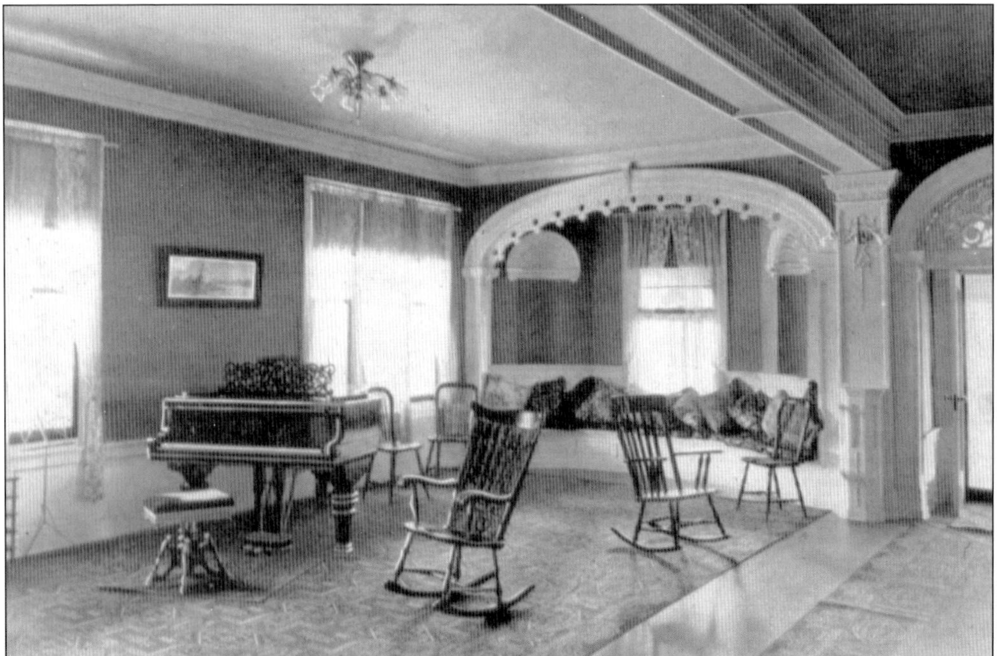

There was plenty of space for lounging and even entertainment, as evidenced by this view of a piano and sitting area. Rooms also had large windows to allow ample ambient lighting. (Courtesy of the Bill Dreggors family.)

The dining room was almost as massive in length as the front porch. Tables were fully furnished with tablecloths and tableware. (Courtesy of the Bill Dreggors family.)

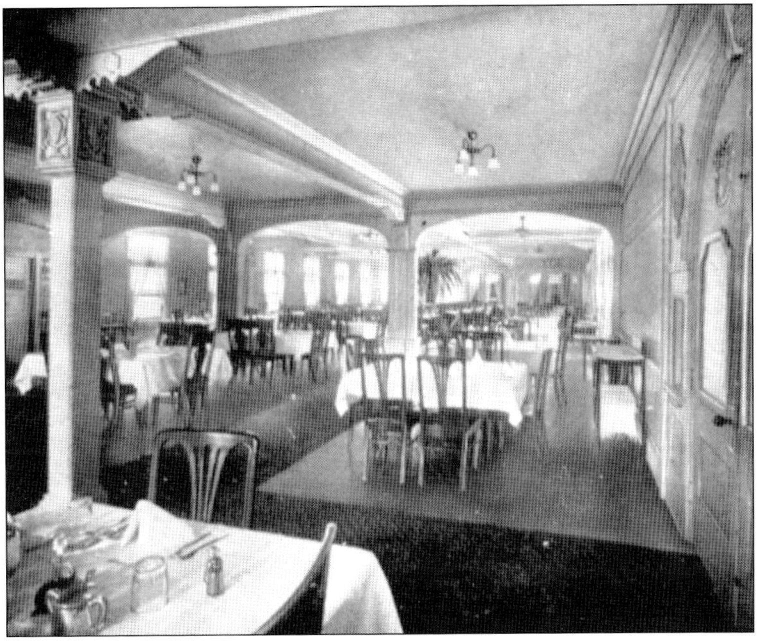

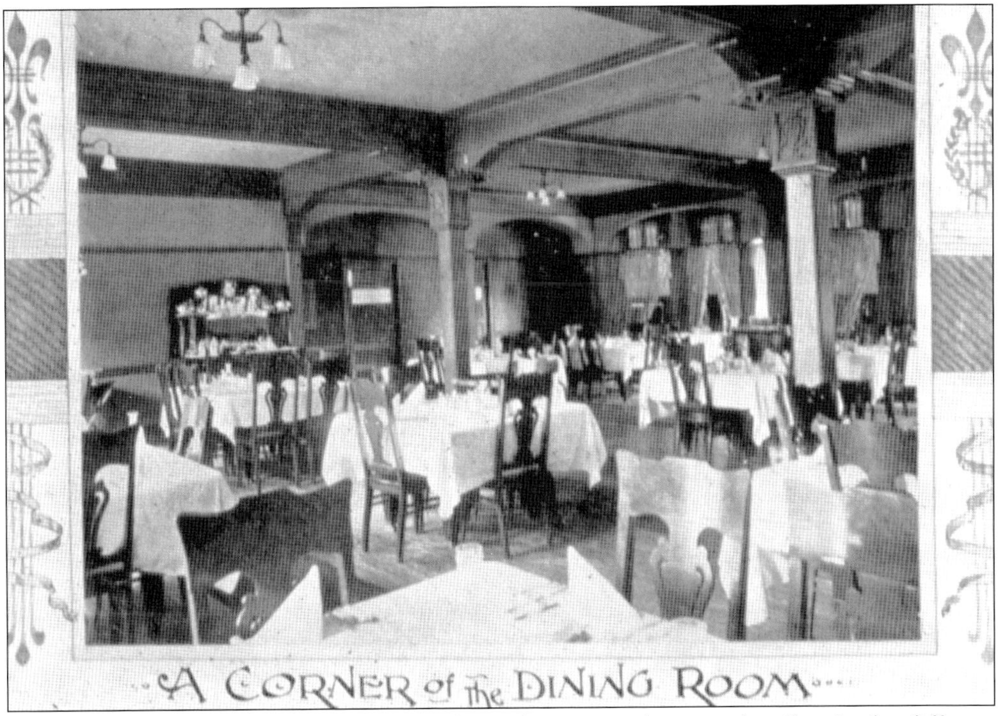

Rooms were designed with high ceilings and open breezeways for natural airflow. In this different angled view of the dining room, some of the serving bureaus and entries to the kitchen are visible to the left. (Courtesy of the Bill Dreggors family.)

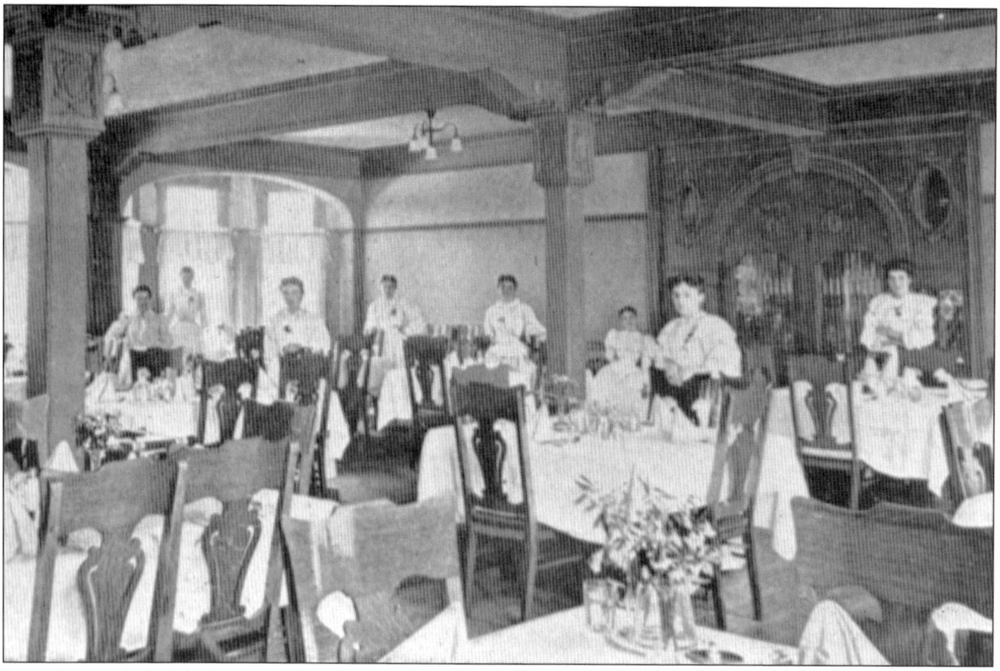

Members of the dining room staff await guests in this 1930s view of the College Arms Hotel dining room. Flower arrangements adorn some of the set tables in the picture. (Courtesy of the Bill Dreggors family.)

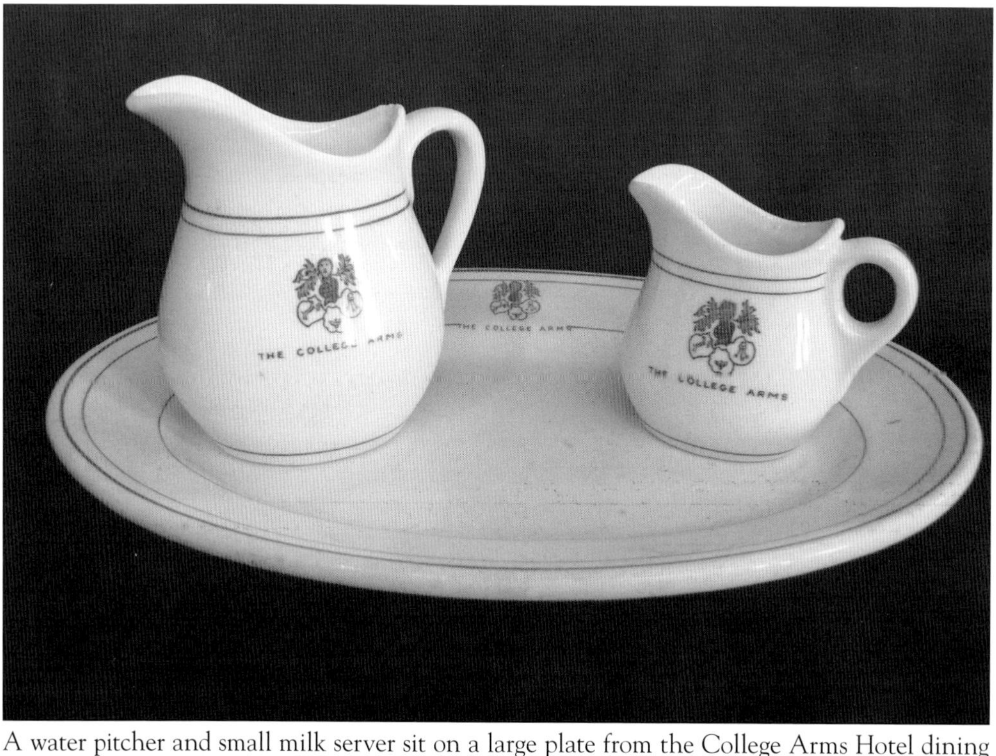

A water pitcher and small milk server sit on a large plate from the College Arms Hotel dining room. (Courtesy of Jim Cara.)

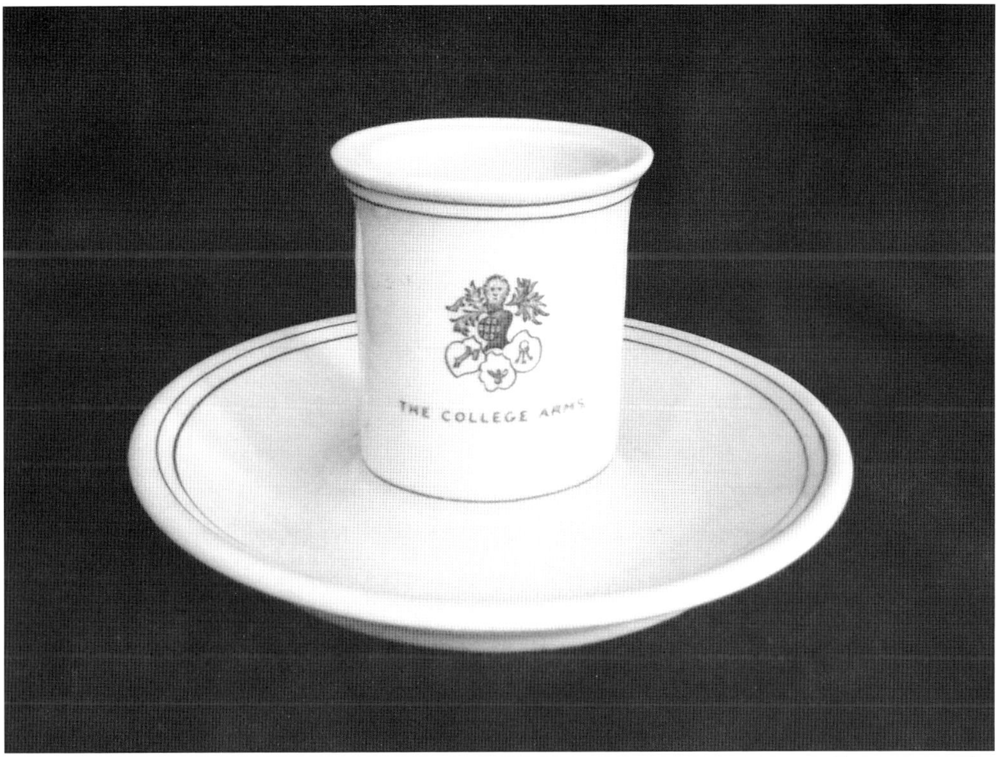

A small bowl and saucer from the College Arms Hotel dining room is pictured here. Note the distinctive coat-of-arms seal found on this plate ware. (Courtesy of Jim Cara.)

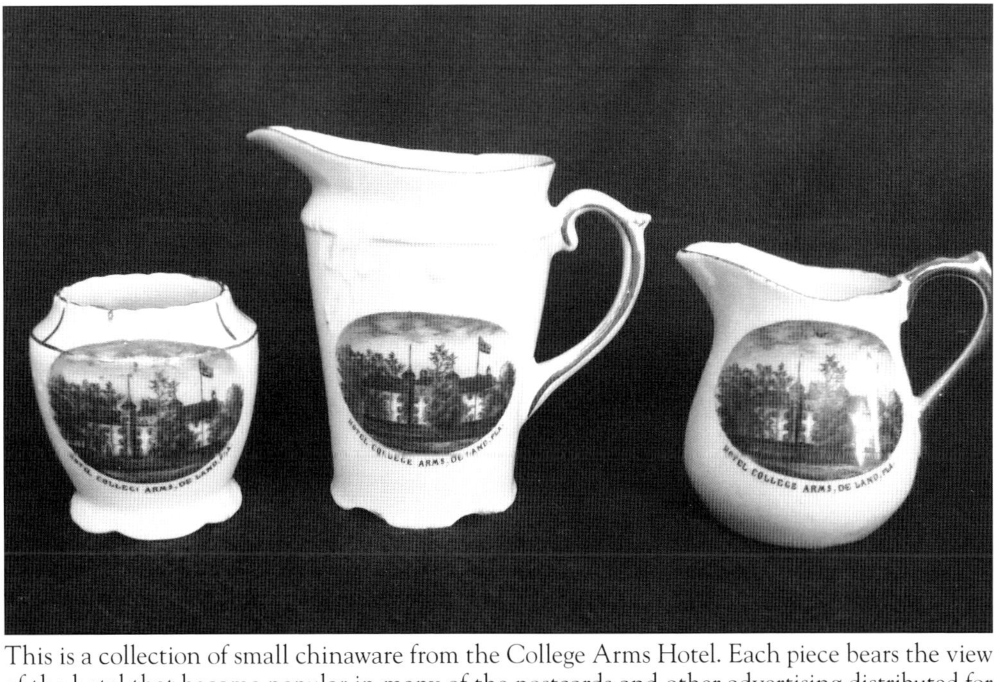

This is a collection of small chinaware from the College Arms Hotel. Each piece bears the view of the hotel that became popular in many of the postcards and other advertising distributed for the hotel. (Courtesy of Jim Cara.)

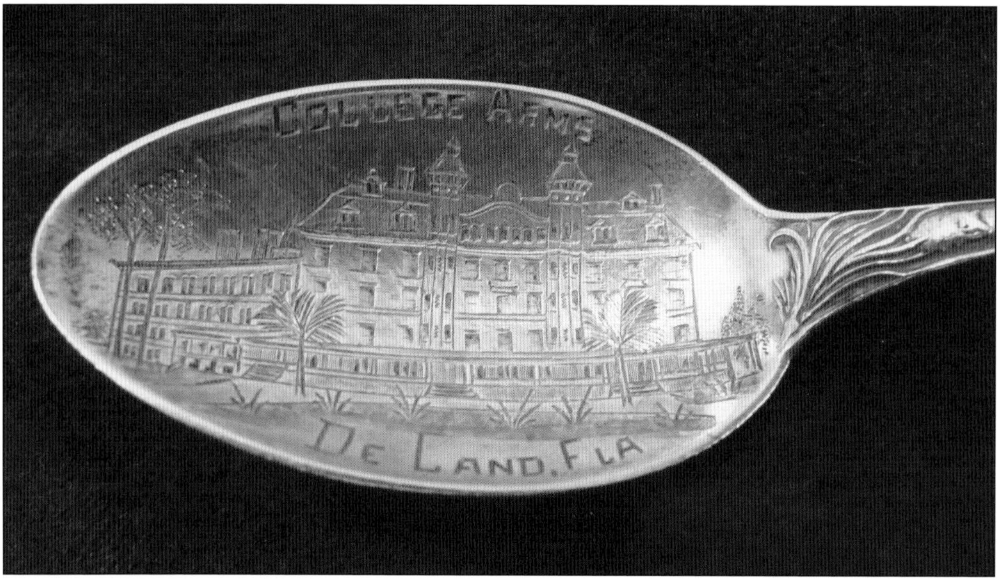

The College Arms Hotel also had ornately designed utensils like this engraved spoon. This kind of unique tableware was also used by other hotels of the time. (Courtesy of Jim Cara.)

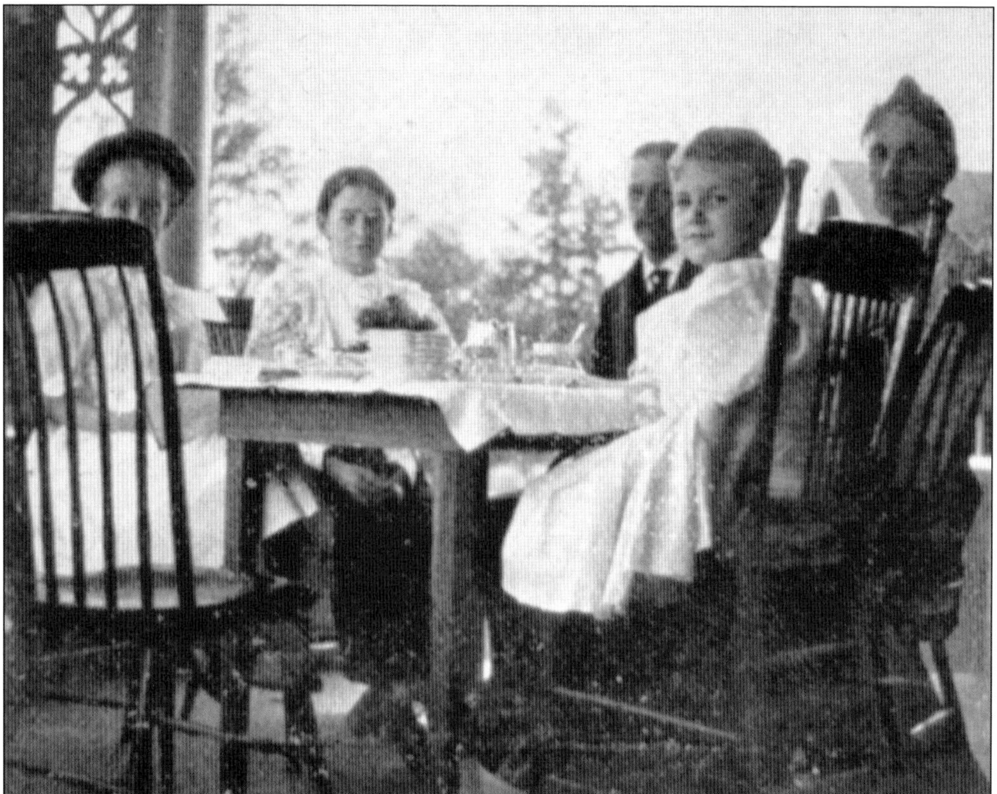

The dining room was not the only place at the College Arms Hotel where guests could take their meals. This family is dining on a balcony with what may be some of the same tableware previously pictured. (Courtesy of the Bill Dreggors family.)

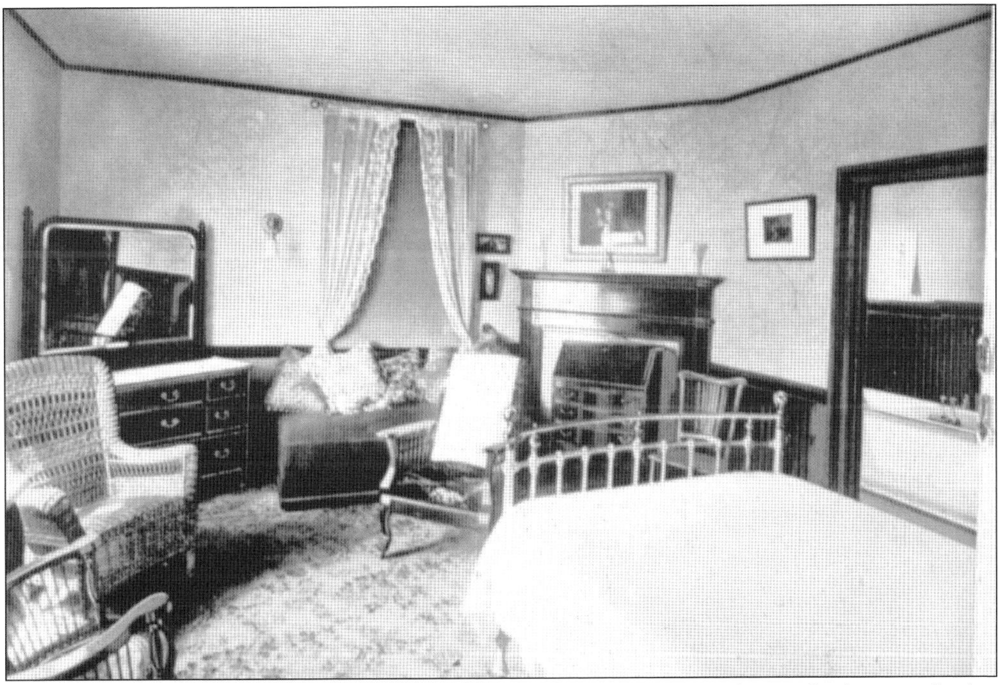

Most rooms at the College Arms Hotel came with a window view, and some had private baths. This corner room features cross ventilation from windows on two sides and came with heating and electric lighting. (Courtesy of the Bill Dreggors family.)

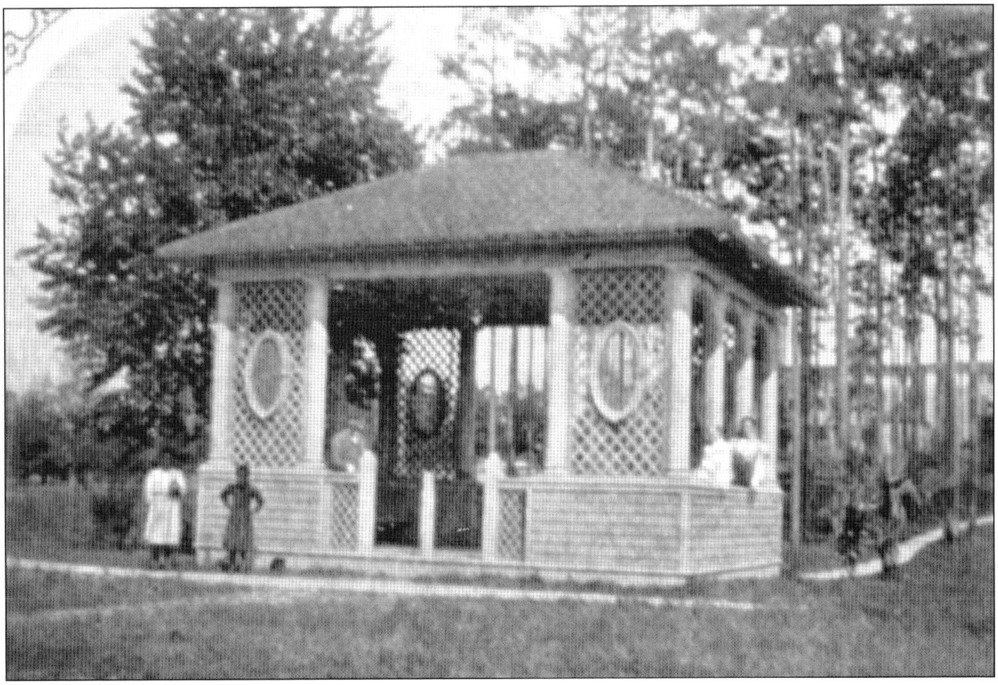

The grounds of the College Arms Hotel were even more massive than the hotel. This large gazebo stood just beyond the stand of pines, with the main hotel in the background. (Courtesy of the Bill Dreggors family.)

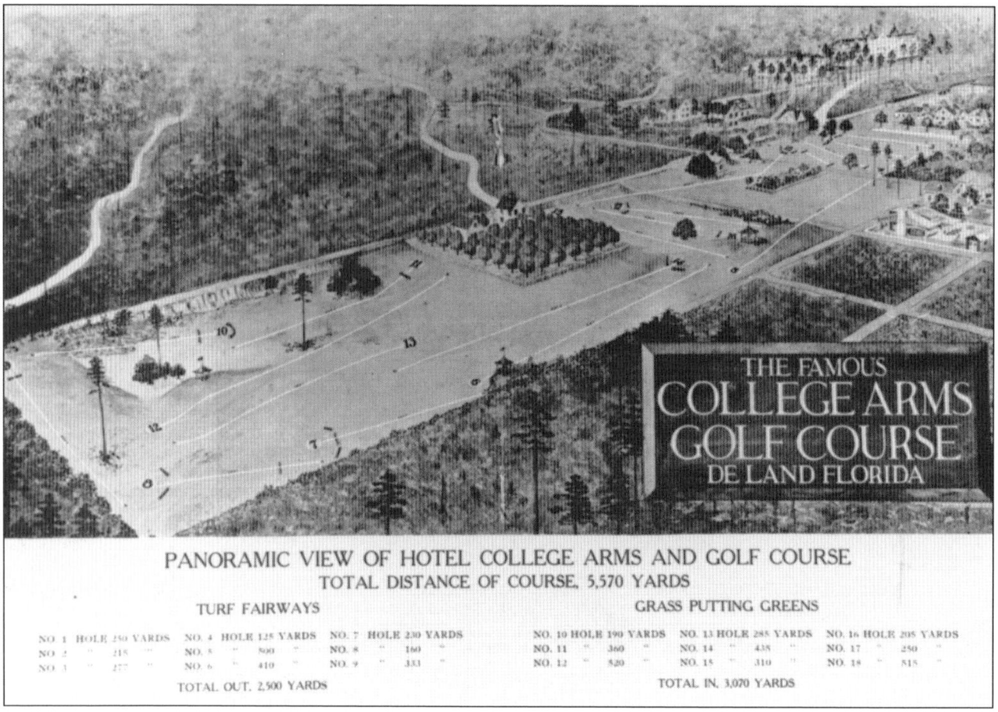

Another popular feature of the College Arms Hotel was its golf course. This map lays out the huge course with the hotel located in the upper right hand corner. (Courtesy of the Bill Dreggors family.)

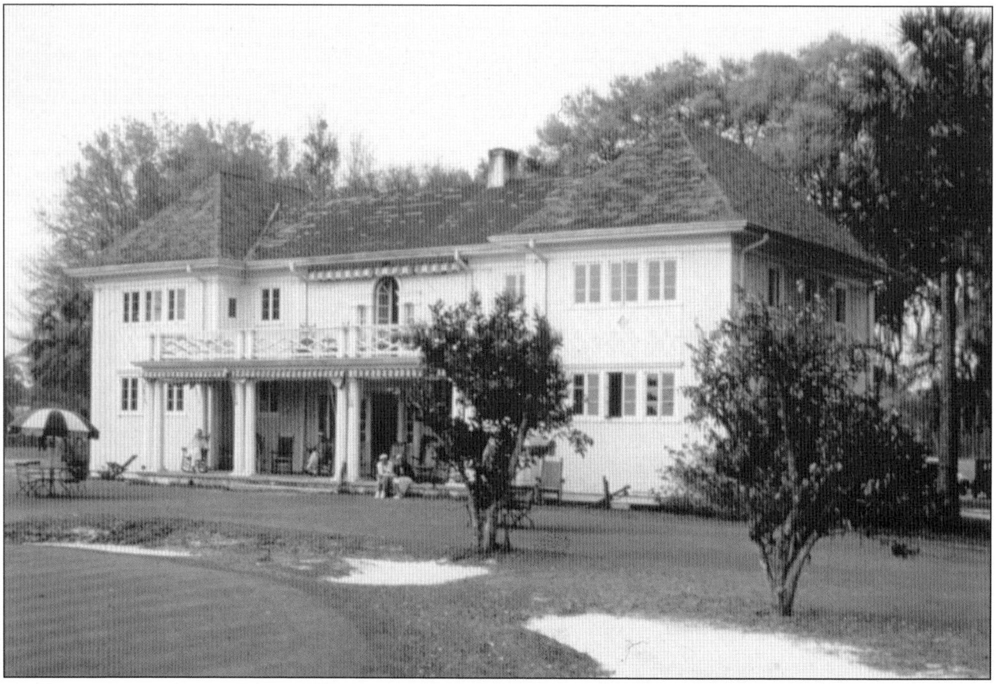

Golf was quite a draw at the College Arms Hotel. The course included a large clubhouse for the use of players and visitors of the College Arms Golf Club. (Courtesy of the Bill Dreggors family.)

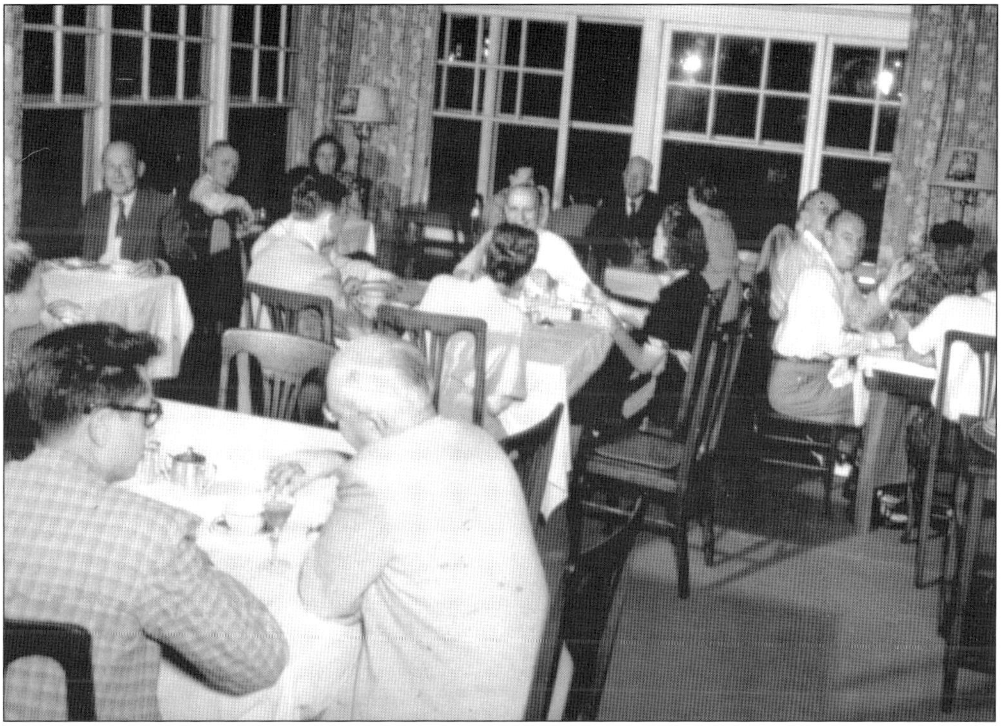

Visitors to the clubhouse could enjoy dining in the clubhouse restaurant. This image from the 1940s shows a number of people in attendance for an evening meal. (Courtesy of the Bill Dreggors family.)

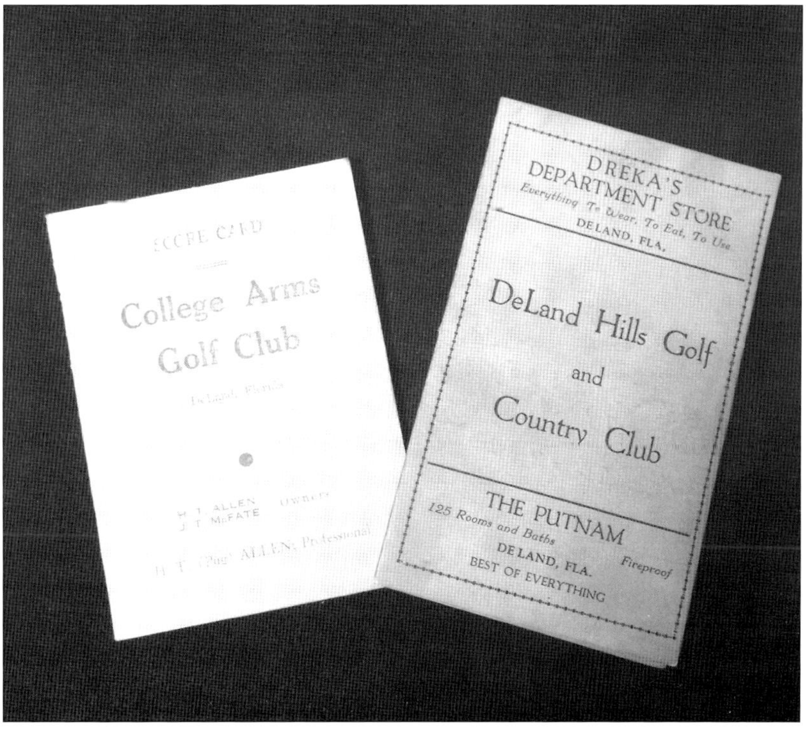

A pair of score cards from the College Arms Golf Club. Note the advertising on the card to the right for Dreka's (formerly the Carrollton Hotel) and the Putnam, two of DeLand's other hotels. (Courtesy of Jim Cara.)

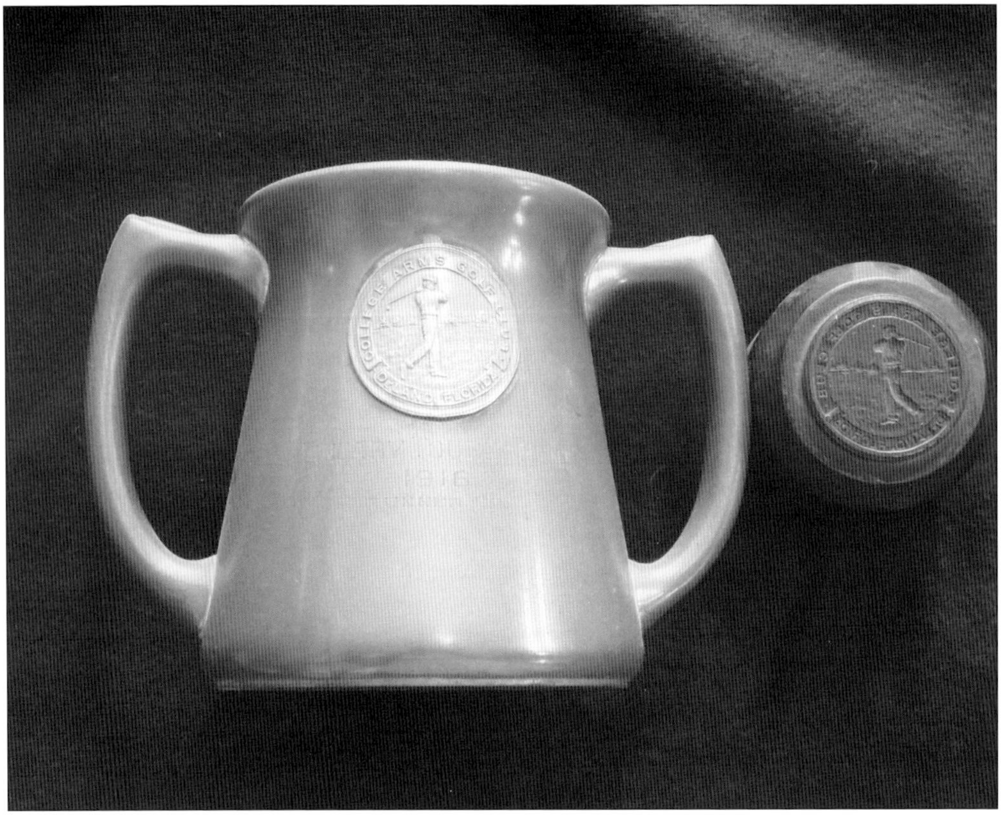

The College Arms Golf Club was also the host to a number of professional golf tournaments. This award trophy and stamp from 1916 attest to the popularity of golf at the hotel. (Courtesy of Jim Cara.)

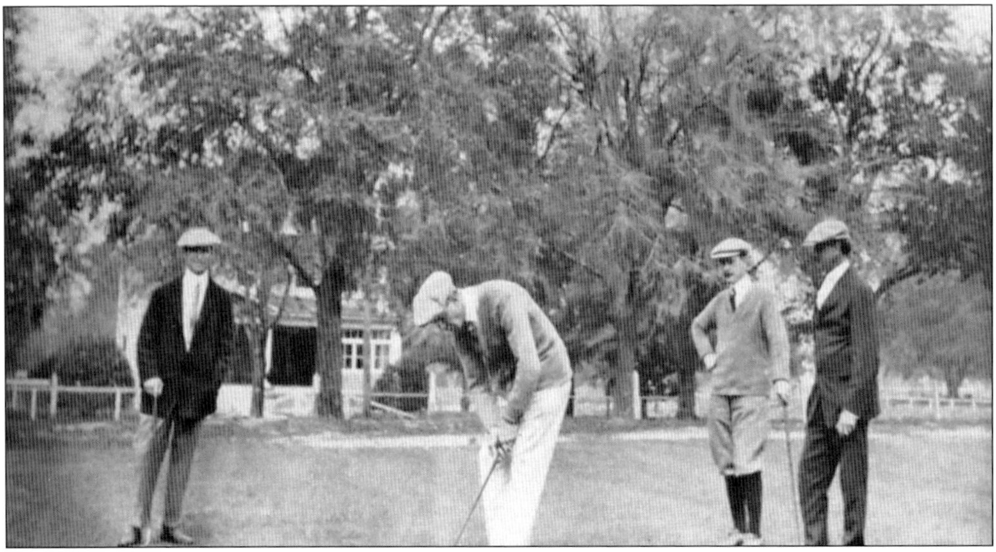

The College Arms Golf Club has its own separate history. In this 1900s photograph of a group of golfers, Jack Jolly, inventor of the liquid-core golf ball, stands second from the right. (Courtesy of Jim Cara.)

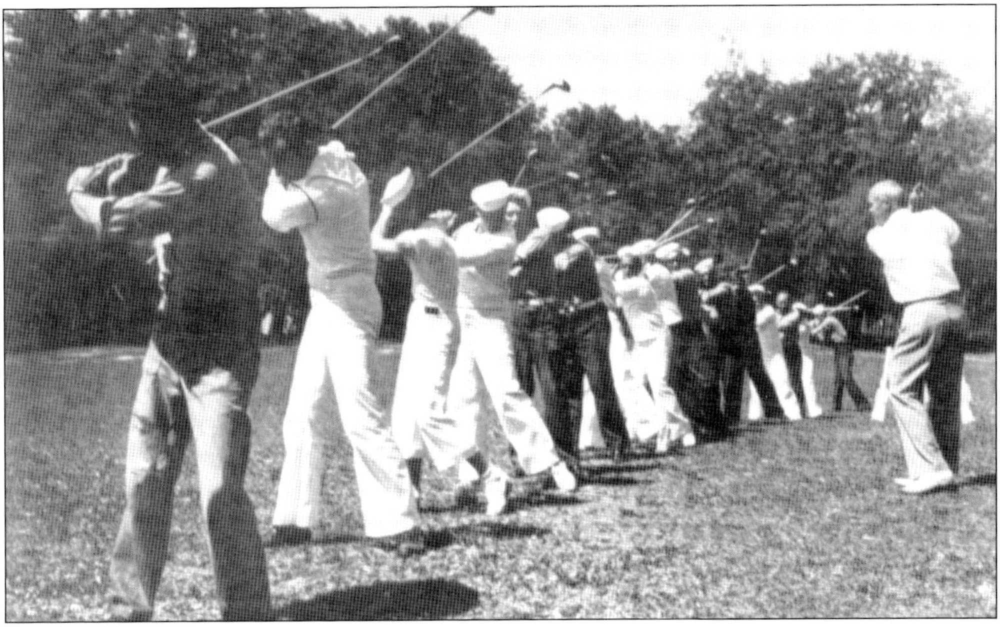

The hotel survived the war years and, for a time, was under lease to the US Navy and used as a rehabilitation center. Servicemen learning and playing golf were quite a common sight at the College Arms and around town during the 1940s. (Courtesy of the Bill Dreggors family.)

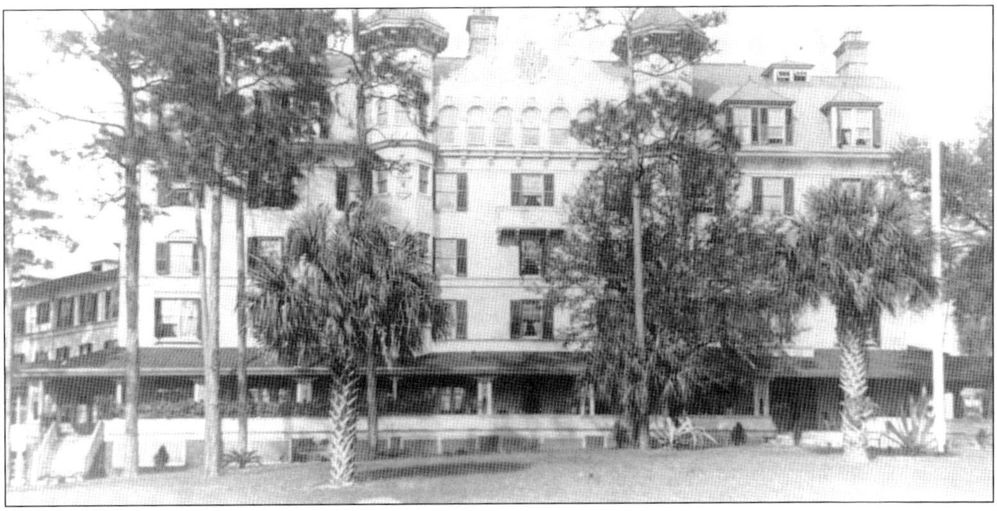

The College Arms Hotel never regained its former popularity following the war years. It declined, and the grand hotel that used to front along Amelia Avenue became disposable in the new economy. (Courtesy of Stetson University, duPont-Ball Library, Memorabilia Collection.)

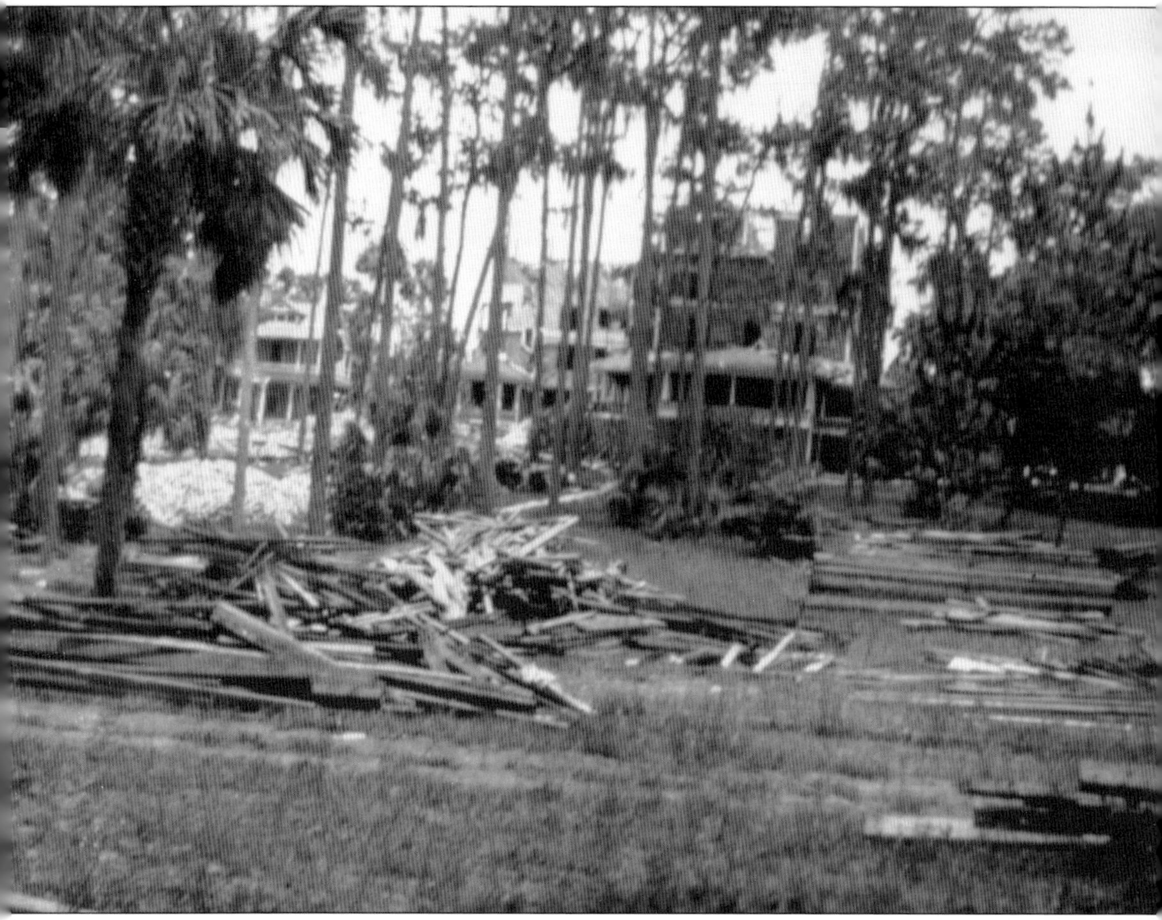

In the 1950s, the College Arms Hotel was torn down, and a hospital took its place for a number of years until DeLand's new courthouse replaced it. The only hint of the hotel's existence today is the College Arms Towers high-rise across the street where Stetson's railroad depot used to be. (Courtesy of the Bill Dreggors family.)

Four

DeLand

DeLand Hotel

The growing volume of tourists to Florida in the winter months brought about the building of the DeLand Hotel. In 1913, Edwin D. Barnhill and his wife, Jeanette, came to Florida and managed a hotel in Daytona Beach. Barnhill came up with the idea for a modest hotel in DeLand. He contracted architect Medwin Peek, who had designed a number of stylish homes in the University Terrace area of town near Stetson University, to draft plans for the hotel. DeLand contractor Andrew Bradshaw, who built the Athens Theater, then supervised the hotel's construction. In February 1927, the DeLand Hotel opened for business.

The DeLand Hotel had more than 40 rooms. Each room contained a bed, a sink, and closet. A bathroom was available for every two rooms, which for the time was considered a luxury. Most hotel accommodations had several guests sharing the same bath and toilet. Barnhill started the first bus line from DeLand to Daytona Beach. An open-air bus shuttle was provided to his guests for day trips to the beach. It was a great way to enjoy the Florida weather, but guests had to bring along umbrellas in case of rain.

Unfortunately, Jeanette died in 1928. Edwin continued the business but was declared insane a year later. The hotel later declined in use as the tourist trade shifted. The building began to deteriorate and became vacant for several years in the 1980s. Fortunately, in 1997, the hotel was purchased, and restoration began. Guest rooms were remodeled to include separate baths and suites. The hotel reopened as the DeLand Artisan Inn in 1999.

During the restoration process, some of the windows on the south side of the building had to be eliminated. The restorers of the hotel had each of these windows painted with a life-sized mural depicting winter visitors standing at their hotel windows. Artist Courtney Canova, who painted several of the murals in DeLand, depicted the people in each window clothed for the 1930s and 1940s during the hotel's popular years.

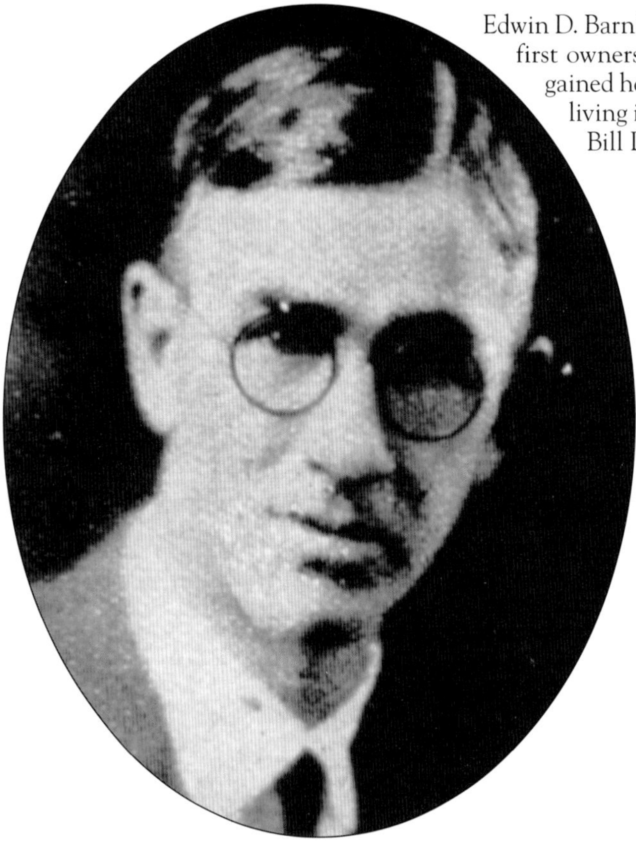

Edwin D. Barnhill and his wife, Jeanette, were the first owners of the DeLand Hotel. They had gained hotel management experience while living in Daytona Beach. (Courtesy of the Bill Dreggors family.)

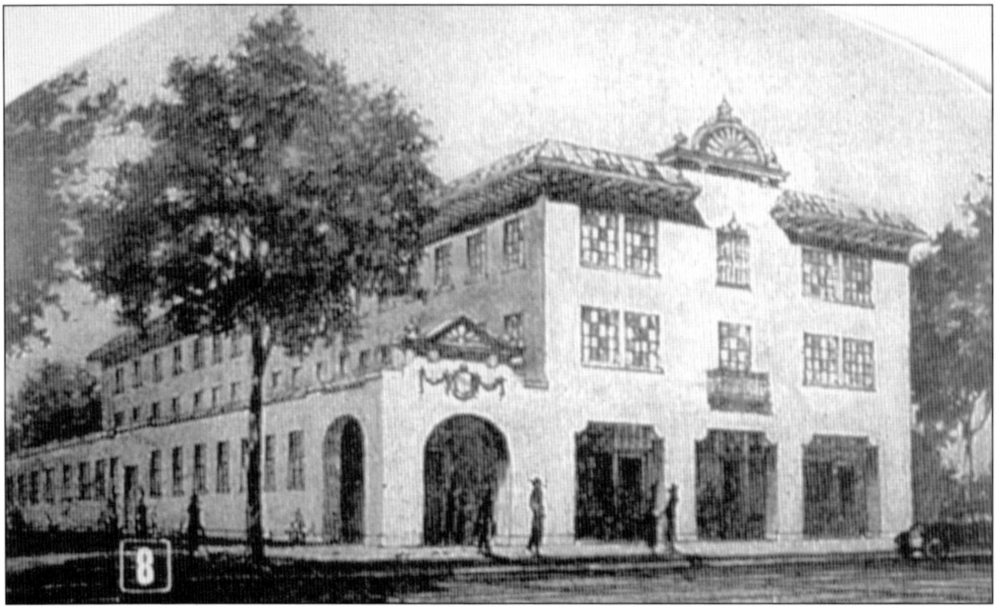

The DeLand Hotel was another of the fine architecturally designed new buildings built of concrete and masonry in DeLand. The hotel features some of the same style included in other structures in the downtown area crafted by architect Medwin Peek. (Courtesy of the Bill Dreggors family.)

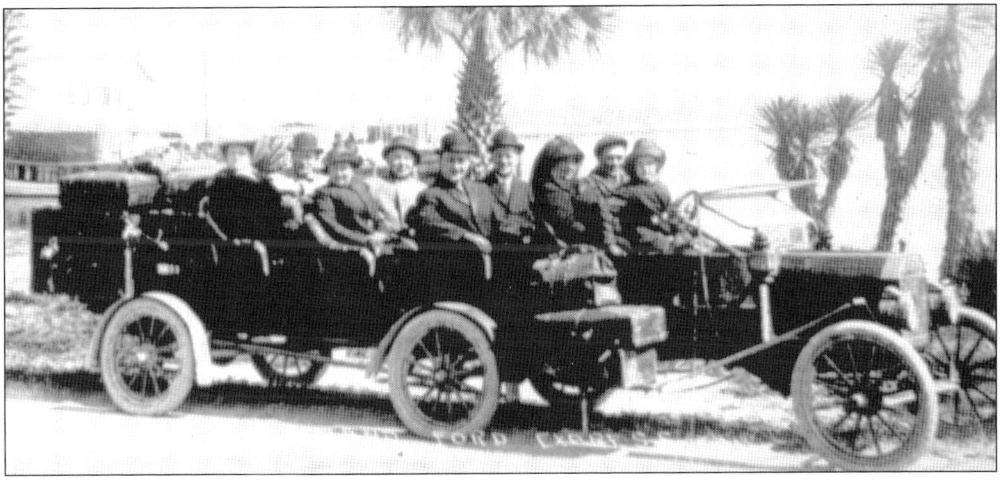

Like other hotel owners, the Barnhills provided their guests with transportation for excursions. Note the unusual design of this vehicle similar to some stretch vehicles of today. (Courtesy of the Bill Dreggors family.)

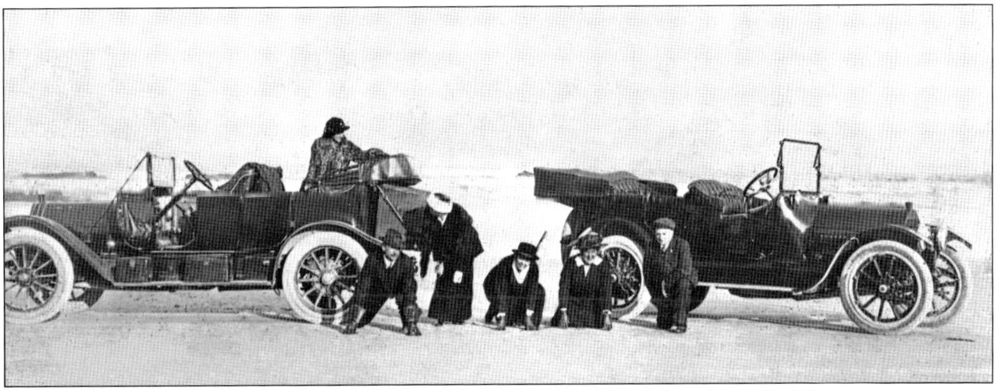

Visitors to Florida liked to see the sites while spending time at local hotels. The transportation furnished to guests of the DeLand Hotel would take them on day trips to the beach. (Courtesy of State Archives of Florida, Florida Memory.)

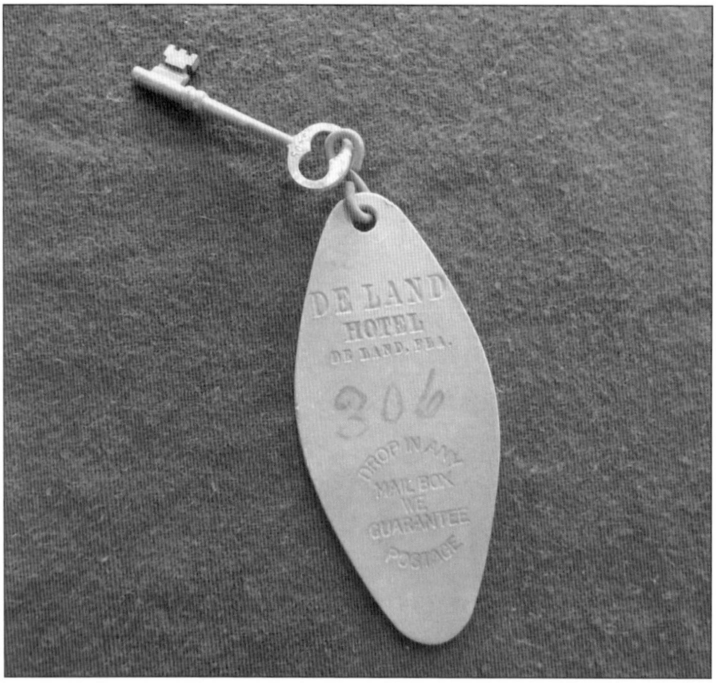

This room key is a relic of the early years of the DeLand Hotel. Mary Stewart Howarth-Hewitt owned and operated the hotel after the Barnhills in the 1930s. (Courtesy of Jim Cara.)

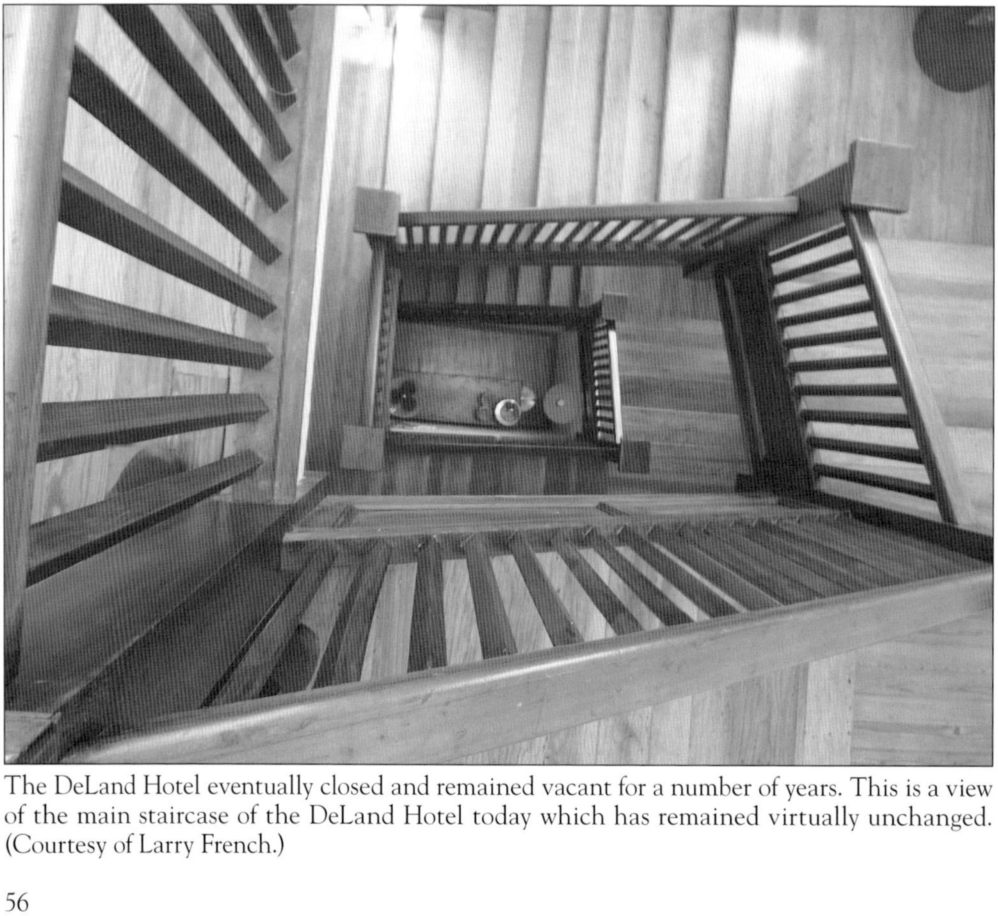

The DeLand Hotel eventually closed and remained vacant for a number of years. This is a view of the main staircase of the DeLand Hotel today which has remained virtually unchanged. (Courtesy of Larry French.)

The hotel was purchased by two brothers from Pennsylvania, John and Brett Soety, in 1999. They completely renovated the hotel, adding necessary upgrades like the emergency stairway lighting, seen here near the sprinkler system. (Courtesy of Larry French.)

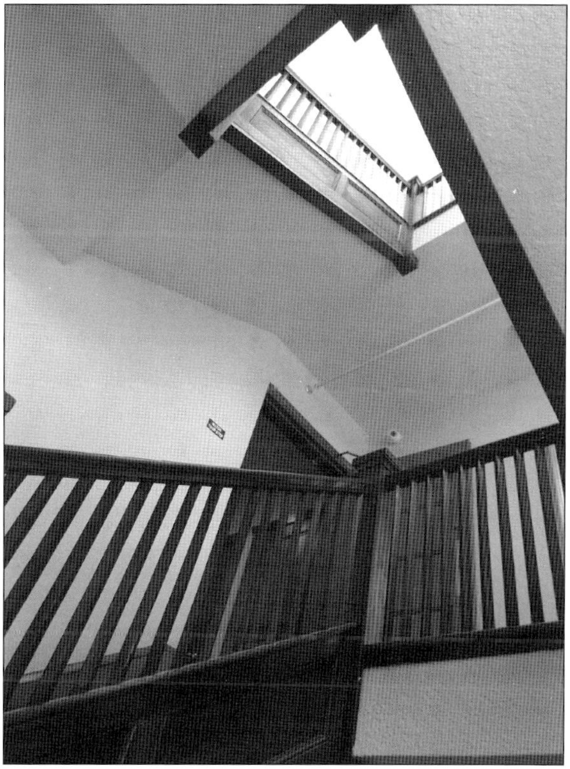

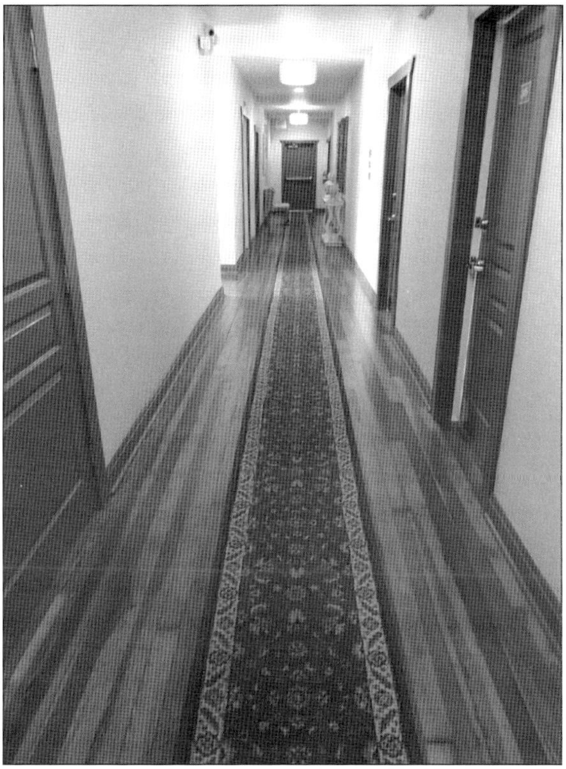

The DeLand Hotel was reopened in 1999 as the DeLand Artisan Inn. The Patel sisters Sara and Hina later bought the hotel, renamed it the Artisan Downtown, and have maintained its original décor. (Courtesy of Larry French.)

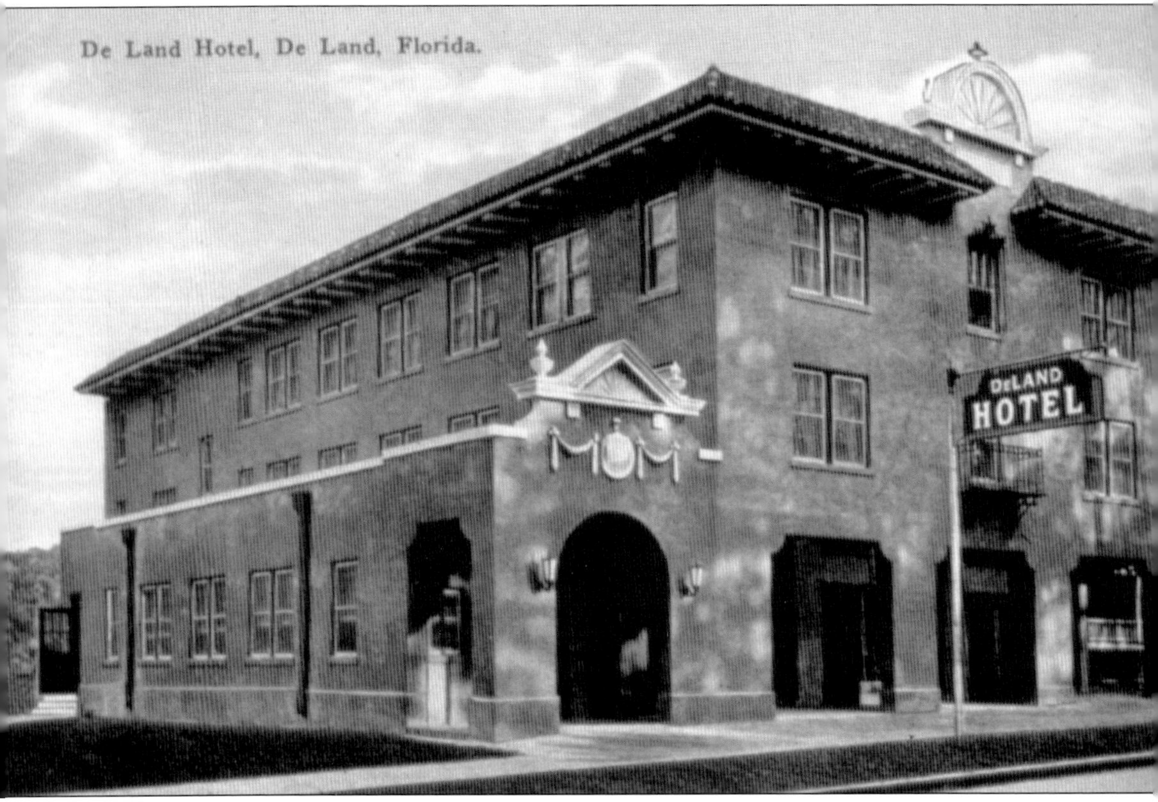

The Artisan Downtown continues as a hotel today. The hotel is presently undergoing another renovation to change back a large space used as a banquet room into additional guest rooms. (Courtesy of the Bill Dreggors family.)

Five

DeLand

Putnam Hotel

In 1885, the Grove House Hotel was built. It was a three-story wooden structure with 85 rooms surrounded by an orange grove. Arthur Putnam bought the hotel and renamed it Putnam House and added improvements. Putnam in 1888, sold the hotel to Gardener D. Gould who then renamed it the Putnam Inn. Gould later sold the Putnam Inn to B.E. Brown. An explosion in the basement burned down the hotel in 1921. The new Hotel Putnam was designed by architect William J. Carpenter, who specialized in fireproof buildings, Carpenter used reinforced poured concrete, and the rebuild was completed in 1923.

The new hotel was six stories high, with towers and 128 guest rooms. Business was good until the Great Depression. There was an upsurge in activity during the war years with the presence of the US Navy. Following the war, more guests returned and the hotel was a venue for all kinds of community occasions such as, weddings, graduation celebrations, and parties. The Red Sox baseball team even spent time there. But the surge in business was a short-lived. Florida visitors no longer used steamboats and trains to bring them to town. Instead, they drove themselves elsewhere.

Hotel Putnam's ownership changed over the decades, as did the building itself. The lounge became a bar. The number of guest hotel rooms were reduced to 26 to provide apartments. By the 1970s, there were 46 apartments equipped with kitchen, living room, separate bedroom and a bathroom. The building was in disrepair and becoming an eyesore. Police also were responding frequently to illegal activity at the hotel. In 2011, the site was closed, the tenants evicted, and the property was put up for sale. Over six years, two separate developers bought the hotel and found the cost of restoration too costly.

On June 6, 2017, the DeLand City Commission accepted an offer from Sarasota historic developer Tony Collins to purchase Hotel Putnam with the aid of $500,000 of city funding and tax exemptions. Collins will work under an agreement with the city over the next five years to restore the Hotel Putnam.

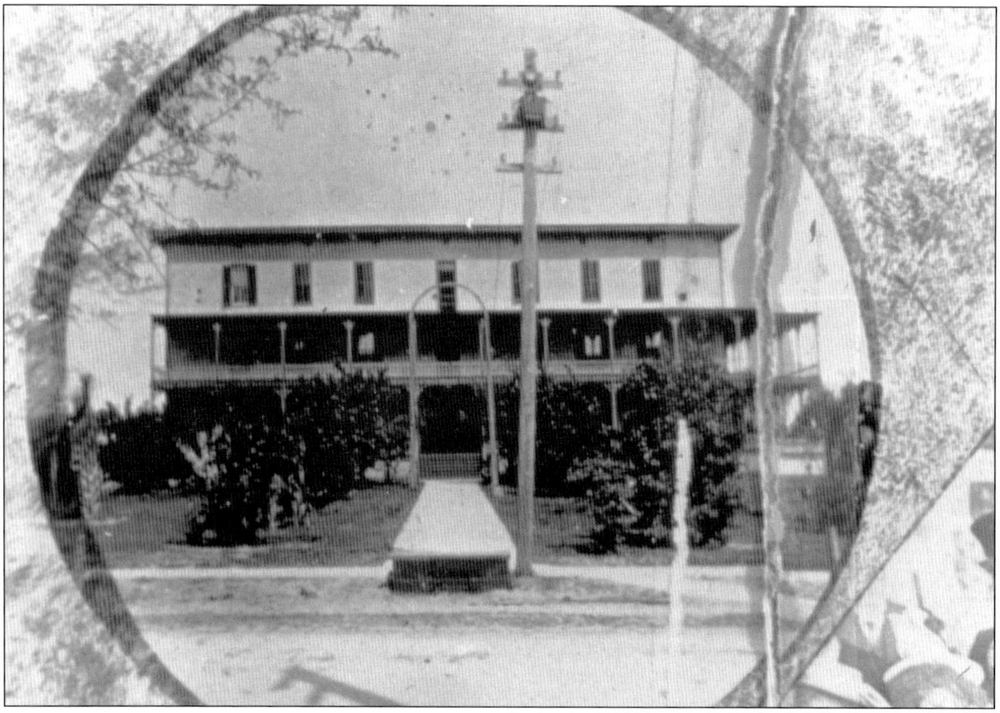

Built in 1885 as the Grove House Hotel, this hotel was three stories high and had 85 rooms. The hotel was sold to Alfred Putnam in the 1880s, and he renamed it the Putnam House. (Courtesy of the Bill Dreggors family.)

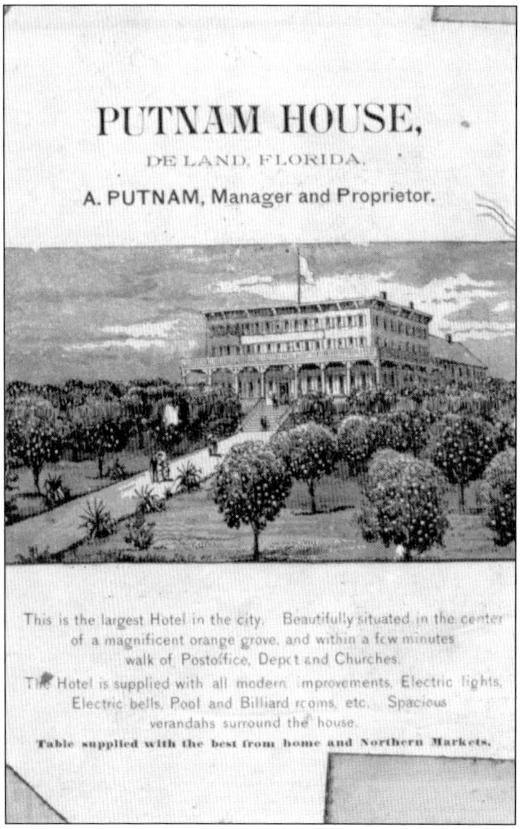

At first, Putnam House was the largest hotel in DeLand and boasted a number of modern features as seen in this handbill from the 1880s. Putnam House was originally an all-wood structure surrounded by a large orange grove. (Courtesy of the Bill Dreggors family.)

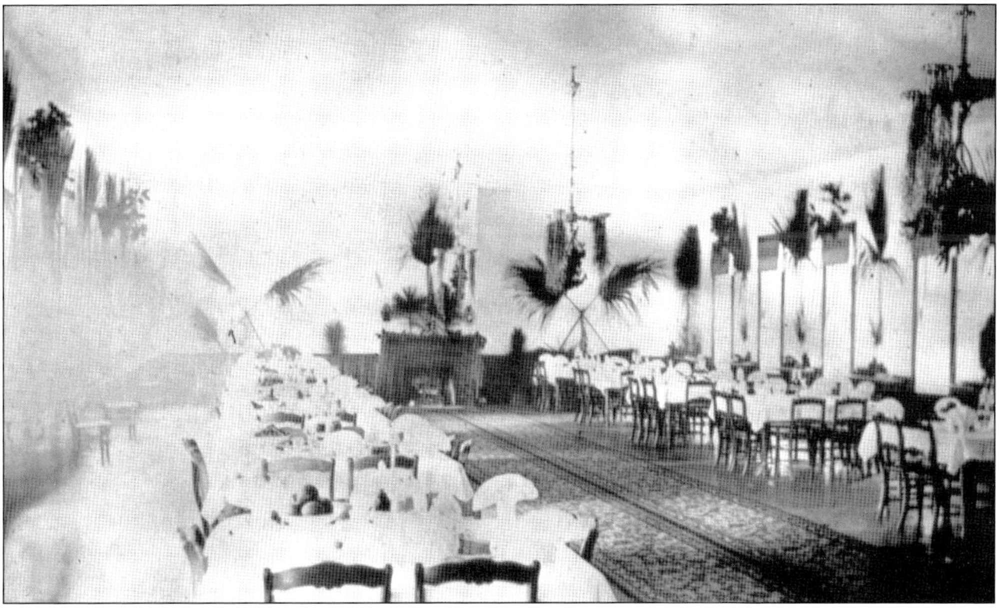

This view of the expansive dining room of the Putnam House from 1885 gives an impression of the size of the hotel. Note the use of native foliage in the form of palm fronds for wall decorations. (Courtesy of the Bill Dreggors family.)

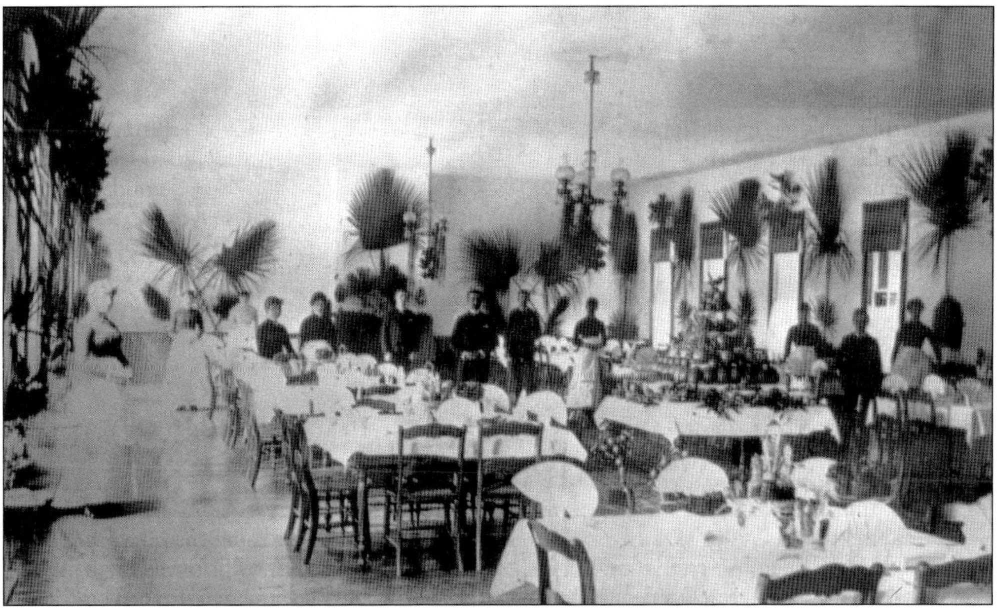

Here is another view of the hotel dining room filled with serving staff. Off to the right, a large pyramid shaped display of various fruits can be seen. (Courtesy of the Bill Dreggors family.)

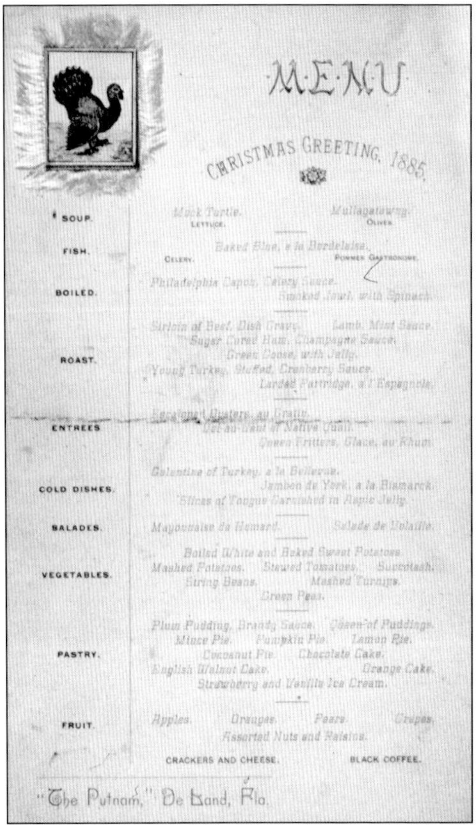

M·E·N·U

CHRISTMAS GREETING, 1885.

SOUP.	Mock Turtle. Mullagatawny. LETTUCE. OLIVES.
FISH.	Baked Blue, a la Bordelaise. CELERY. POMMES GASTRONOME.
BOILED.	Philadelphia Capon, Celery Sauce. Smoked Jowl, with Spinach.
ROAST.	Sirloin of Beef, Dish Gravy. Lamb, Mint Sauce. Sugar Cured Ham, Champagne Sauce. Green Goose, with Jelly. Young Turkey, Stuffed, Cranberry Sauce. Larded Partridge, a l'Espagnole.
ENTREES	Escaloped Oysters, au Gratin. Vol-au-Vent of Native Quail. Queen Fritters, Glace, au Rhum.
COLD DISHES.	Galantine of Turkey, a la Bellevue. Jambon de York, a la Bismarck. Slices of Tongue Garnished in Aspic Jelly.
SALADES.	Mayonnaise de Homard. Salade de Volaille.
VEGETABLES.	Boiled White and Baked Sweet Potatoes. Mashed Potatoes. Stewed Tomatoes. Succotash. String Beans. Mashed Turnips. Green Peas.
PASTRY.	Plum Pudding, Brandy Sauce. Queen of Puddings. Mince Pie. Pumpkin Pie. Lemon Pie. Cocoanut Pie. Chocolate Cake. English Walnut Cake. Orange Cake. Strawberry and Vanilla Ice Cream.
FRUIT.	Apples. Oranges. Pears. Grapes. Assorted Nuts and Raisins.
	CRACKERS AND CHEESE. BLACK COFFEE.

"The Putnam," De Land, Fla.

Guests had a wide selection of dinner choices to select from while staying at the Putnam House. Here is the dinner menu from around Christmas in 1885. (Courtesy of the Bill Dreggors family.)

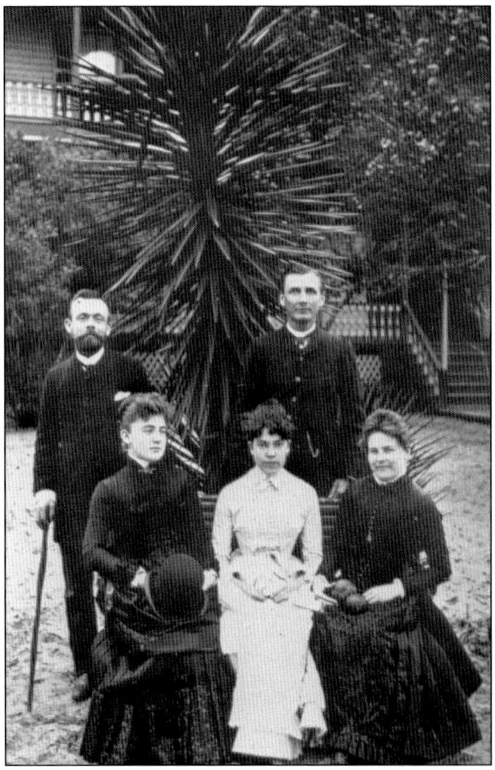

The grounds around the Putnam House lent themselves well to picture taking. In this 1885 photograph, three ladies sit while the gentleman stand behind them framing a large yucca plant. (Courtesy of the Bill Dreggors family.)

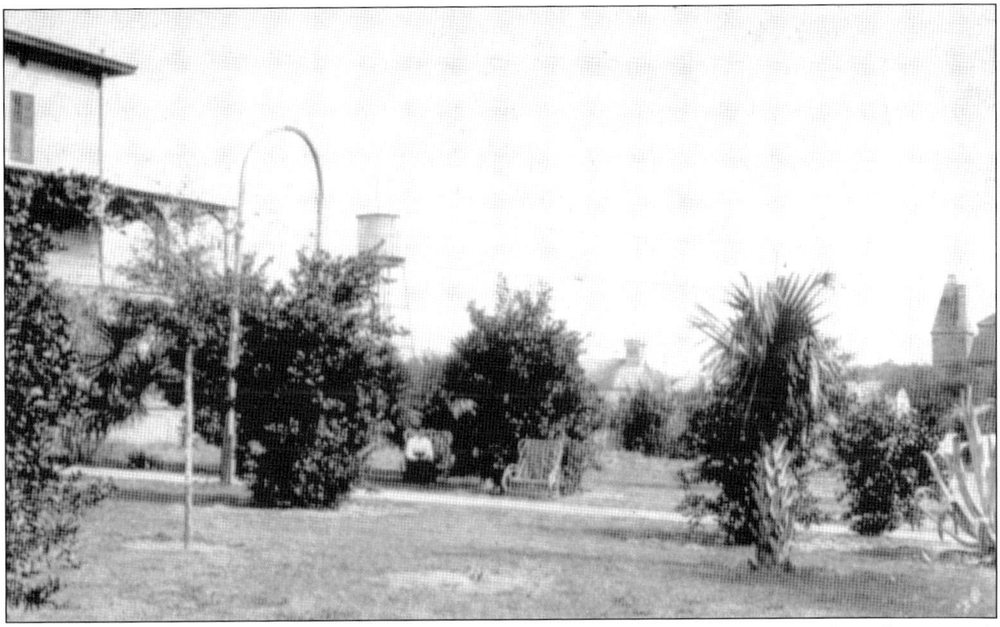

This closer view of the orange grove surrounding the Putnam Inn gives an idea of its size. A woman seated near the base of one of the fruit trees (center) in this picture gives a comparative scale. (Courtesy of the Bill Dreggors family.)

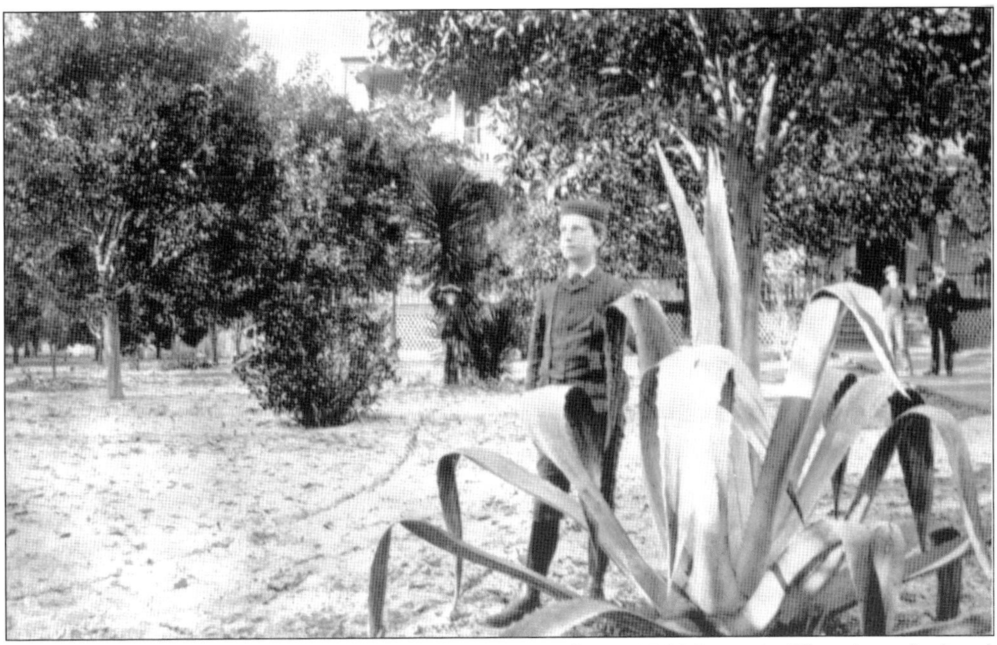

A picture of the grounds in front of the Putnam House from 1885. Here, a bell hop from the hotel poses next to a large cycad plant. (Courtesy of the Bill Dreggors family.)

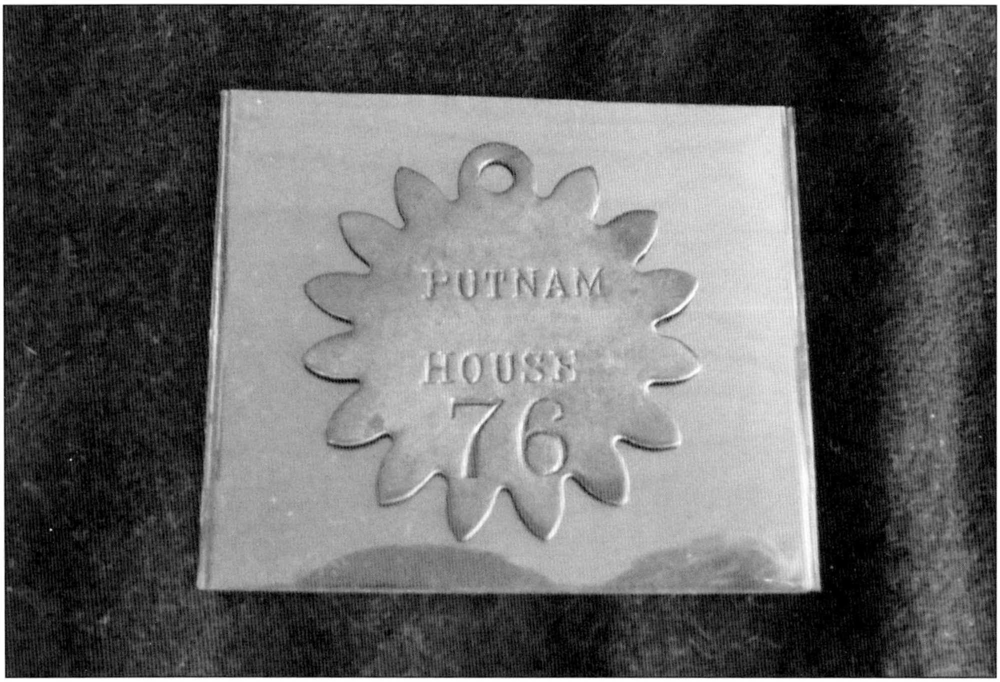

Part of a room key from the Putnam House. In 1889, Alfred Putnam sold the hotel to Gardner Gould, who renamed it the Putnam Inn and managed it with his family until 1896. (Courtesy of Jim Cara.)

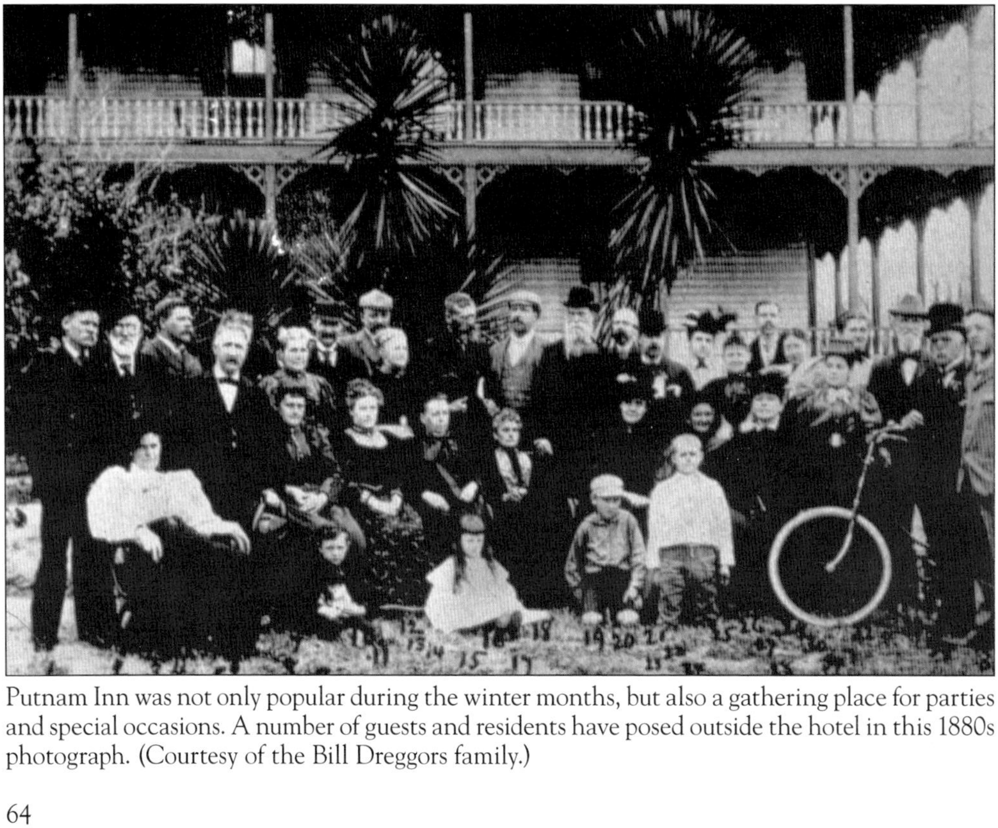

Putnam Inn was not only popular during the winter months, but also a gathering place for parties and special occasions. A number of guests and residents have posed outside the hotel in this 1880s photograph. (Courtesy of the Bill Dreggors family.)

Putnam Inn was also a source for long-term lodging. One notable resident of the hotel was Bert Fish, former ambassador to Egypt and namesake of the hospital that replaced the College Arms Hotel. (Courtesy of Stetson University, duPont-Ball Library, Memorabilia Collection.)

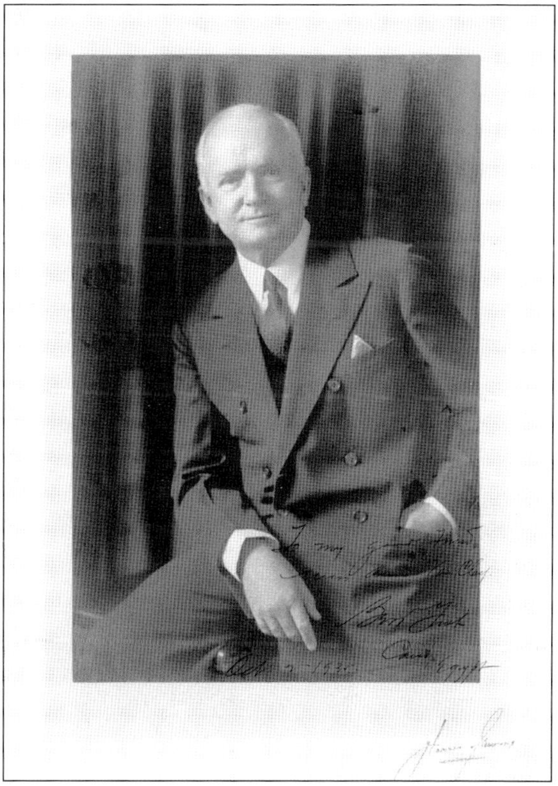

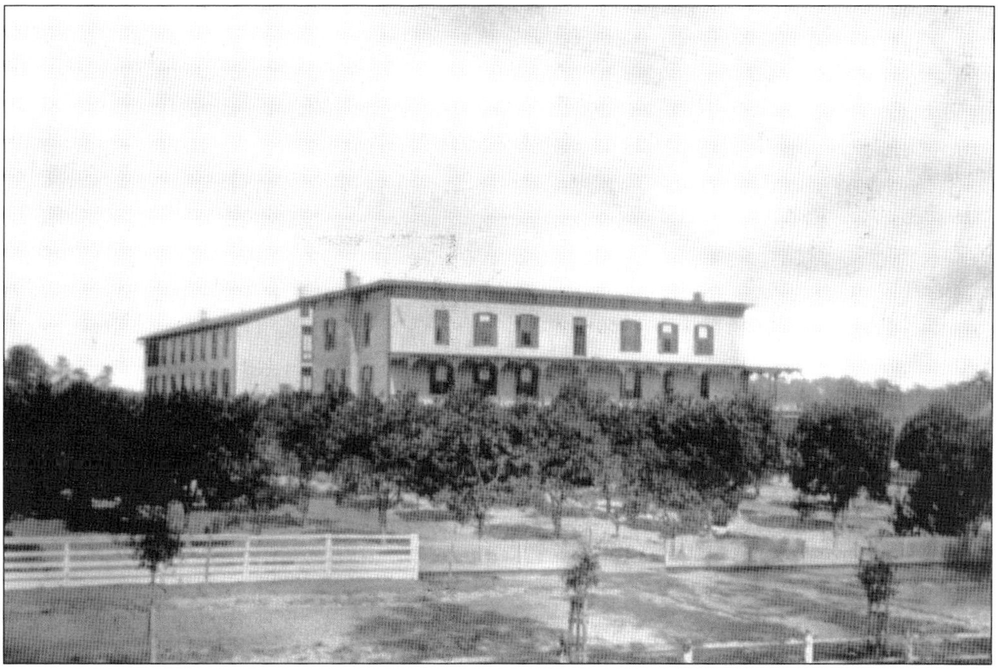

Ten acres of citrus trees originally surrounded the Putnam Inn. This image shows how the hotel fronted New York Avenue, facing south with newly planted oak trees lining DeLand's main east-west roadway in the foreground. (Courtesy of the Bill Dreggors family.)

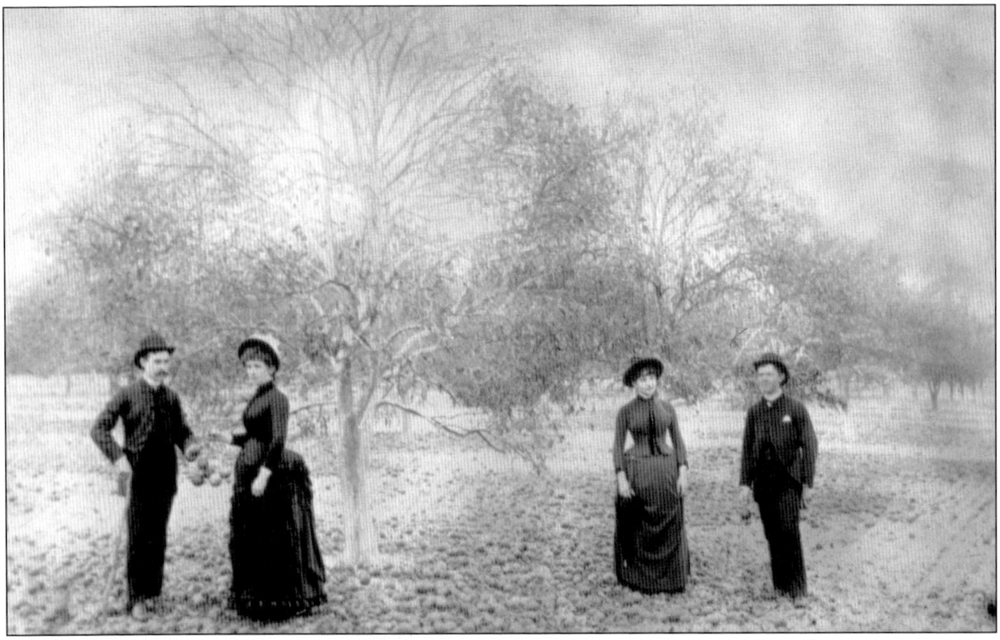

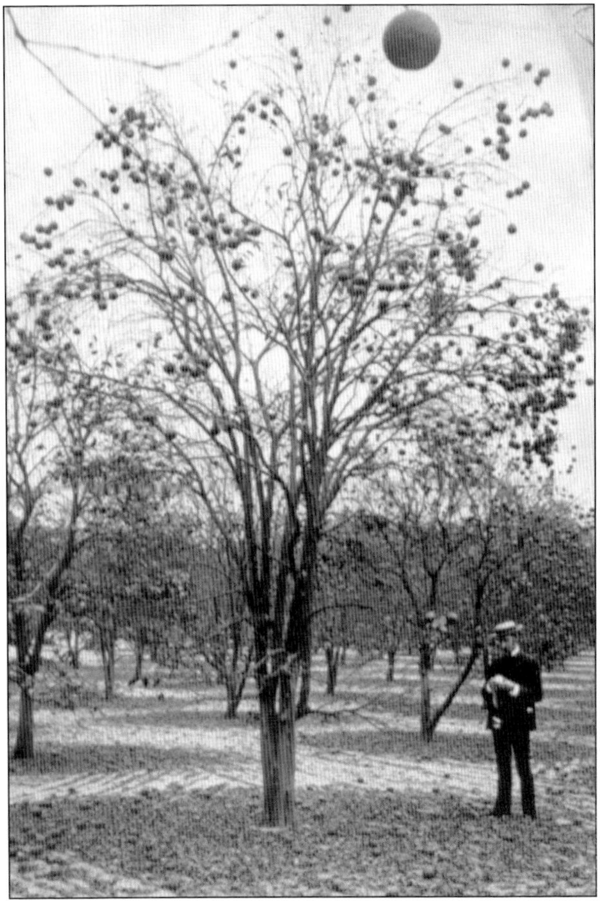

Citrus was an industry that brought economic growth to DeLand. In December 1894, there was a freeze that caused major damage to the orange trees. (Courtesy of the Bill Dreggors family.)

The freeze in December 1894 caused a great deal of concern. Residents, however, became hopeful when the trees sprouted new growth and showed signs of recovery. (Courtesy of the Bill Dreggors family.)

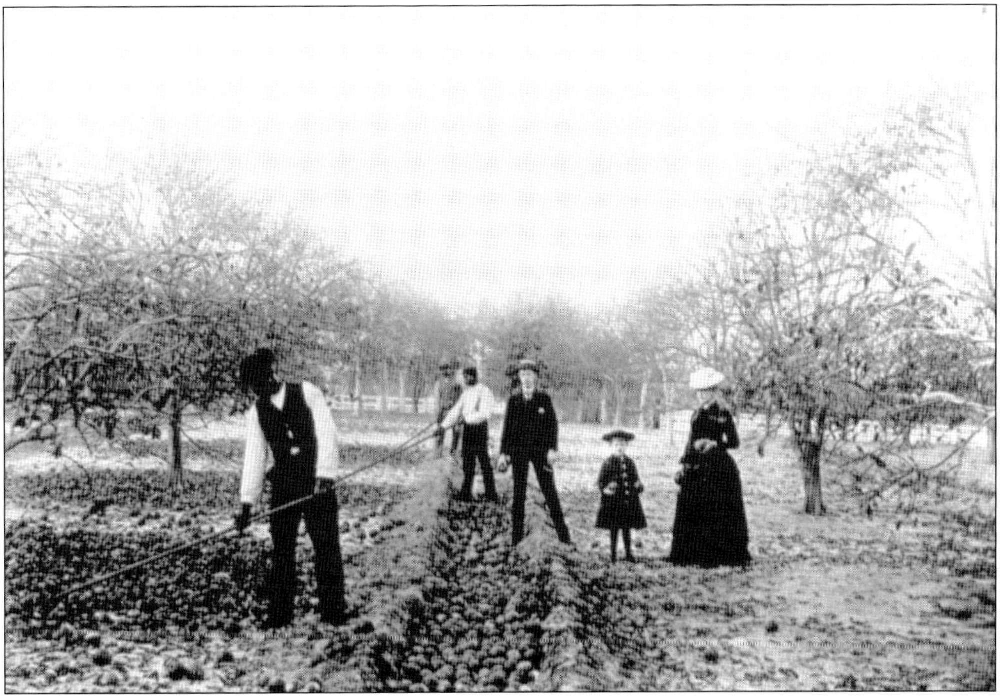

There was a second freeze two months later in February 1895. This freeze was much colder and lasted longer than the first virtually overnight killing much of the locally established citrus industry, like the grove around the Putnam Inn, pictured here. (Courtesy of the Bill Dreggors family.)

HOTEL - PUTNAM,

FIRST HOTEL.

DeLAND, - - FLA.

Largest in the place. Situated in the midst of a ten-acre grove in full bearing.

Is homelike. Table supplied with the best. Amusements for old and young.

No Pleasanter Quarters to be Found.

In 1896, Gardner Gould sold the Putnam Inn to B.E. Brown and another name change to the hotel took place. This ad from the *Stetson Collegiate* newspaper briefly describes the hotel. (Courtesy of Stetson University, duPont-Ball Library, Memorabilia Collection.)

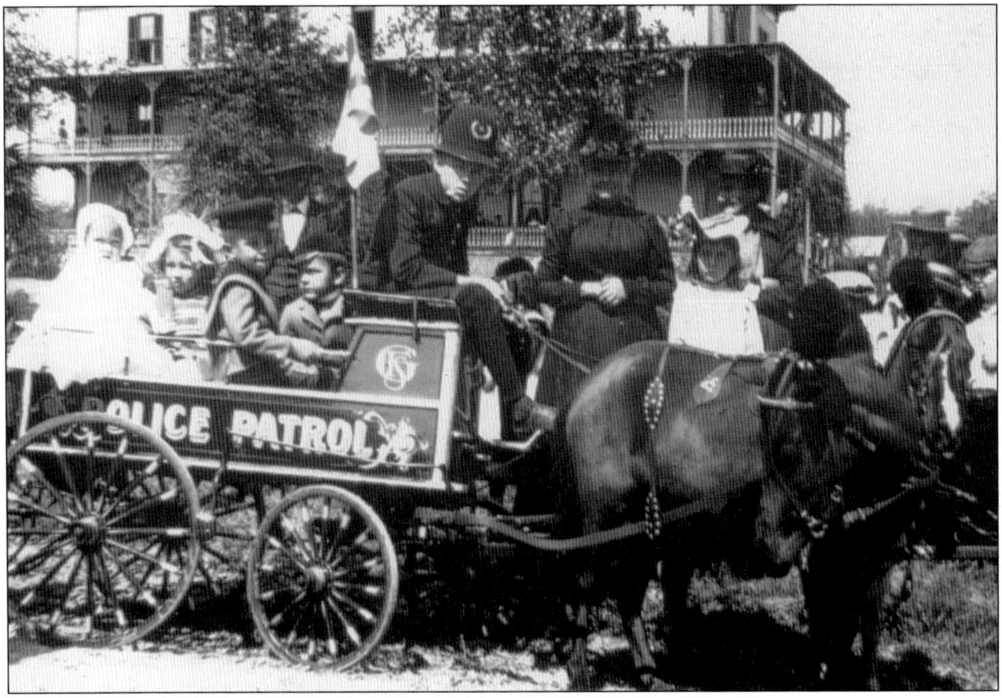

The town slowly recovered though Henry Addison DeLand went broke, honoring the agreement he had made to purchasers of land developed for citrus to buy back the property if people could not maintain it. Tourism continued to bring people to the area, and the Putnam Inn participated in community celebrations. (Courtesy of the Bill Dreggors family.)

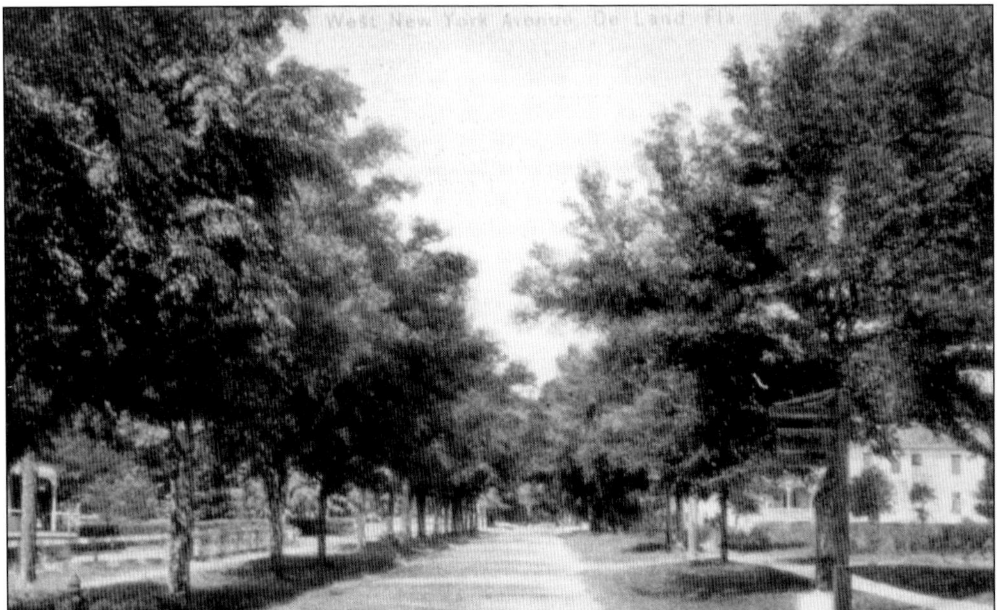

This postcard image from the 1890s shows New York Avenue looking westward out of town. In the foreground right, along the row of maturing oak trees, is a sign post for the Putnam Inn. (Courtesy of the Bill Dreggors family.)

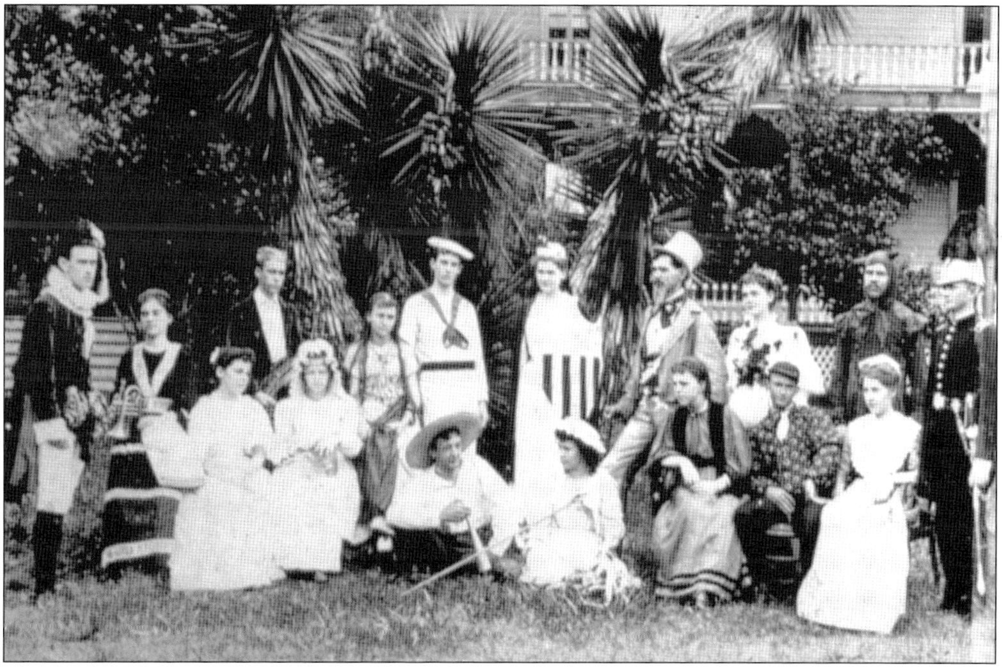

DeLand continued to grow, and the Putnam Inn stayed a gathering place for many activities. In this 1905 photograph near the same spot seen on page 64, a costumed group of college students pose for an event. (Courtesy of the Bill Dreggors family.)

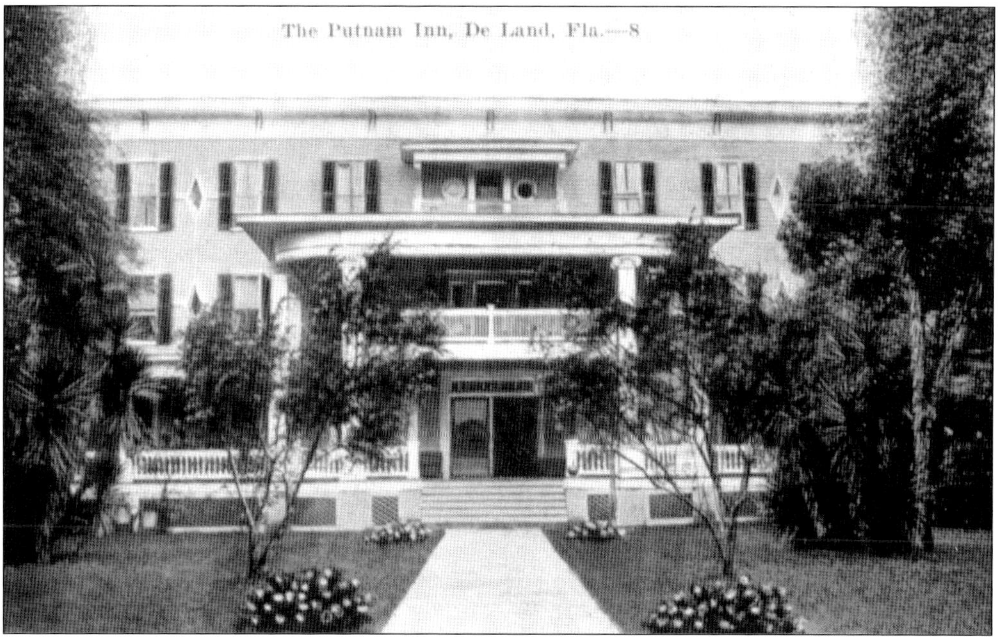

Putnam Inn went through a renovation that changed its original construction. Despite that, on November 4, 1921, the wooden Putnam Inn burned down. (Courtesy of the Bill Dreggors family.)

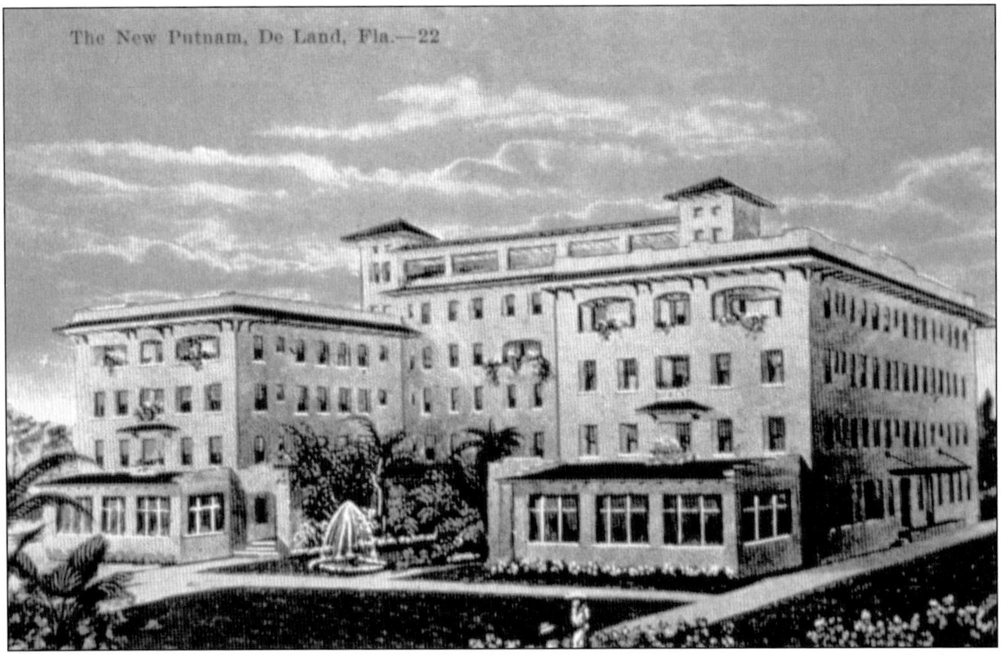

A new concrete fire-proofed version of the hotel was rebuilt to replace the Putnam Inn. Architect William James Carpenter designed the new hotel, and it was renamed the Hotel Putnam. (Courtesy of the Bill Dreggors family.)

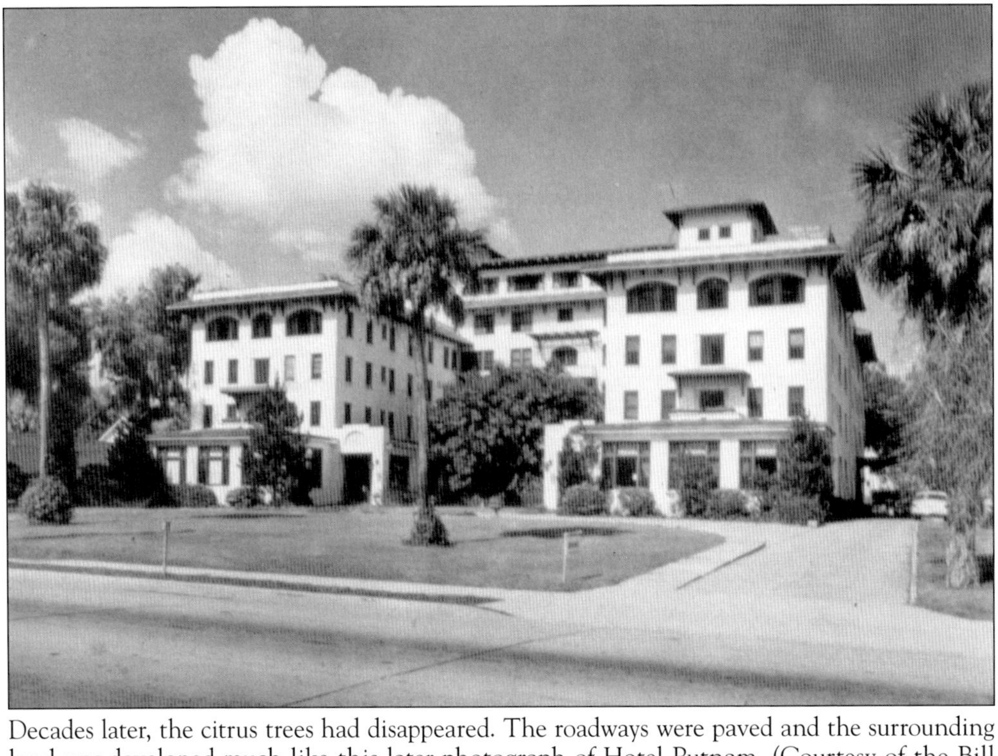
Decades later, the citrus trees had disappeared. The roadways were paved and the surrounding land was developed much like this later photograph of Hotel Putnam. (Courtesy of the Bill Dreggors family.)

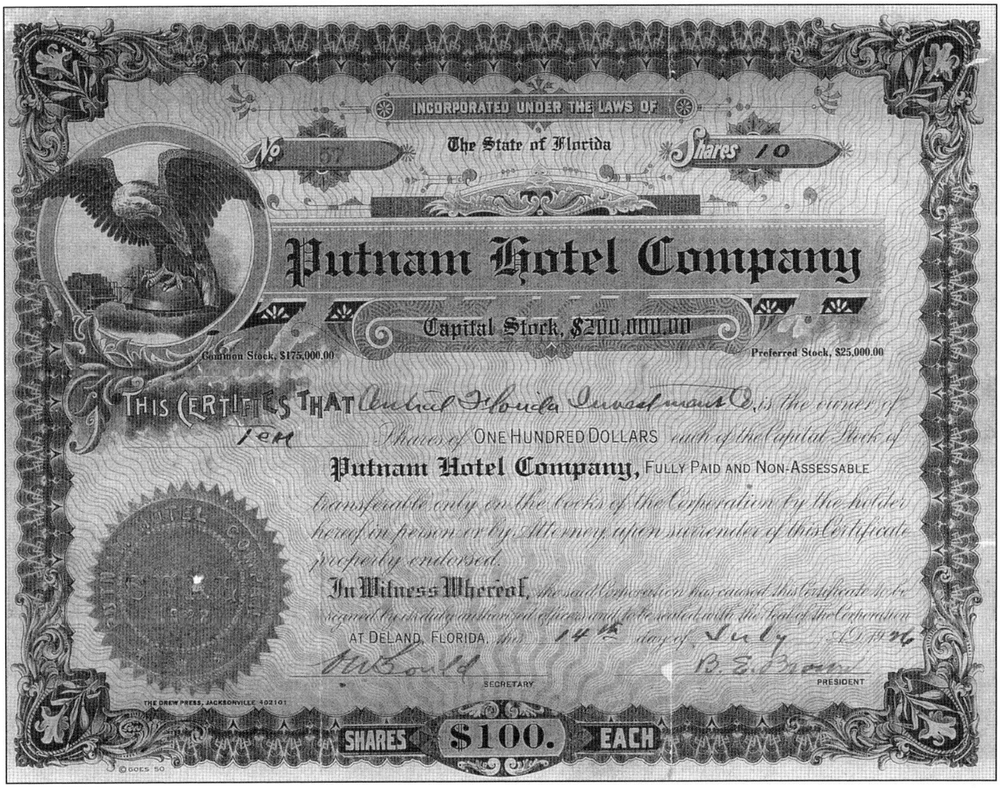

Newer hotels were supported by the sale of shares in the management company financing the hotel. This certificate from 1926 for 10 shares represents an investment of $1,000 in Hotel Putnam. (Courtesy of the Bill Dreggors family.)

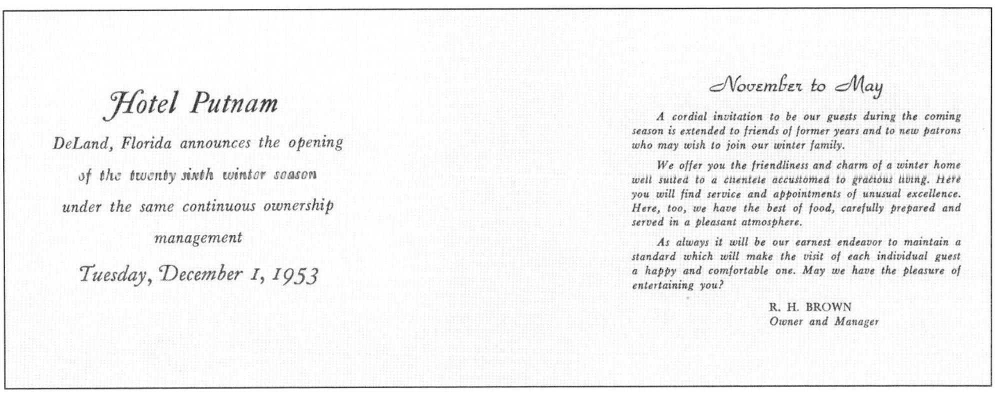

Hotel Putnam

DeLand, Florida announces the opening

of the twenty sixth winter season

under the same continuous ownership

management

Tuesday, December 1, 1953

November to May

A cordial invitation to be our guests during the coming season is extended to friends of former years and to new patrons who may wish to join our winter family.

We offer you the friendliness and charm of a winter home well suited to a clientele accustomed to gracious living. Here you will find service and appointments of unusual excellence. Here, too, we have the best of food, carefully prepared and served in a pleasant atmosphere.

As always it will be our earnest endeavor to maintain a standard which will make the visit of each individual guest a happy and comfortable one. May we have the pleasure of entertaining you?

R. H. BROWN
Owner and Manager

Here is a seasonal announcement from Hotel Putnam in 1953. The new Hotel Putnam was designed to have up to 200 rooms, 112 bedrooms, four floors, stairways, elevator, parlors, and sunrooms among its amenities. (Courtesy of the Bill Dreggors family.)

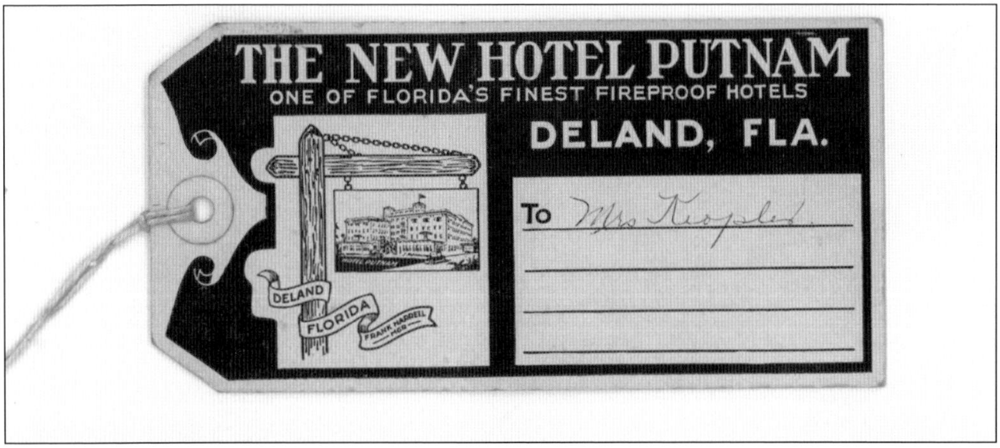

A luggage tag from the new Hotel Putnam. Fires were often a concern in earlier buildings so the new fire safety features of this hotel were prominently advertised. (Courtesy of the Bill Dreggors family.)

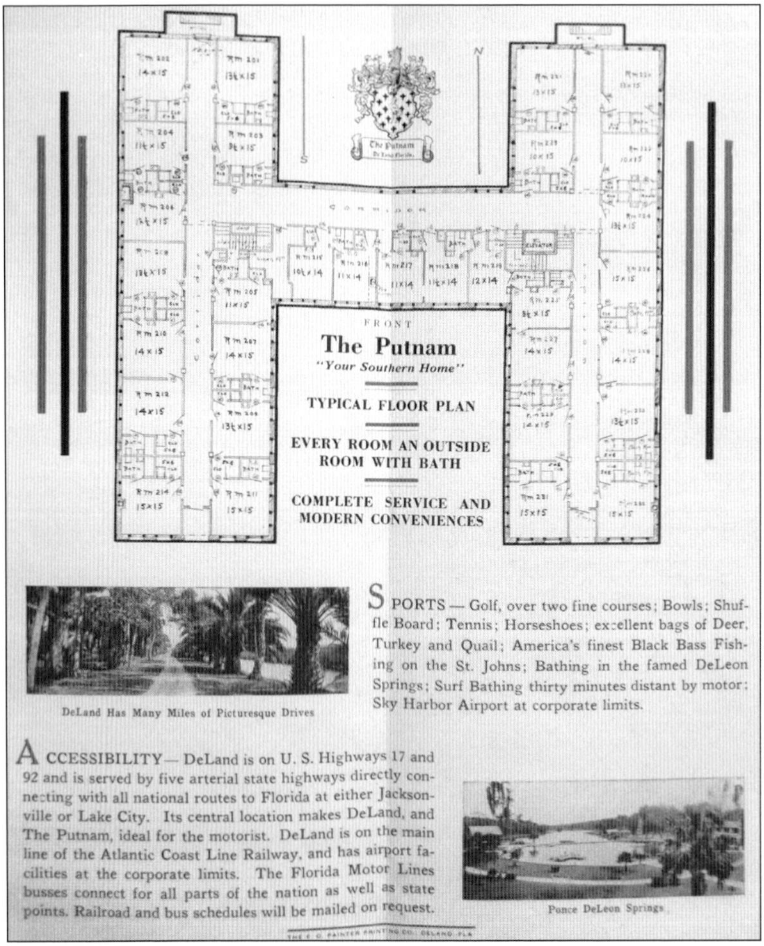

This is a guest brochure displaying the floor plan for Hotel Putnam and some of the area's points of interest. One of the features of the hotel was that all rooms had an outside view and a bath. (Courtesy of Jim Cara.)

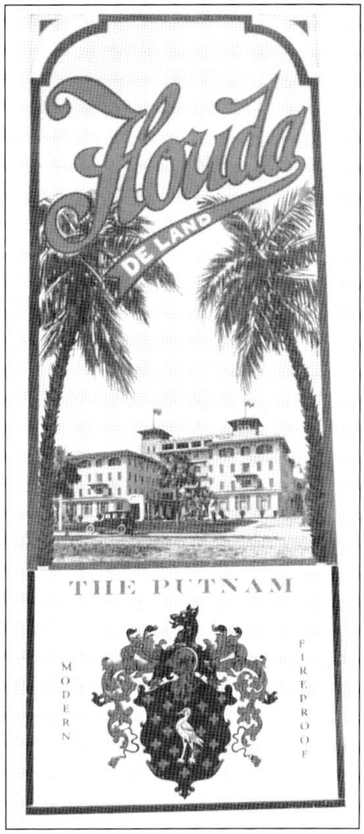

The outside cover of a Hotel Putnam brochure with its distinctive crest. These printed brochures provided guests with important information on the hotel and area. (Courtesy of Jim Cara.)

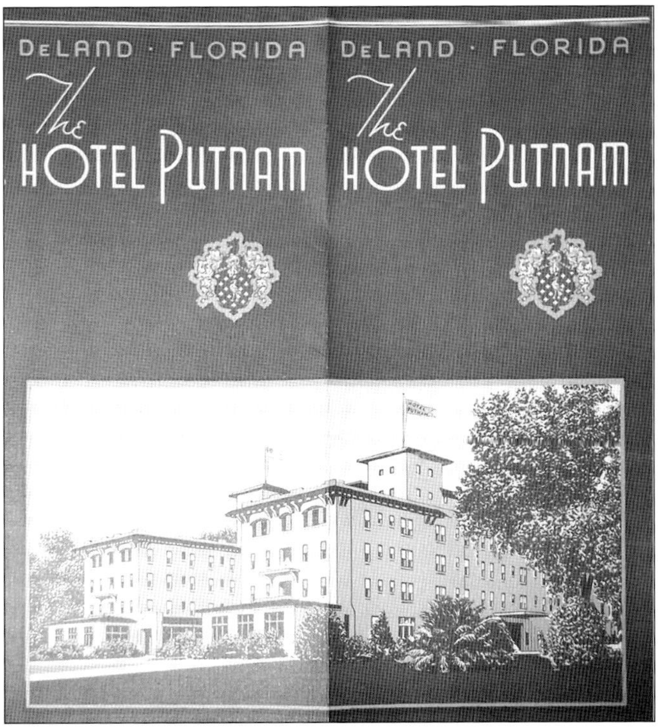

Another brochure for the Hotel Putnam. As the hotel industry and tourism continued to grow in Florida, publications like this became a vital part of the marketing hotels engaged in to attract guests. (Courtesy of Jim Cara.)

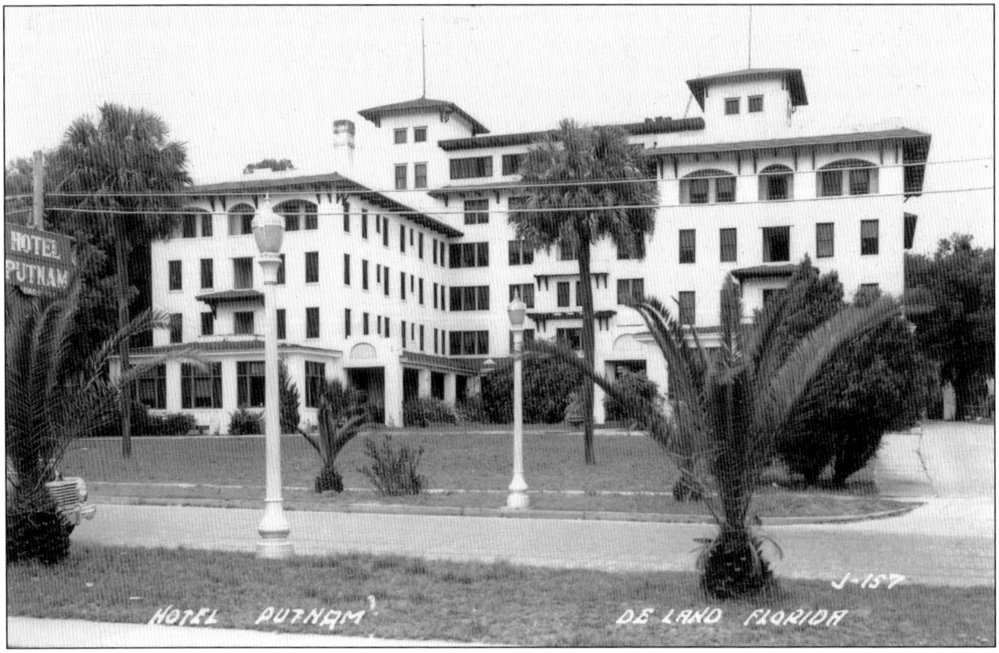

Over the years, the volume of seasonal visitors to DeLand declined as did the number of guests at the hotel. This image of Hotel Putnam is from a postcard used to advertise the hotel. (Courtesy of Stetson University, duPont-Ball Library, Memorabilia Collection.)

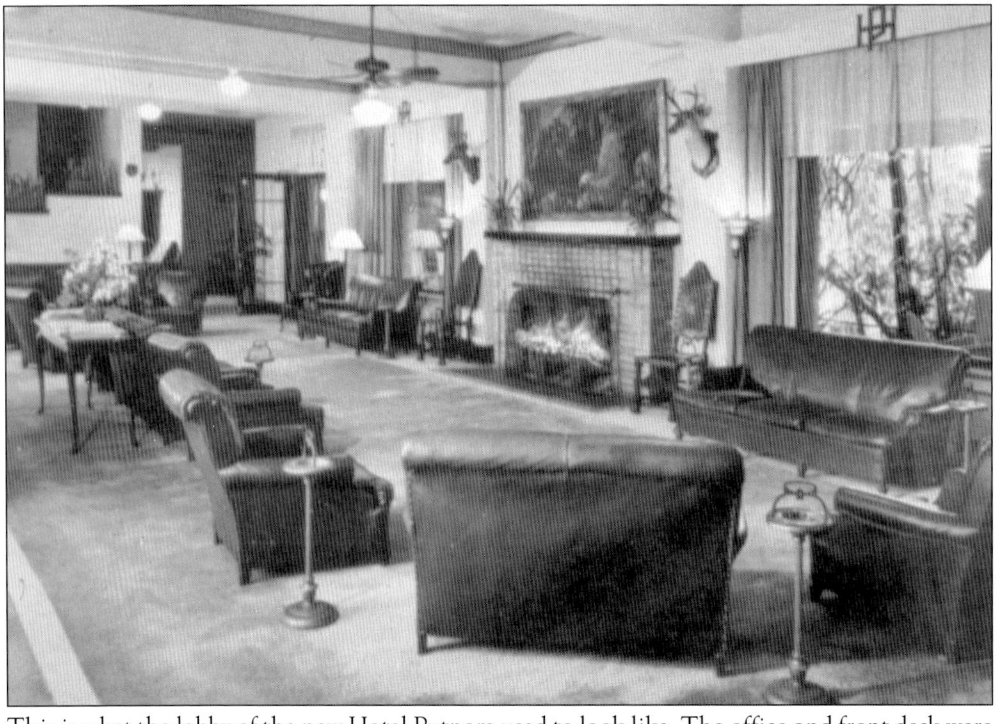

This is what the lobby of the new Hotel Putnam used to look like. The office and front desk were located to the left in this image outside of view. (Courtesy of the Bill Dreggors family.)

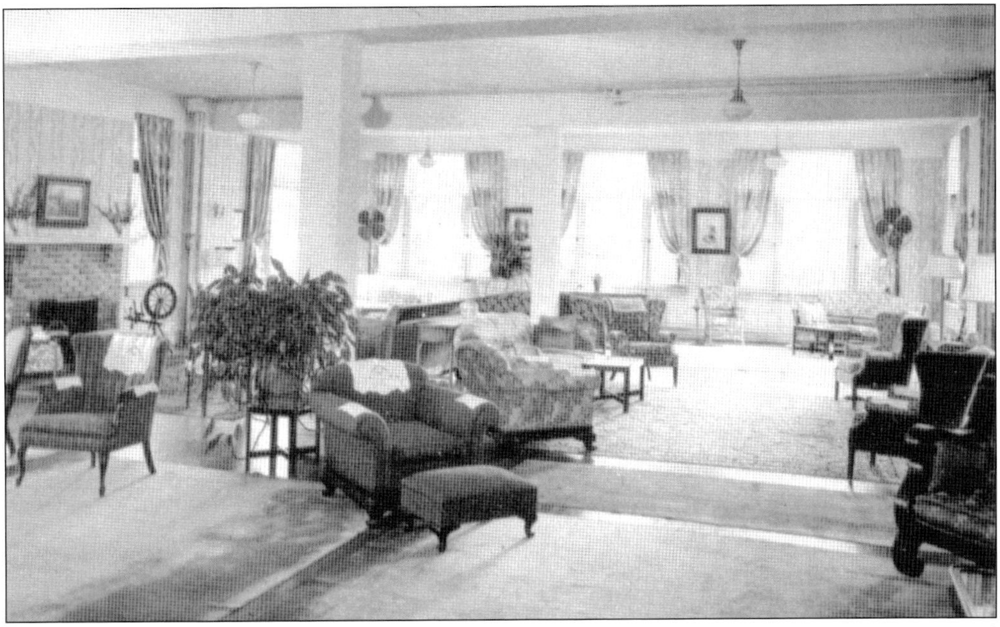

The hotel was spacious. In this image of the reception room, ample room with a view and comfortable seating are arranged to offer a relaxing area to congregate. (Courtesy of the Bill Dreggors family.)

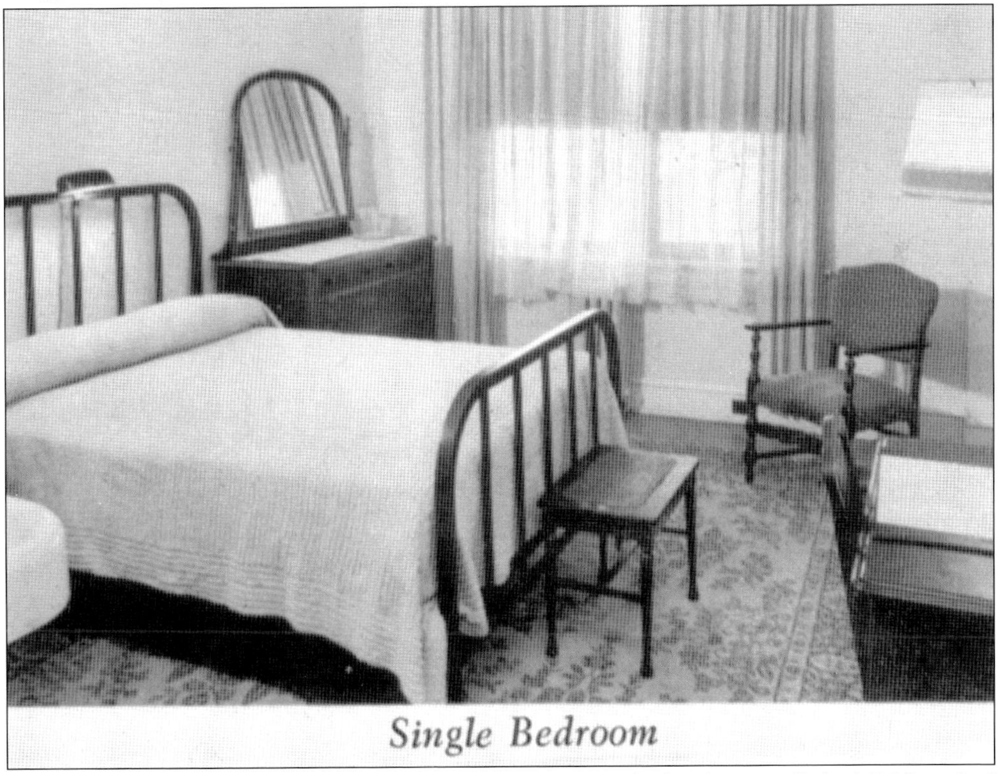

This is a how a single bedroom was furnished in Hotel Putnam. The hotel eventually had 125 furnished guest rooms in addition to its parlors and public areas. (Courtesy of the Bill Dreggors family.)

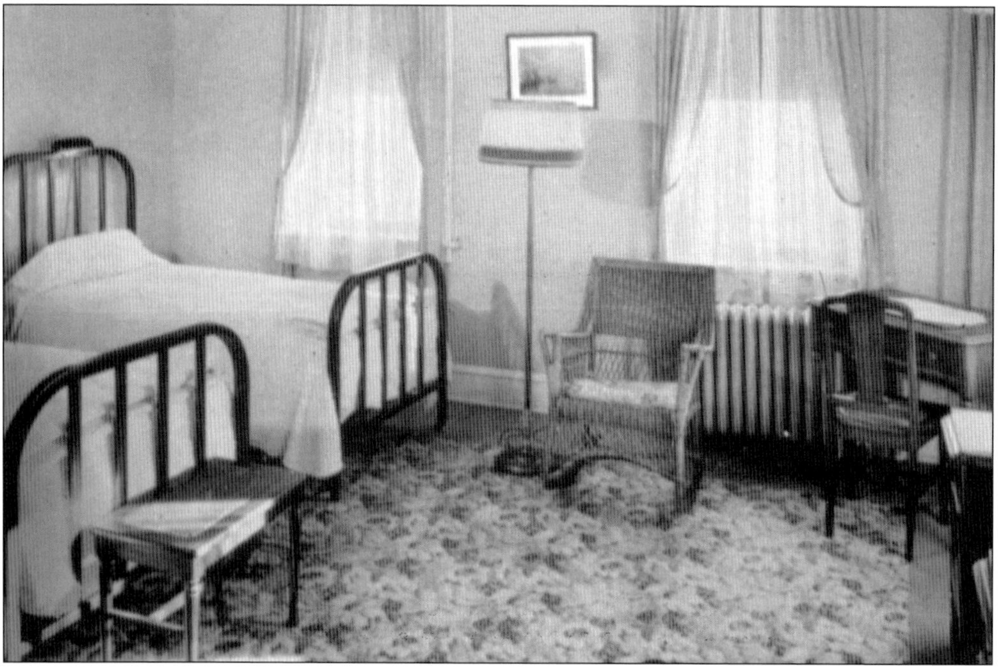

Seen here is how a double bedroom was furnished in Hotel Putnam. Each room had a tiled bath, steam heat, comfortable bed, mirror, large closet, and stylish furnishings. (Courtesy of the Bill Dreggors family.)

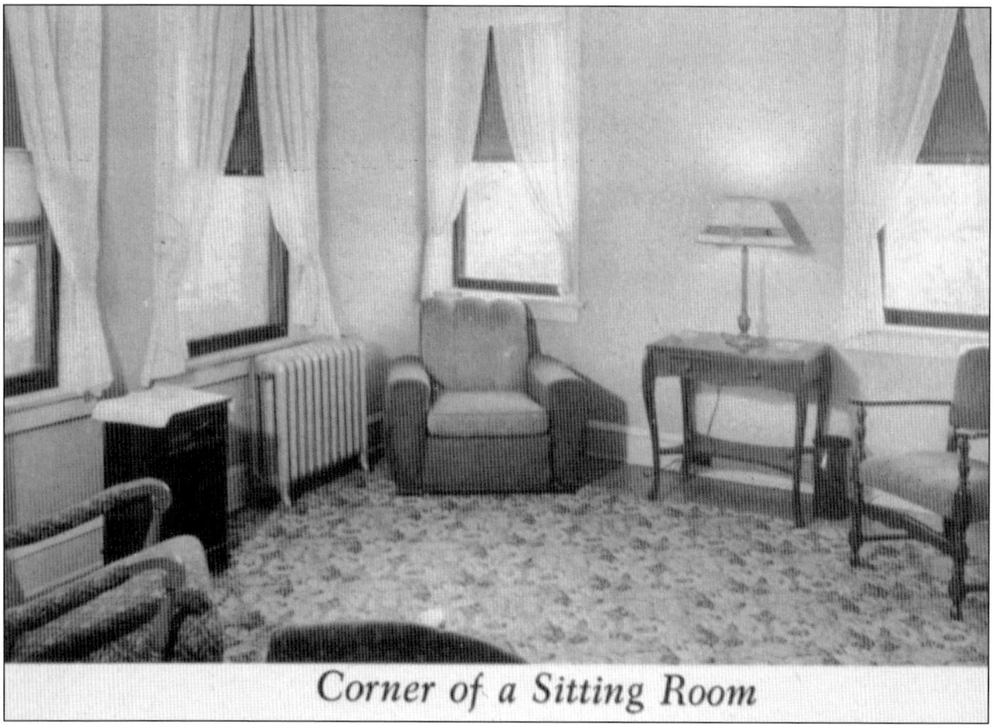

This is what the sitting area in some rooms looked like. A corner room in the hotel offered even better views and the added benefit of a cross breeze. (Courtesy of the Bill Dreggors family.)

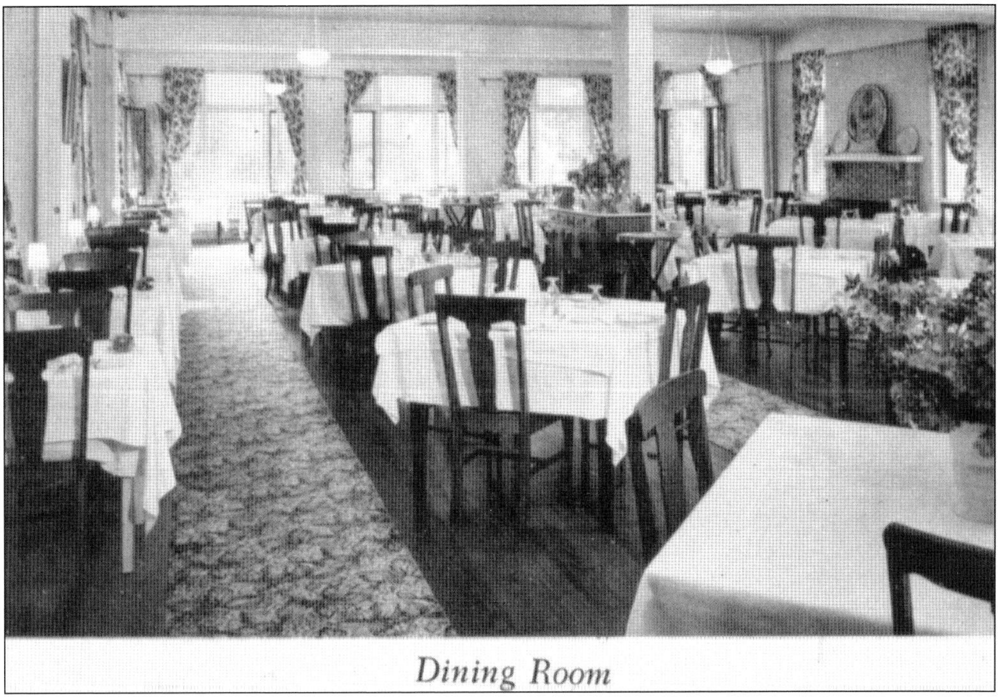

The dining room of Hotel Putnam was another finely furnished room. The room was well lit, and tables were carefully set for diners. (Courtesy of the Bill Dreggors family.)

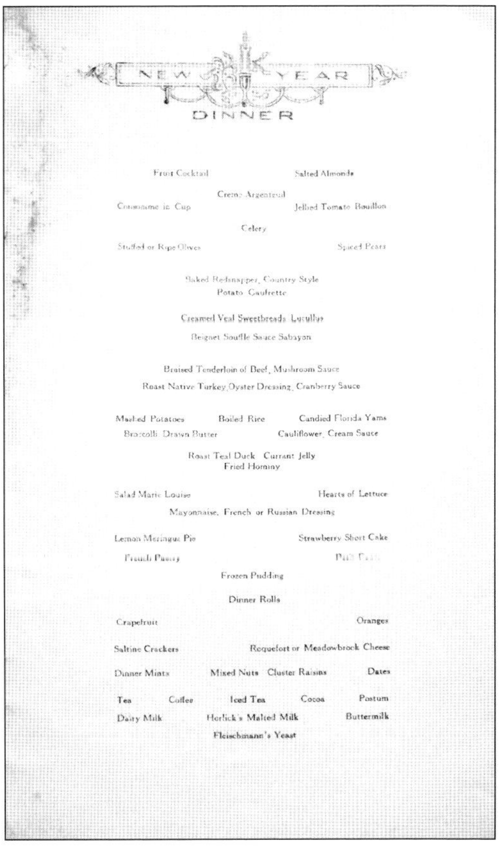

NEW YEAR DINNER

Fruit Cocktail   Salted Almonds

Creme Argenteuil

Consomme in Cup   Jellied Tomato Bouillon

Celery

Stuffed or Ripe Olives   Spiced Pears

Baked Redsnapper, Country Style
Potato Gaufrette

Creamed Veal Sweetbreads Lucullus

Beignet Souffle Sauce Sabayon

Braised Tenderloin of Beef, Mushroom Sauce

Roast Native Turkey, Oyster Dressing, Cranberry Sauce

Mashed Potatoes   Boiled Rice   Candied Florida Yams
Broccolli Drawn Butter   Cauliflower, Cream Sauce

Roast Teal Duck Currant Jelly
Fried Hominy

Salad Marie Louise   Hearts of Lettuce

Mayonnaise, French or Russian Dressing

Lemon Meringue Pie   Strawberry Short Cake

French Pastry   [illegible]

Frozen Pudding

Dinner Rolls

Grapefruit   Oranges

Saltine Crackers   Roquefort or Meadowbrook Cheese

Dinner Mints   Mixed Nuts   Cluster Raisins   Dates

Tea   Coffee   Iced Tea   Cocoa   Postum
Dairy Milk   Horlick's Malted Milk   Buttermilk
Fleischmann's Yeast

Here is an example of what some of the dining at Hotel Putnam was like. This menu offers a wide assortment of food choices for dinner on New Year's. (Courtesy of Jim Cara.)

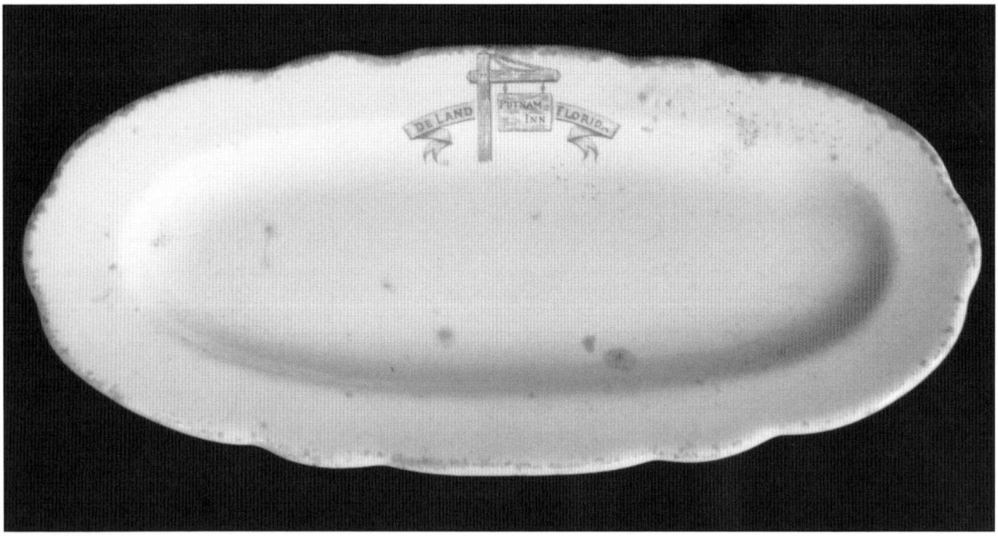

Some relics have survived from the hotel's past. Seen here is a large serving platter from the dining room of the Putnam Inn. (Courtesy of Jim Cara.)

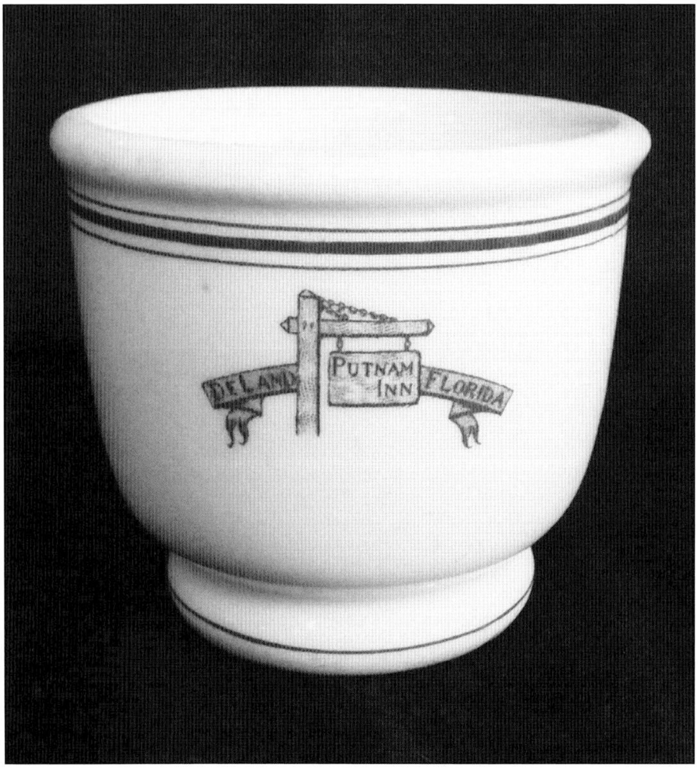

Pictured here is another small artifact that once was part of the hotel. This is a bowl that may have been used for soup or shaving at the Putnam Inn. (Courtesy of Jim Cara.)

This is another item once used in the dining room of the Putnam Inn. The large plate displays the distinctive label used over the years for the hotel. (Courtesy of Jim Cara.)

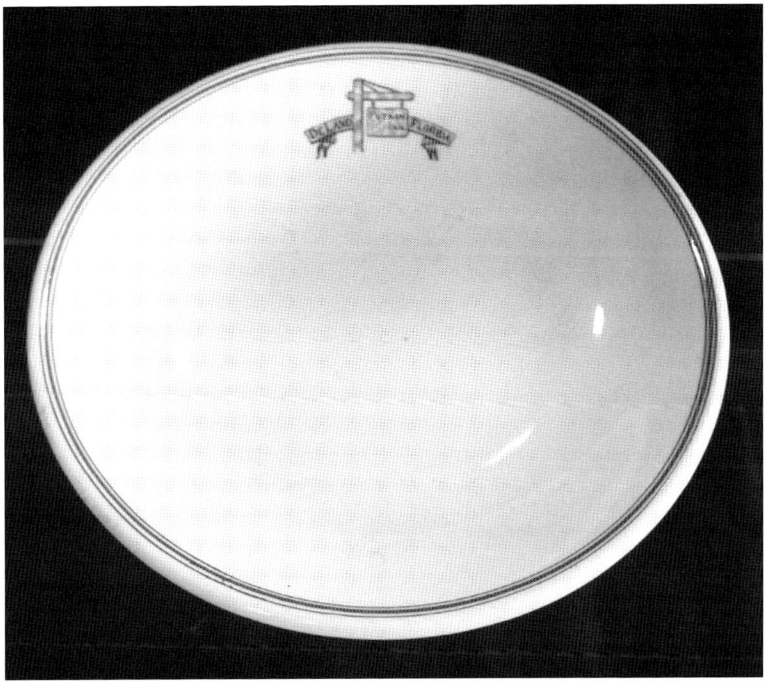

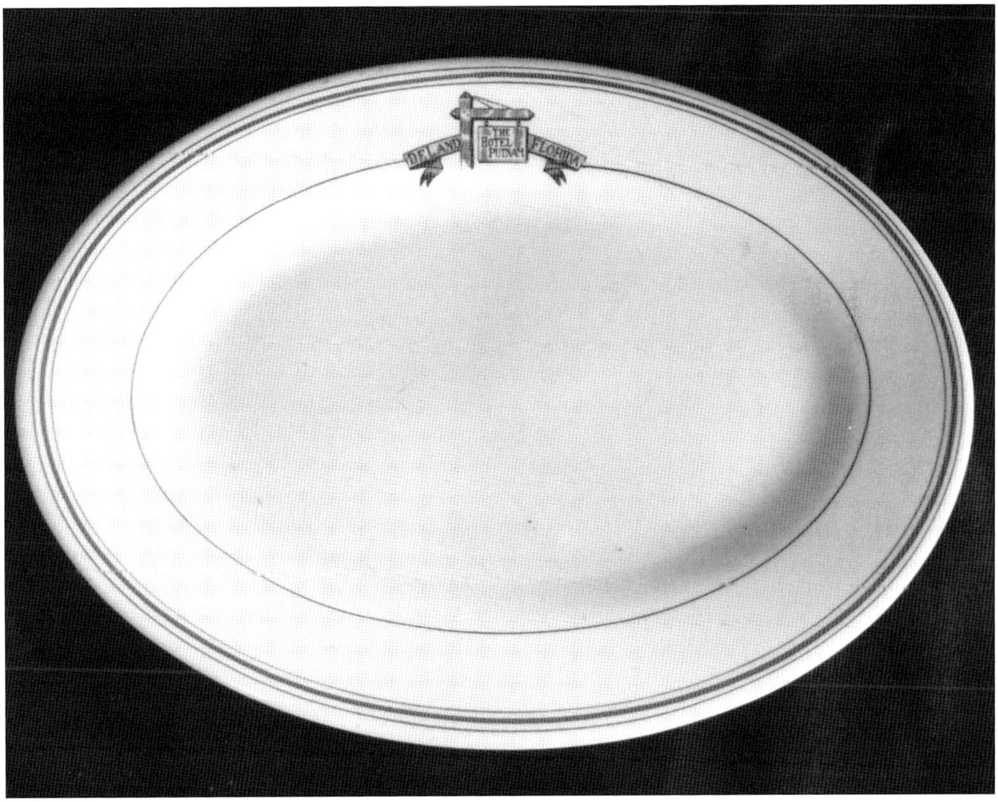

Shown here is another surviving piece of serving ware from the hotel. Note how the label on this plate indicates the change over time in the hotel. (Courtesy of Jim Cara.)

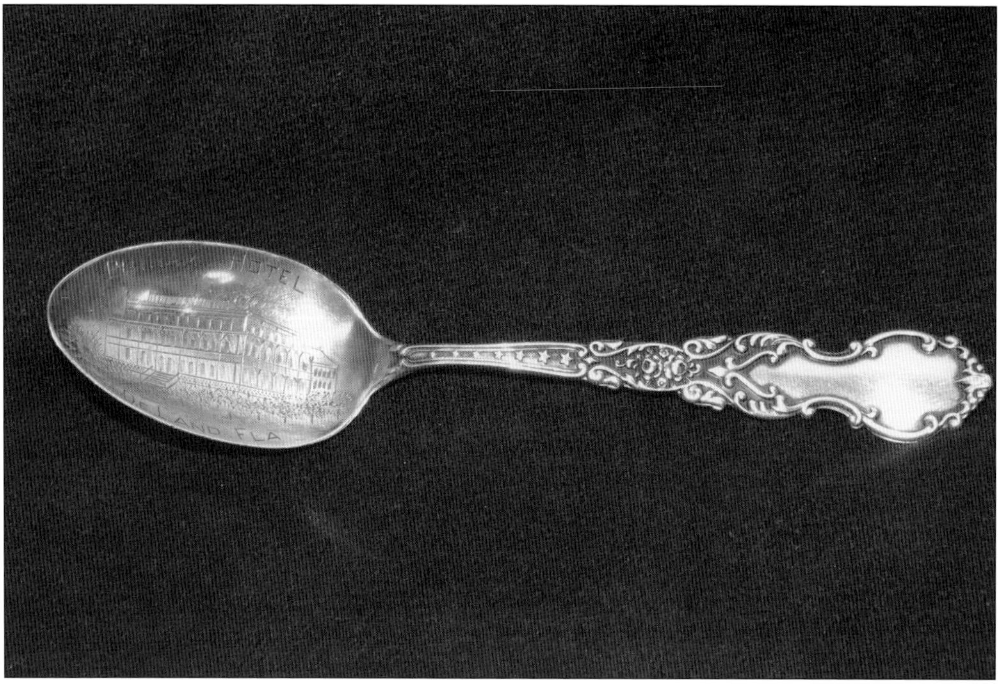

It was common in many of the hotels of the time to have customized fine utensils. Pictured here is an example of some of the craftsmanship that went into furnishings in these hotels. (Courtesy of Jim Cara.)

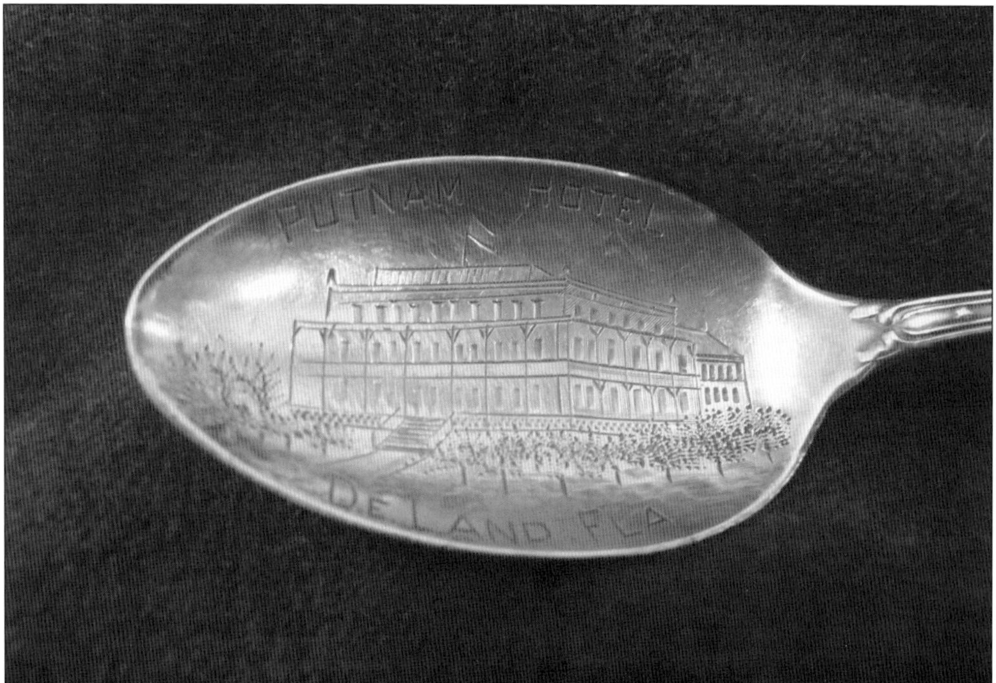

Here is a close-up view of the same spoon. Note the detail that went into making this spoon, which was not uncommon in many of the hotels of the time. (Courtesy of Jim Cara.)

This is what the kitchen of the Hotel Putnam looked like in the 1950s. The hotel had a fully furnished modern kitchen equipped with stoves, refrigerators, and freezers. (Courtesy of the Bill Dreggors family.)

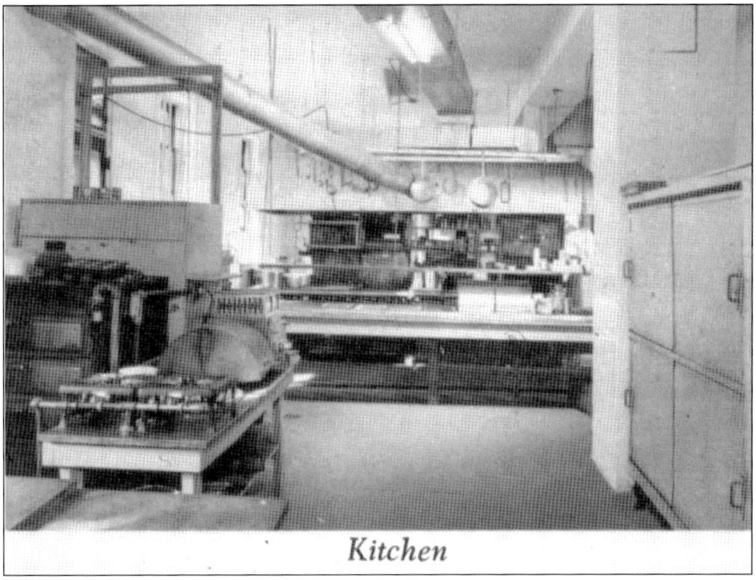

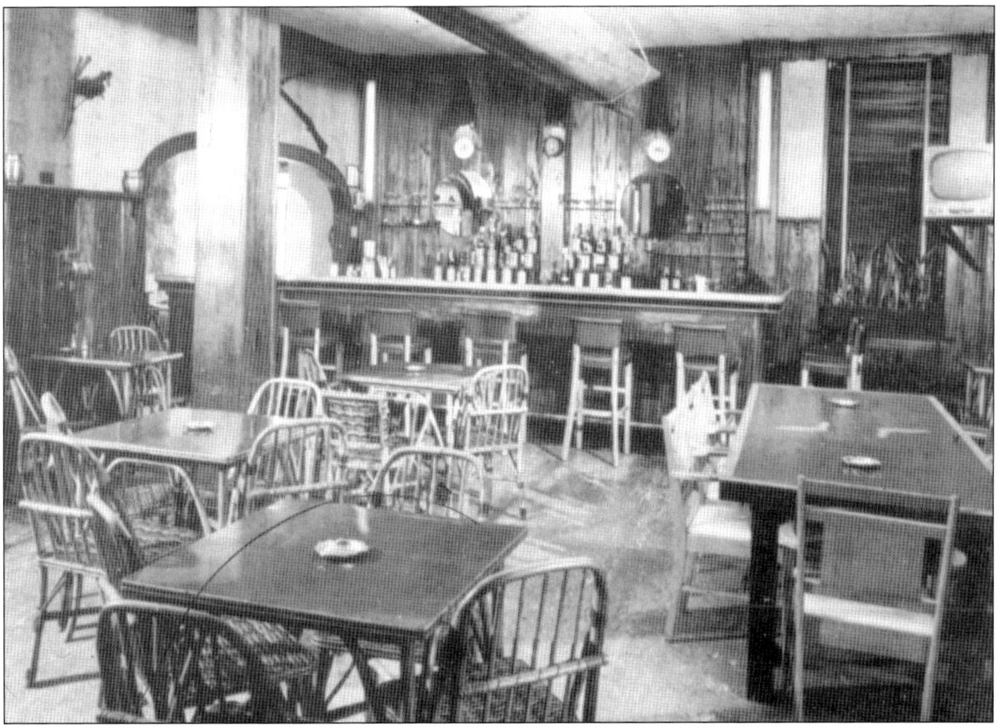

No respectable hotel of the time went without a bar or lounge for its guests. This is a picture of the Cypress Room of the Hotel Putnam. (Courtesy of the Bill Dreggors family.)

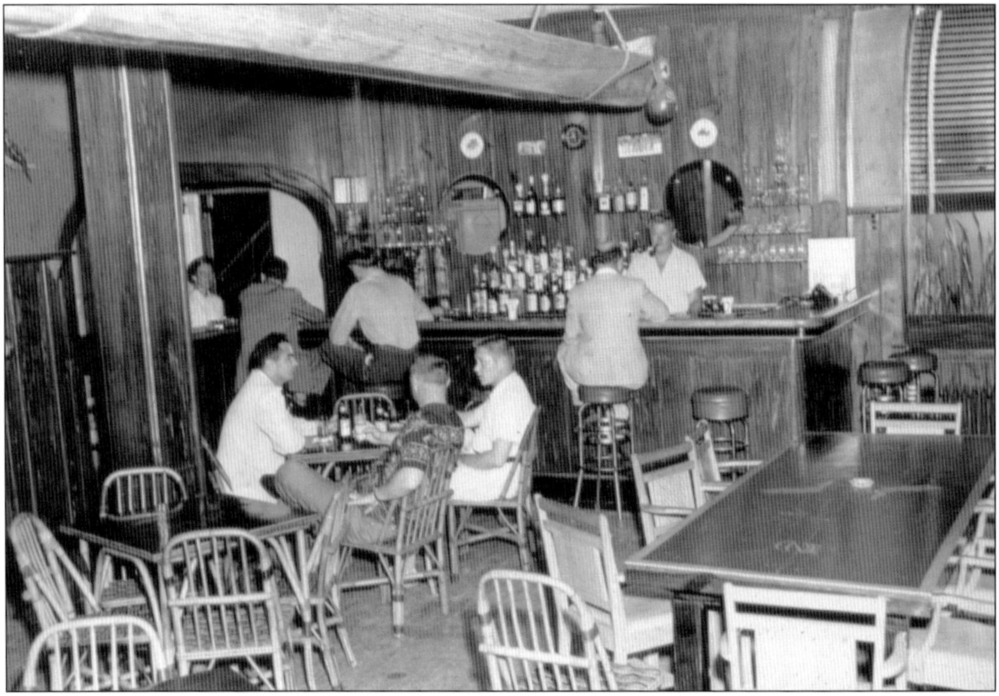

Here is another view of the Cypress Room of the Hotel Putnam with its wood-lined walls. Another interesting feature of this room was the old canoe suspended from the ceiling. (Courtesy of the Bill Dreggors family.)

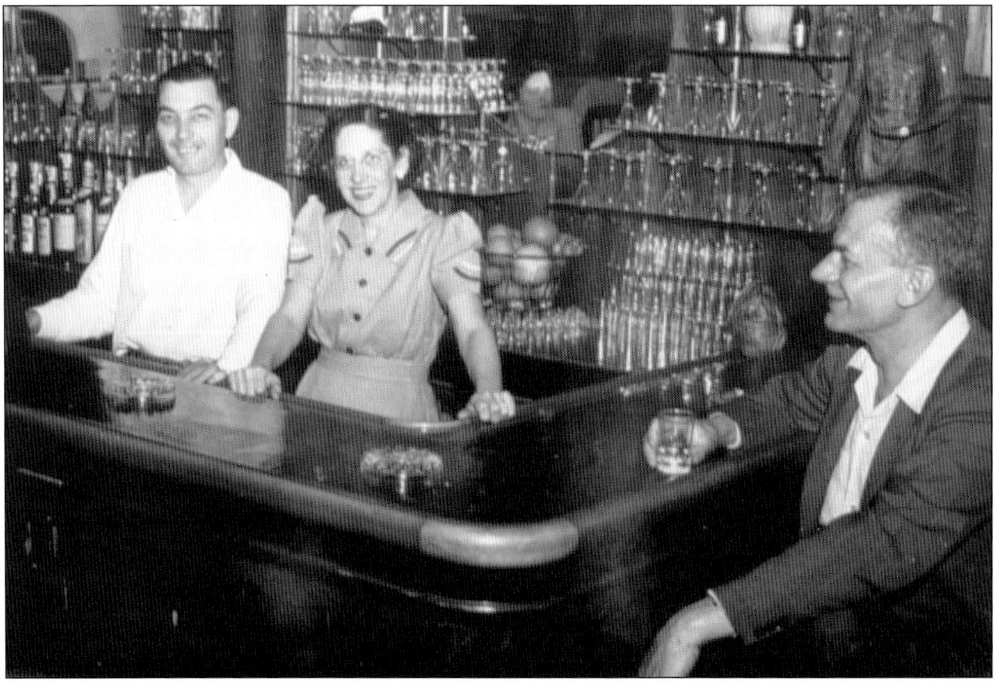

The bar of the Cypress Room was fully stocked with drinks for guests and visitors alike. This close-up provides an even better view of some of the bar features. (Courtesy of the Bill Dreggors family.)

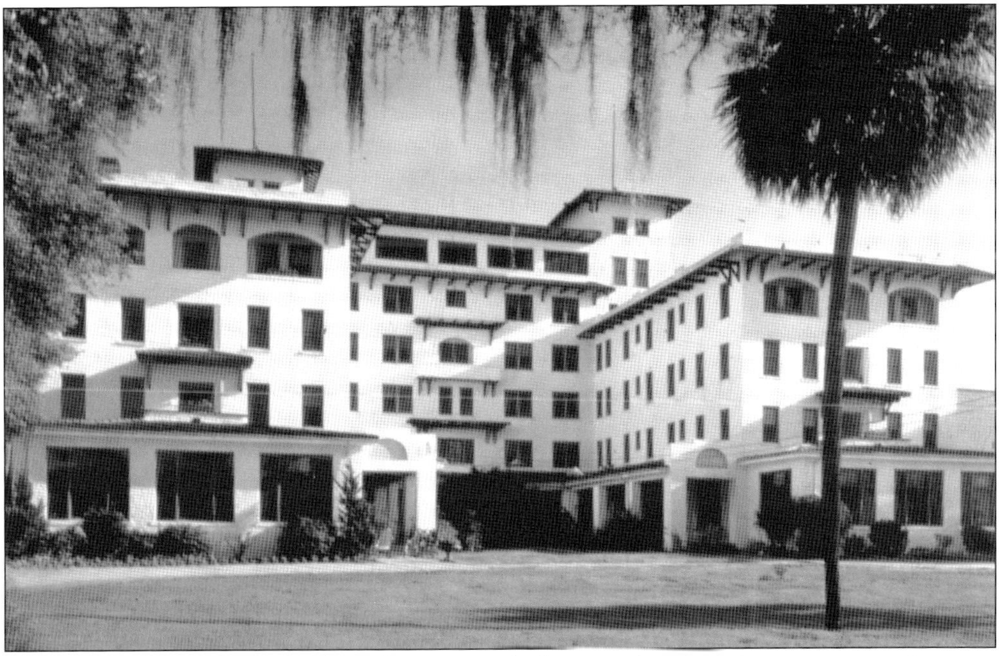

The hotel industry in West Volusia County was declining as hotels and attractions on the coast drew more patrons to the beaches. In 1959, B.E. Brown sold the Hotel Putnam. (Courtesy of the Bill Dreggors family.)

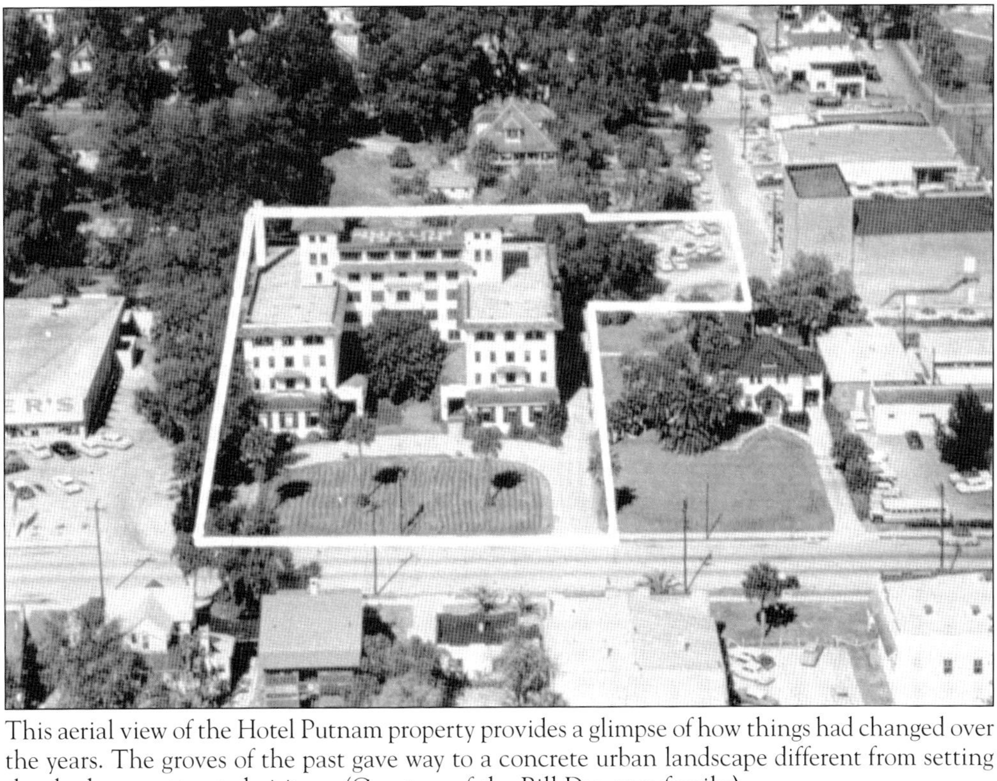

This aerial view of the Hotel Putnam property provides a glimpse of how things had changed over the years. The groves of the past gave way to a concrete urban landscape different from setting that had once attracted visitors. (Courtesy of the Bill Dreggors family.)

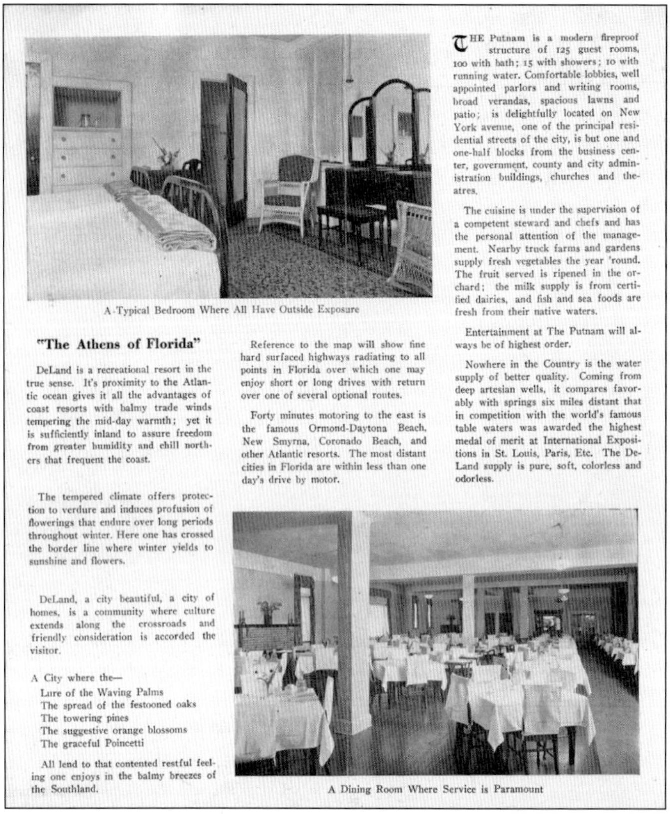

THE Putnam is a modern fireproof structure of 125 guest rooms, 100 with bath; 15 with showers; 10 with running water. Comfortable lobbies, well appointed parlors and writing rooms, broad verandas, spacious lawns and patio; is delightfully located on New York avenue, one of the principal residential streets of the city, is but one and one-half blocks from the business center, government, county and city administration buildings, churches and theatres.

The cuisine is under the supervision of a competent steward and chefs and has the personal attention of the management. Nearby truck farms and gardens supply fresh vegetables the year 'round. The fruit served is ripened in the orchard; the milk supply is from certified dairies, and fish and sea foods are fresh from their native waters.

A Typical Bedroom Where All Have Outside Exposure

Entertainment at The Putnam will always be of highest order.

Nowhere in the Country is the water supply of better quality. Coming from deep artesian wells, it compares favorably with springs six miles distant that in competition with the world's famous table waters was awarded the highest medal of merit at International Expositions in St. Louis, Paris, Etc. The DeLand supply is pure, soft, colorless and odorless.

"The Athens of Florida"

DeLand is a recreational resort in the true sense. It's proximity to the Atlantic ocean gives it all the advantages of coast resorts with balmy trade winds tempering the mid-day warmth; yet it is sufficiently inland to assure freedom from greater humidity and chill northers that frequent the coast.

The tempered climate offers protection to verdure and induces profusion of flowerings that endure over long periods throughout winter. Here one has crossed the border line where winter yields to sunshine and flowers.

DeLand, a city beautiful, a city of homes, is a community where culture extends along the crossroads and friendly consideration is accorded the visitor.

A City where the—
Lure of the Waving Palms
The spread of the festooned oaks
The towering pines
The suggestive orange blossoms
The graceful Poincetti

All lend to that contented restful feeling one enjoys in the balmy breezes of the Southland.

Reference to the map will show fine hard surfaced highways radiating to all points in Florida over which one may enjoy short or long drives with return over one of several optional routes.

Forty minutes motoring to the east is the famous Ormond-Daytona Beach, New Smyrna, Coronado Beach, and other Atlantic resorts. The most distant cities in Florida are within less than one day's drive by motor.

A Dining Room Where Service is Paramount

Hotel Putnam began to change along with the times and the elegance once advertised in this brochure began to fade away. After its sale in 1959, Hotel Putnam became a hotel-apartment complex. (Courtesy of Jim Cara.)

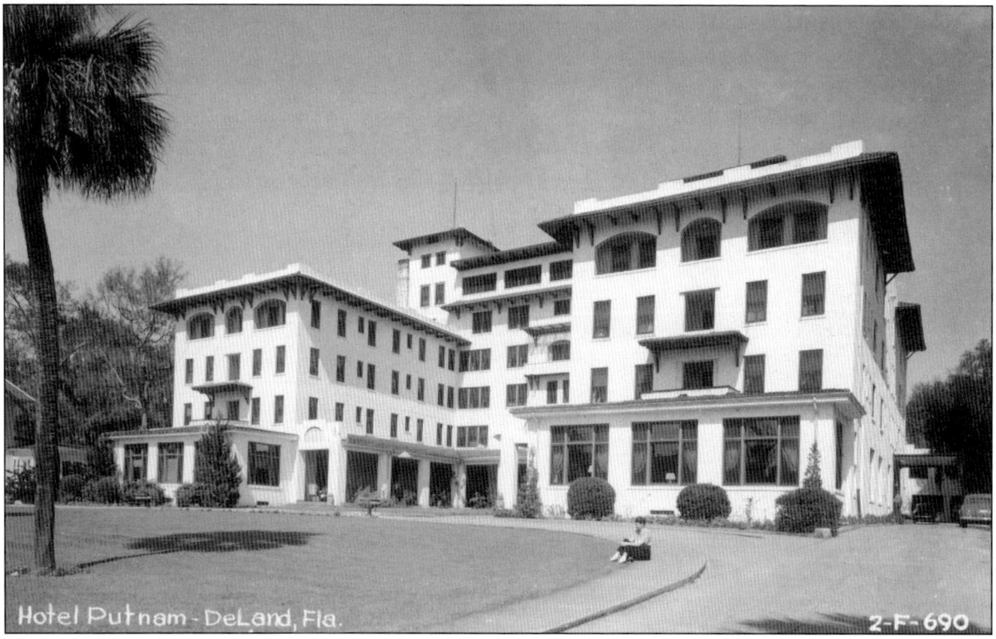

The grandeur of the hotel lost its charm, and the building began to fall into disrepair. The property changed hands and the housing it provided closed down in January 2011. (Courtesy of Stetson University, duPont-Ball Library, Memorabilia Collection.)

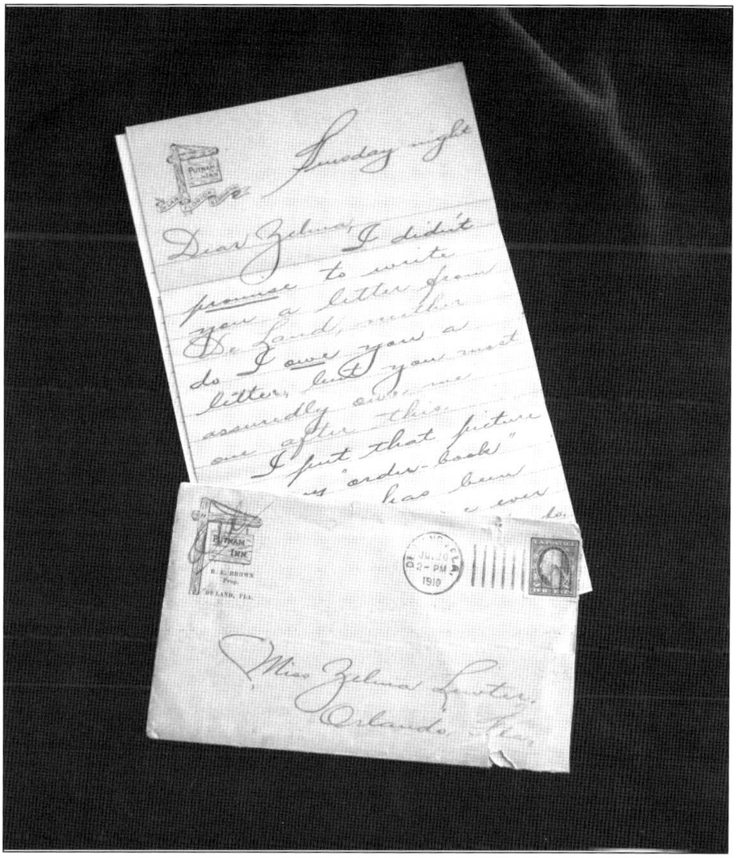

Saved artifacts from the hotel's past, like this letter written on Putnam Inn stationary, is a reminder of how the hotel once was. The hotel property has been sold repeatedly since its closing in attempts by buyers to save and restore the hotel. (Courtesy of Jim Cara.)

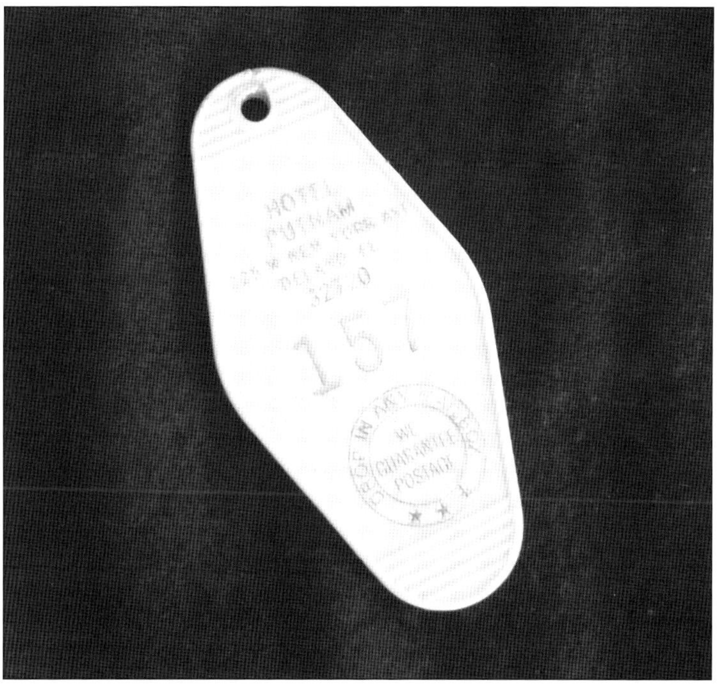

This is part of a room key from the Hotel Putnam. The key to saving the historic hotel today depends upon finding a buyer who can successfully finance the purchase and restoration of the property. (Courtesy of Jim Cara.)

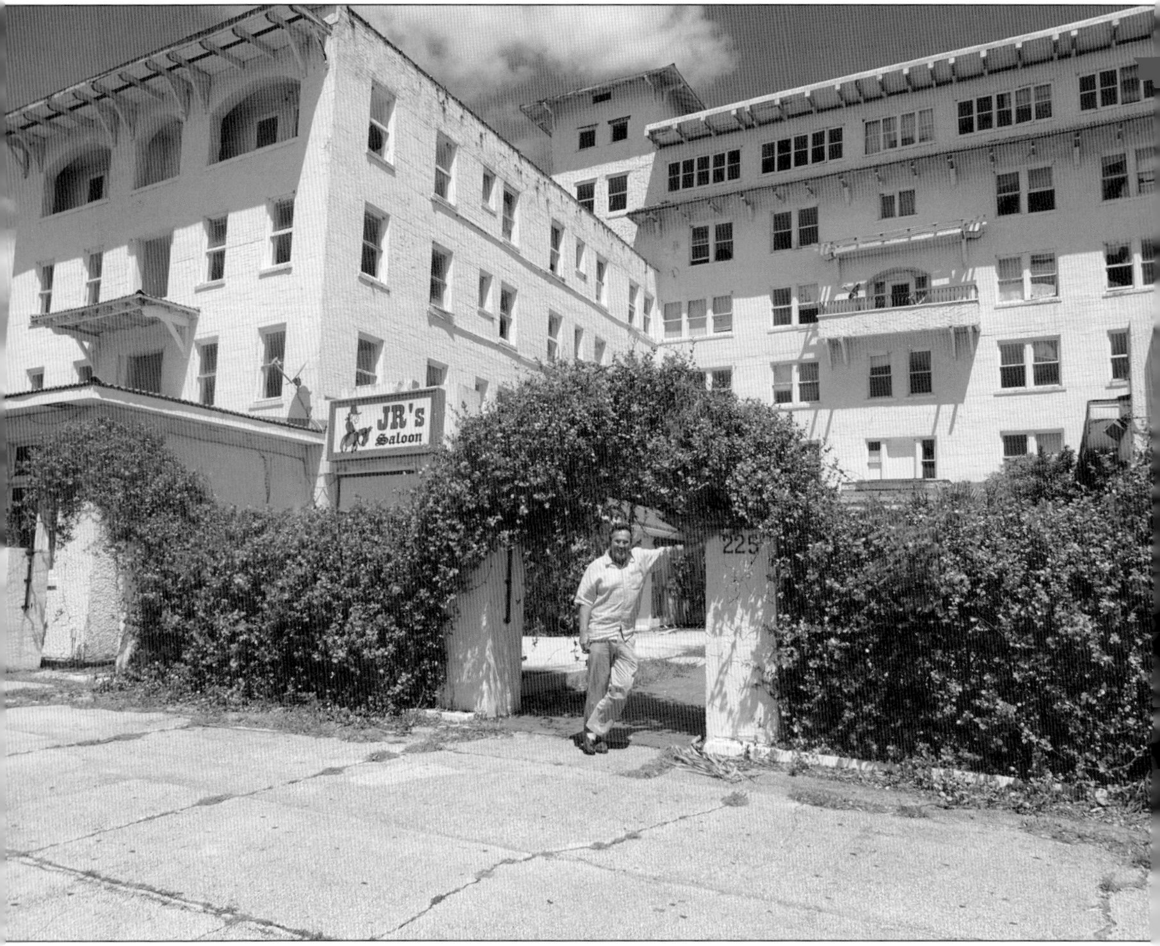

Restoration developer Tony Collins brokered an agreement with the City of DeLand in early 2017 for purchase of Hotel Putnam. Successful purchase of the property to save and restore the historic hotel is still pending as of this printing. (Courtesy of Barb Shepherd, Owner/Publisher/CEO The West Volusia Beacon.)

Six

Lake Helen

Harlan Hotel

The Harlan Hotel was in Lake Helen overlooking the lake. The hotel and the town were named after the children of Henry Addison DeLand, Harlan DeLand, and Helen DeLand. The small community was another winter retreat for northern visitors. The town flourished with orange groves and had a sawmill and a brick company.

The Harlan Hotel used to be situated at the corner of Connecticut and Harlan Avenues. It is said to have been built by Henry Addison DeLand in 1884 among the pines and was two stories high. The manager was Kate A. Wyatt. The Harlan was 170 feet long and 75 feet wide, with verandas on three sides. Additional wings were built on the south side of the hotel in 1886 and on the north side in 1887. There was a boathouse on the lake that offered guests a fleet of boats. During the towns heyday, the Harlan Hotel was a center of social activity in Lake Helen. Travel there was quite a task. Visitors had to disembark from steamships on the St. Johns River and then journey by horse, mule, or wagon. The trip became easier in 1887 when the railroad arrived. The community thrived during the boom era receiving thousands of visitors.

The freeze of the winter of 1894–1895 destroyed most of the citrus. The loss cost many in the community their livelihood. The citrus never recovered like it had been before. Those that did not replant left. The Harlan Hotel burned down on October 31, 1923. The community survived through the following decades and remained virtually undisturbed as the rest of Central Florida changed with development.

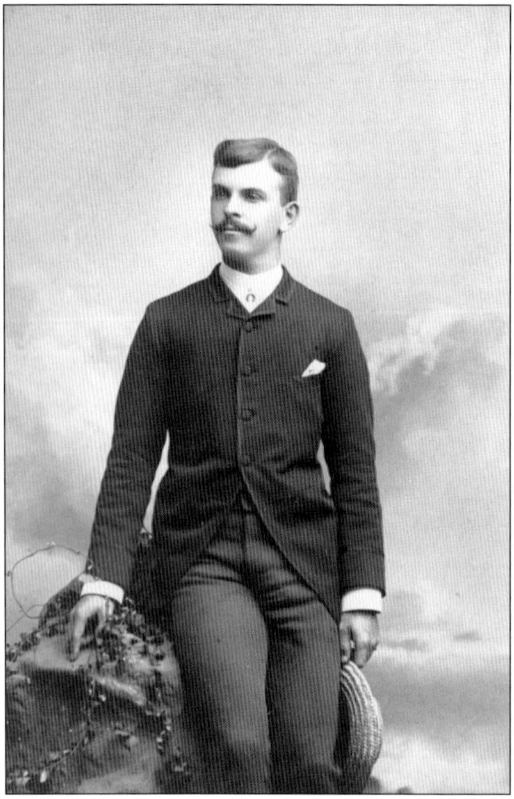

The Harlan Hotel was built in Lake Helen in 1884 and opened on Thanksgiving. It was named after Henry Deland's son Harlan DeLand, pictured here. (Courtesy of Stetson University, duPont-Ball Library, Memorabilia Collection.)

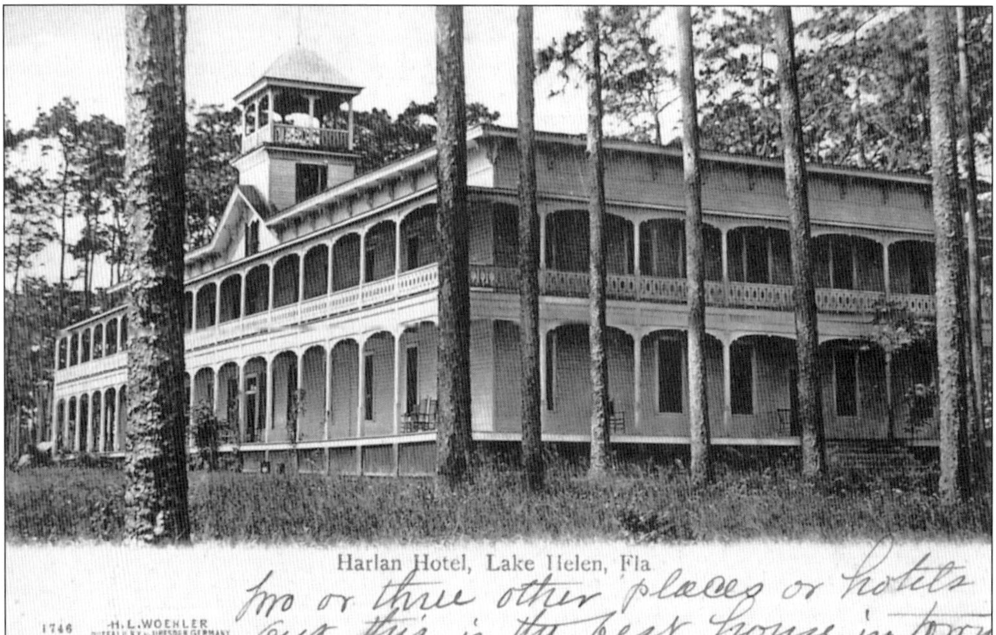

Harlan Hotel was one of two large hotels that were built in Lake Helen. The hilly pine forested land around the lake was quite popular for winter guests who frequented the hotels. (Courtesy of Lake Helen Historical Society and Museum.)

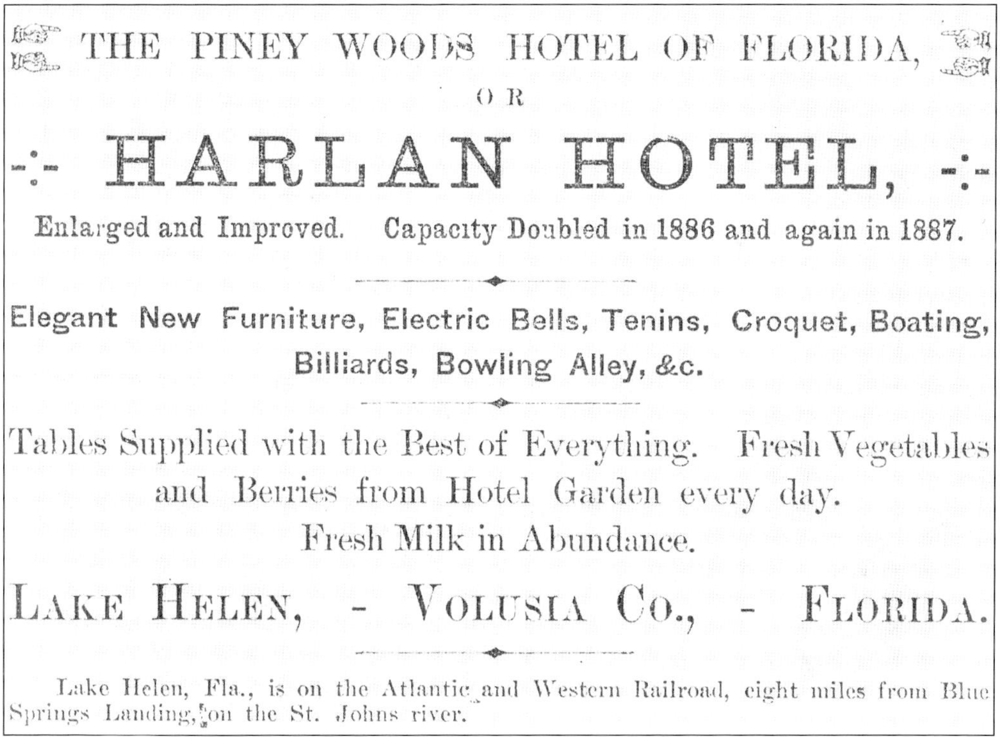
THE PINEY WOODS HOTEL OF FLORIDA,

OR

HARLAN HOTEL,

Enlarged and Improved. Capacity Doubled in 1886 and again in 1887.

Elegant New Furniture, Electric Bells, Tenins, Croquet, Boating, Billiards, Bowling Alley, &c.

Tables Supplied with the Best of Everything. Fresh Vegetables and Berries from Hotel Garden every day. Fresh Milk in Abundance.

LAKE HELEN, - VOLUSIA CO., - FLORIDA.

Lake Helen, Fla., is on the Atlantic and Western Railroad, eight miles from Blue Springs Landing, on the St. Johns river.

In 1892, a room at the Harlan Hotel cost $2 to $2.50 a day. Hotel amenities included bowling, tennis, croquet, horse riding, and a number of other activities as advertised. (Courtesy of Lake Helen Historical Society and Museum.)

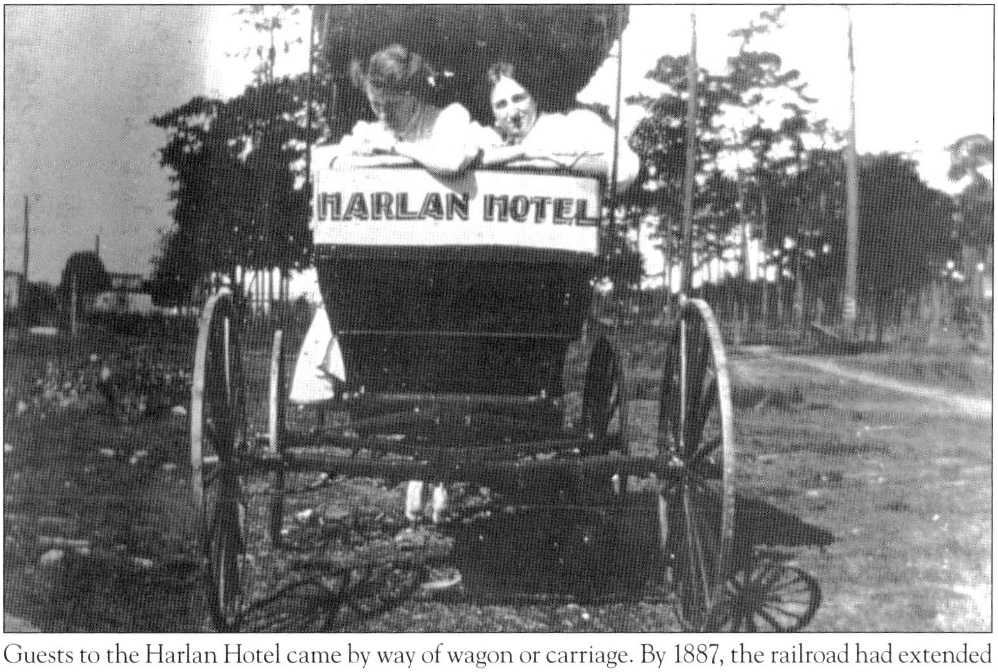

Guests to the Harlan Hotel came by way of wagon or carriage. By 1887, the railroad had extended to Lake Helen and visitors were able to arrive by train. (Courtesy of the City of Lake Helen.)

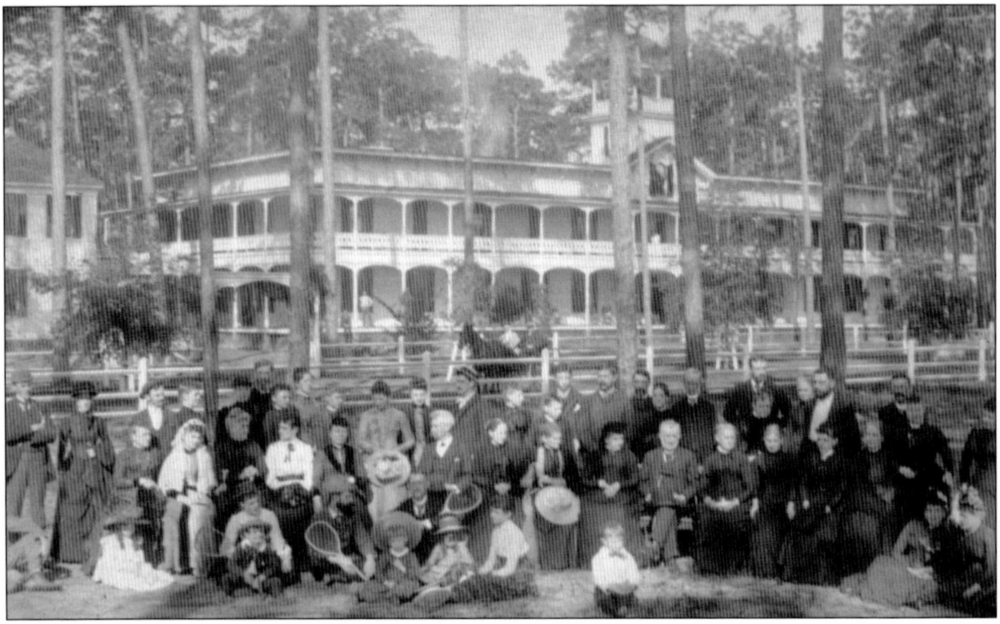

Winter visitors liked the environment around the Harlan Hotel as much as DeLand, and they wintered in Lake Helen by the droves. In this large group photograph in front of the Harlan Hotel, Harlan DeLand can be seen seated in the first row, third from the left, holding a tennis racket and wearing a hat. (Courtesy of the City of Lake Helen.)

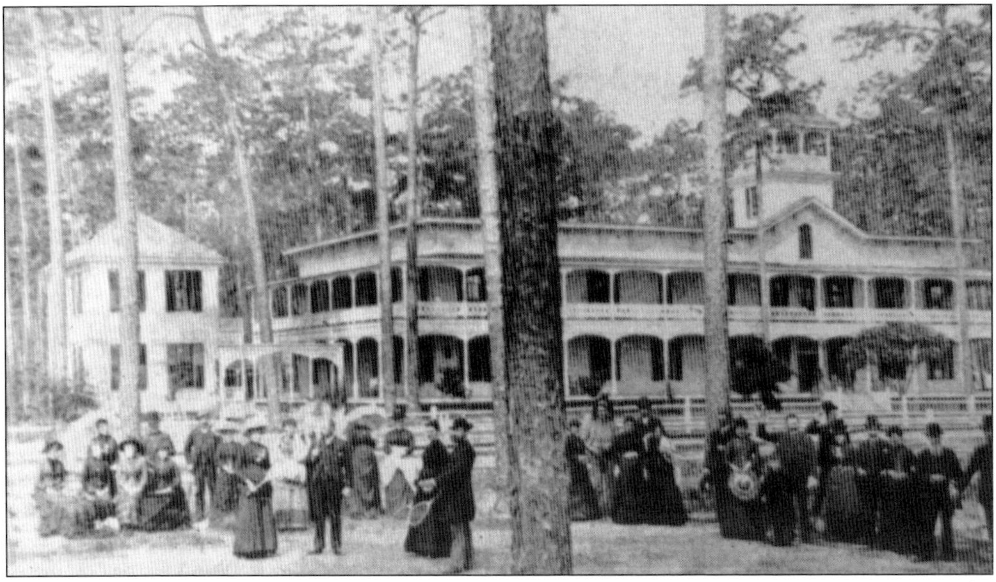

Large gatherings were common at the Harlan Hotel. Another large group of visitors grace the foreground of this 1888 card advertising the hotel in the background. (Courtesy of the City of Lake Helen.)

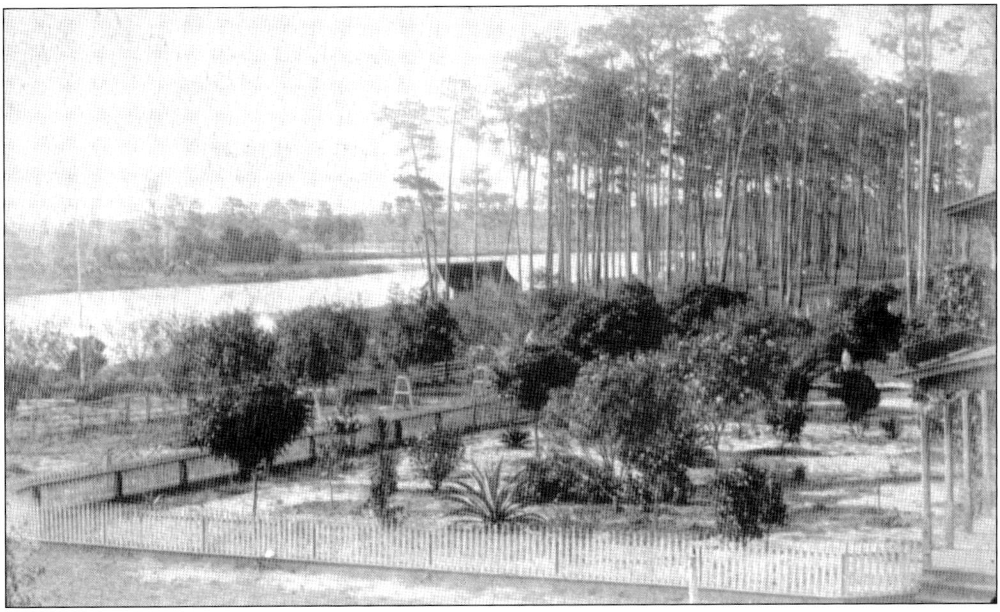

Lake Helen was another facet of the Harlan Hotel that made the location popular. Beyond the orange trees behind the hotel, the boathouse is visible on the lakeshore. (Courtesy of City of Lake Helen.)

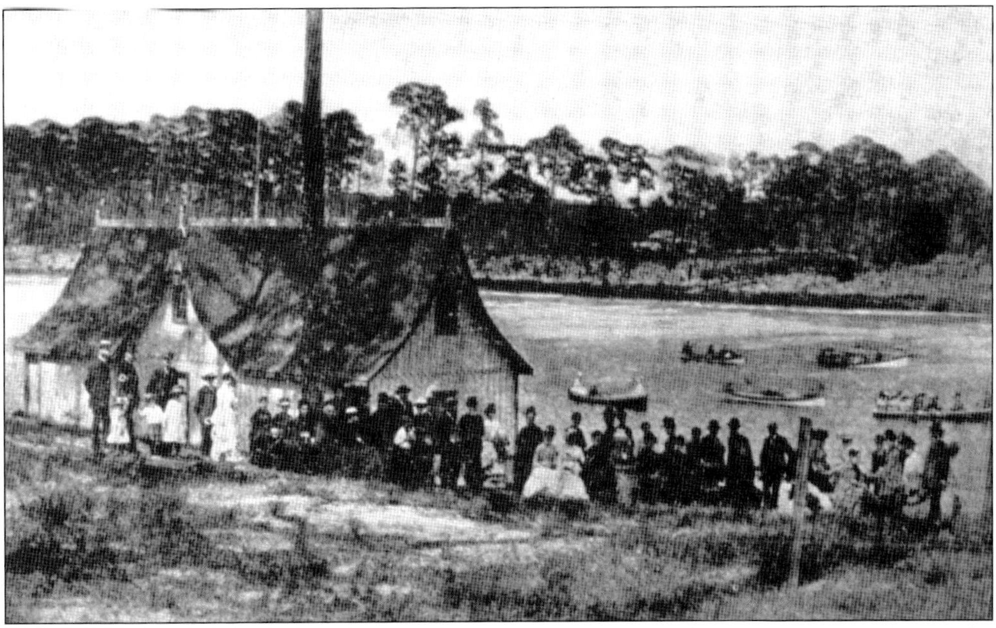

The lake provided a form of recreation for guests at the Harlan Hotel. They would gather at the lake for picnics and other activities, such as taking out rowboats from the boathouse, as pictured here. (Courtesy of the City of Lake Helen.)

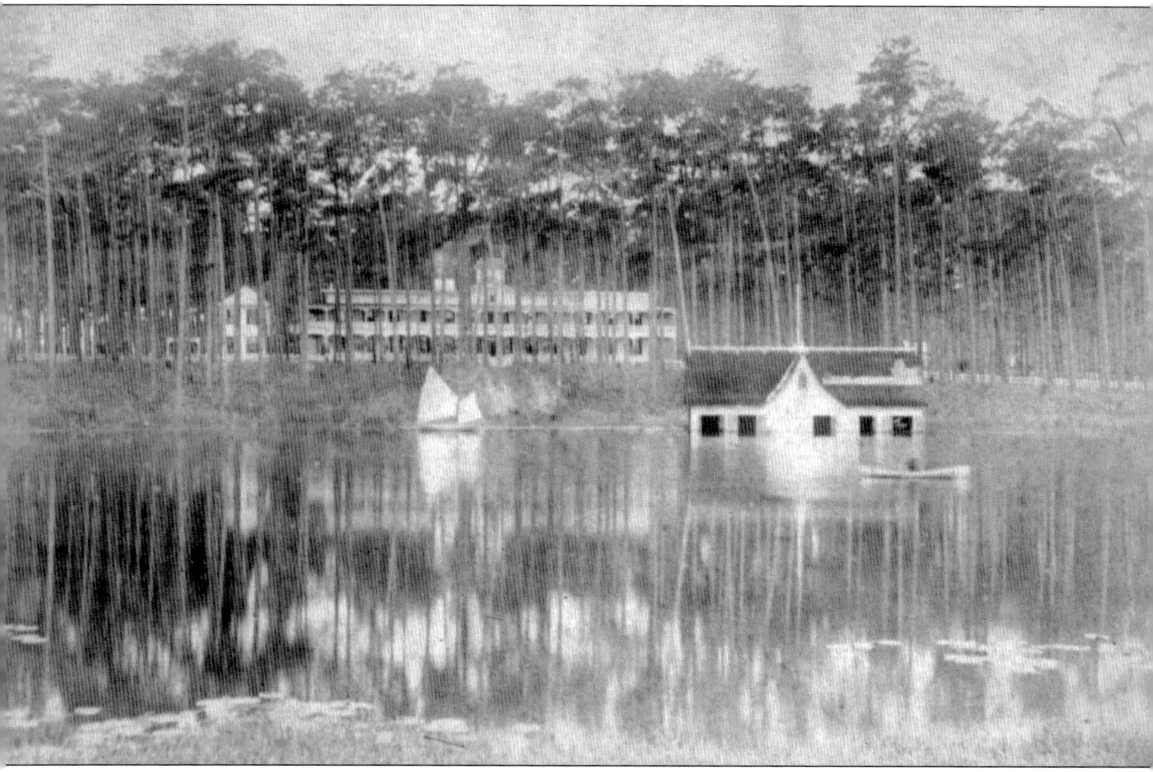

The Harlen Hotel in the pines suffered reduced patronage after the big freezes and over time, as tourism interests shifted, became forgotten. A fire destroyed the hotel in 1922, and there is unfortunately no longer any trace of its existence. (Courtesy of the City of Lake Helen.)

Seven

Cassadaga

Cassadaga Hotel

The first Cassadaga Hotel was built in the late 1800s by the Cassadaga Spiritualist Camp and owned by Emma J. Huff. Like so many of the early hotels, in 1926, the hotel burned down. The residents of Cassadaga had the hotel rebuilt in 1928 using the design of architect William J. Carpenter in the Spanish Mission style still present today. The hotel has 40 rooms and a restaurant. The hotel provided accommodations for guests and visitors to the spiritualist community.

During the Great Depression, ownership of the hotel changed hands and became privately owned. In the 1990s, the Cassadaga Hotel was sold again and renovated. The hotel still offers lodging to guests and maintains a 1920s interior décor, a restaurant, and coffee bar. Visitors seeking to explore the spiritualist camp can find assistance at the hotel.

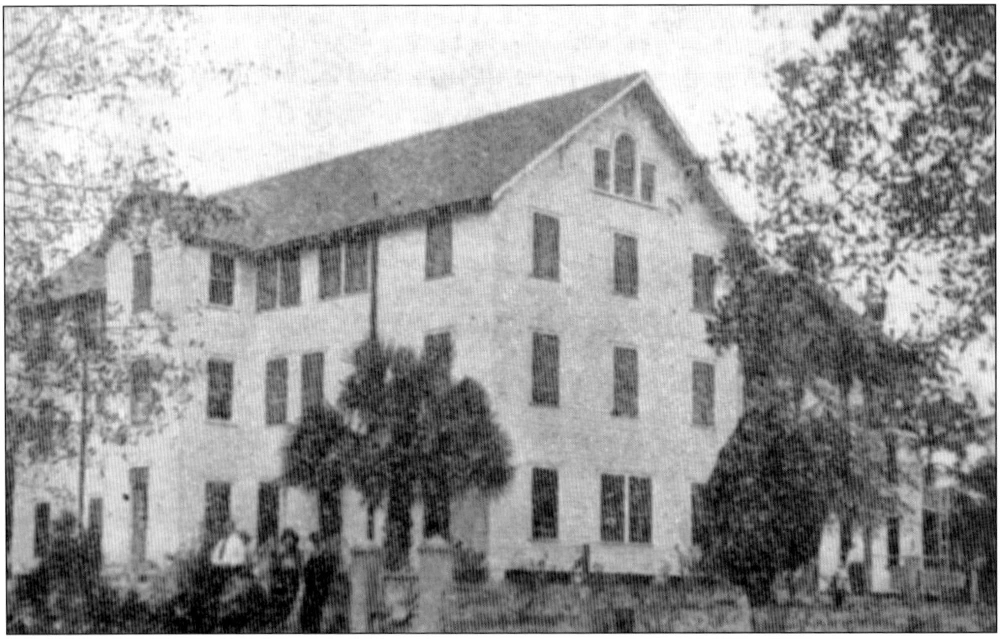

The first Cassadaga Hotel was a three-storied wooden structure. A fire in 1927 destroyed the original building, and the community then sought an expert to design its replacement. (Courtesy of the Bill Dreggors family.)

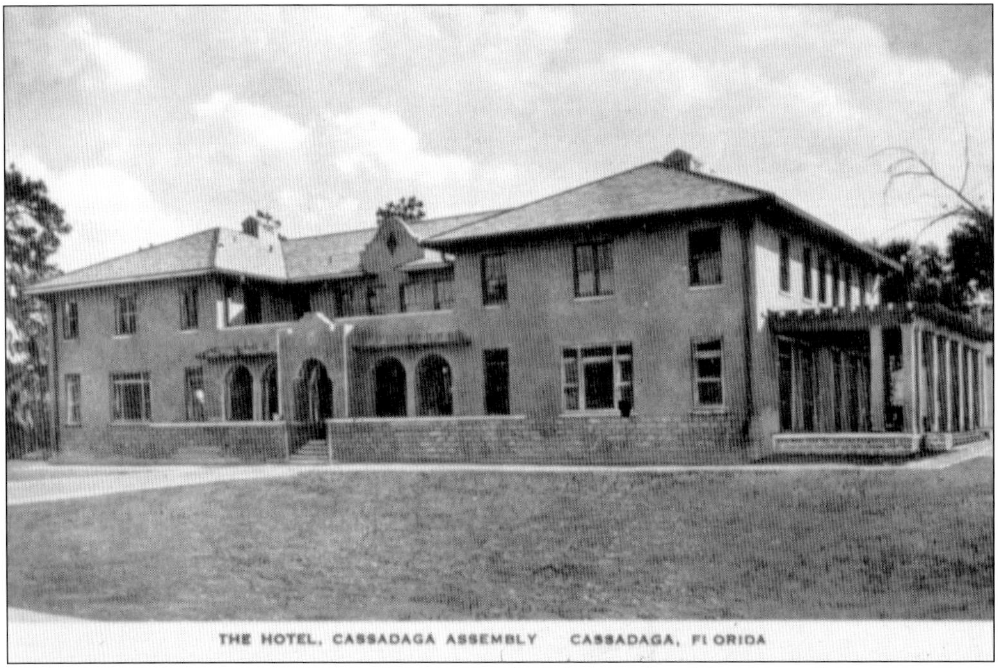

Architect William J. Carpenter was selected to plan the new hotel because of his reputation in designing the fireproof Hotel Putnam. The new concrete Cassadaga Hotel was completed in 1928. (Courtesy of the Bill Dreggors family.)

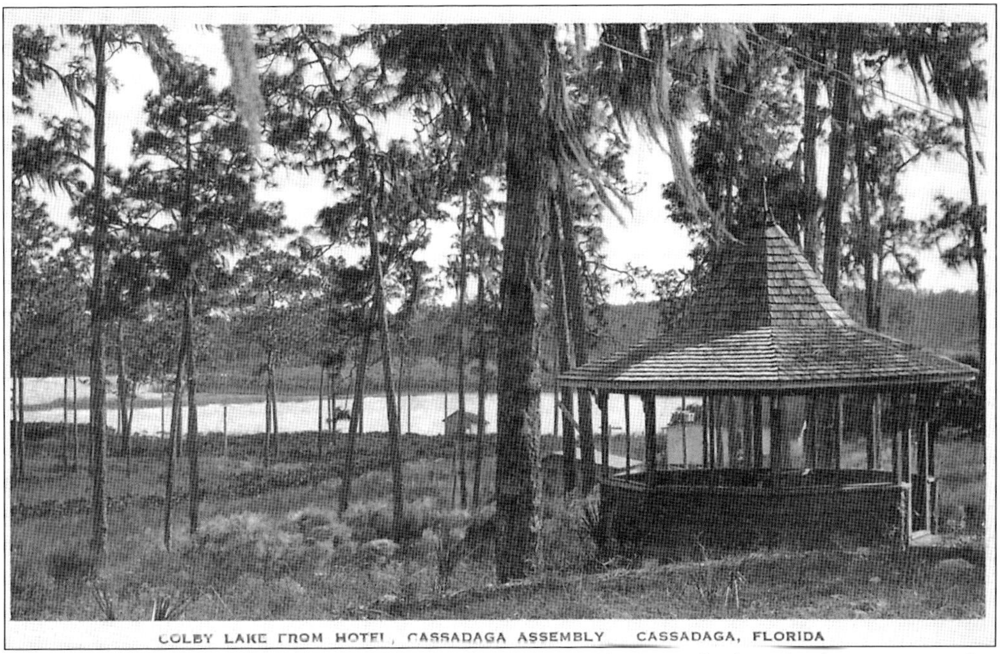

The Cassadaga community had a picturesque lake visible from the hotel. The area was also the home of the Cassadaga Spiritualist Camp, which attracts visitors and frequent gatherings. (Courtesy of the Bill Dreggors family.)

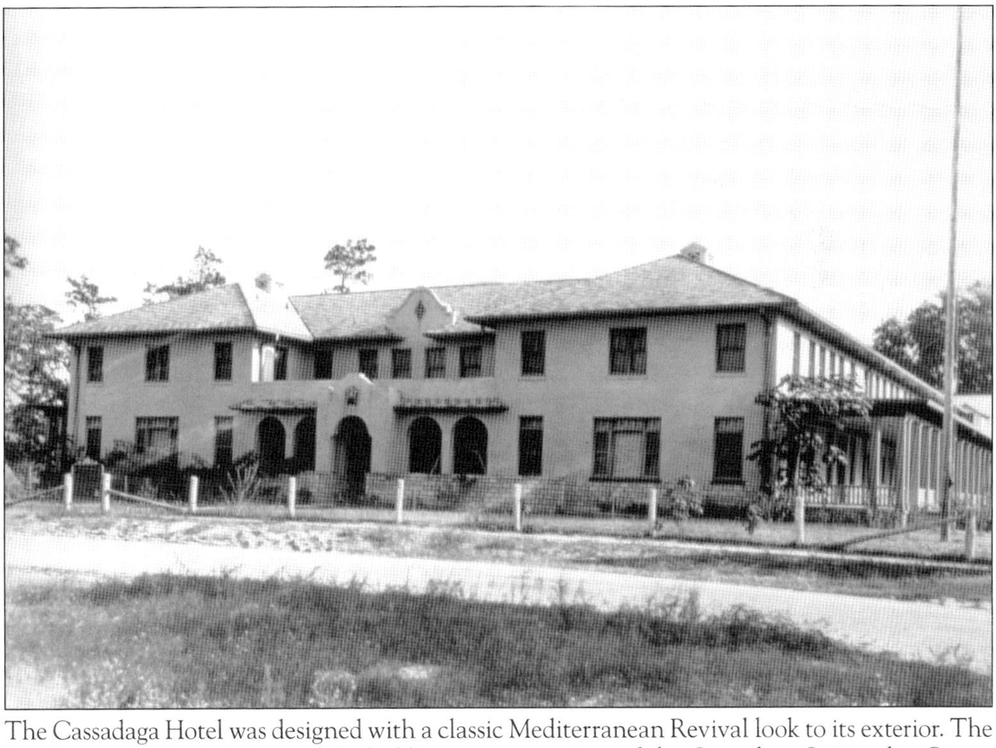

The Cassadaga Hotel was designed with a classic Mediterranean Revival look to its exterior. The hotel was used for lodging and for holding camp meetings of the Cassadaga Spiritualist Camp. (Courtesy of the Bill Dreggors family.)

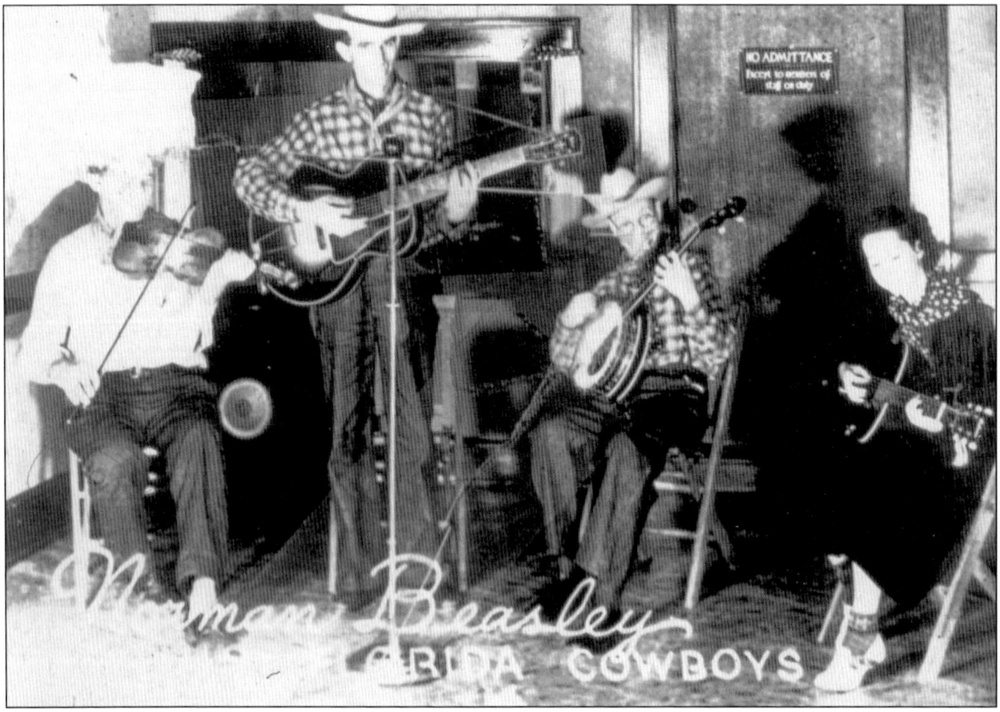

The new hotel featured a one-story veranda to welcome guests and shaded visitors along the west facing side of the building. Besides being a location for meetings of the spiritualist camp, the hotel also provided guests restaurant dining and entertainment. (Courtesy of the Bill Dreggors family.)

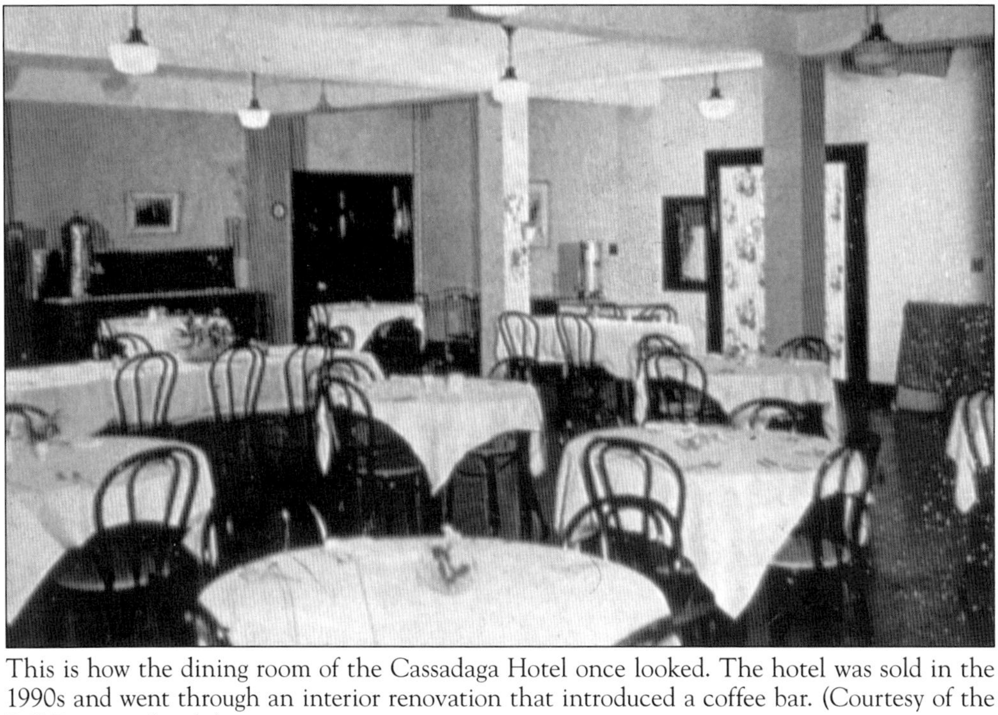

This is how the dining room of the Cassadaga Hotel once looked. The hotel was sold in the 1990s and went through an interior renovation that introduced a coffee bar. (Courtesy of the Bill Dreggors family.)

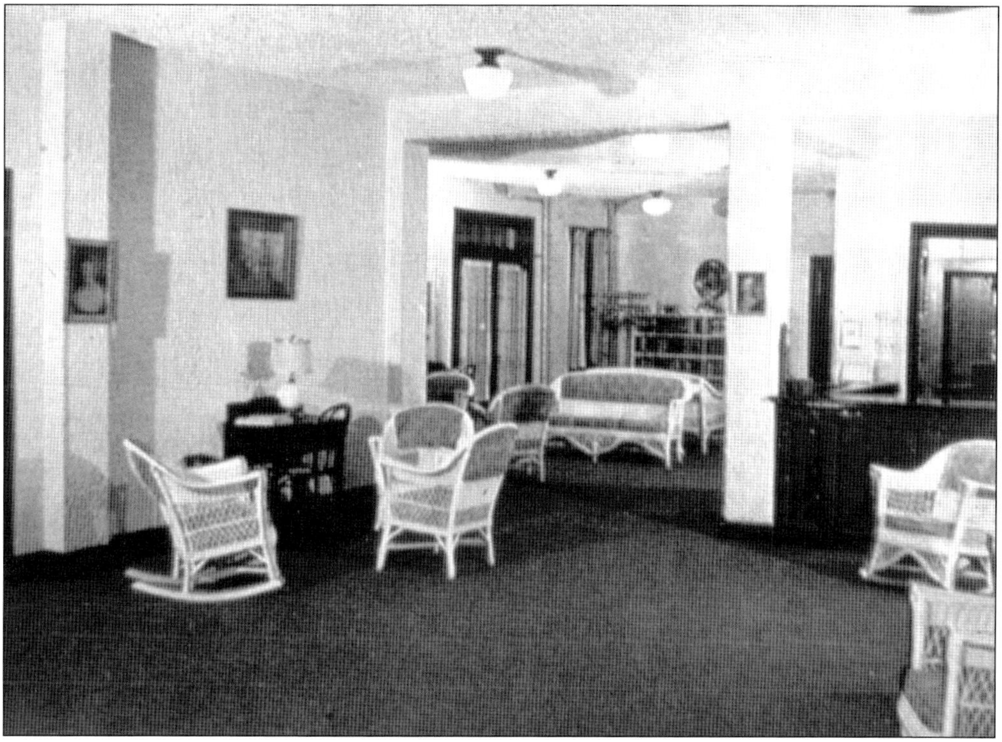

The lobby area is seen here before it was renovated in the 1990s. The owners of the Cassadaga Hotel restored the interior with a 1920s décor to preserve its elegance. (Courtesy of the Bill Dreggors family.)

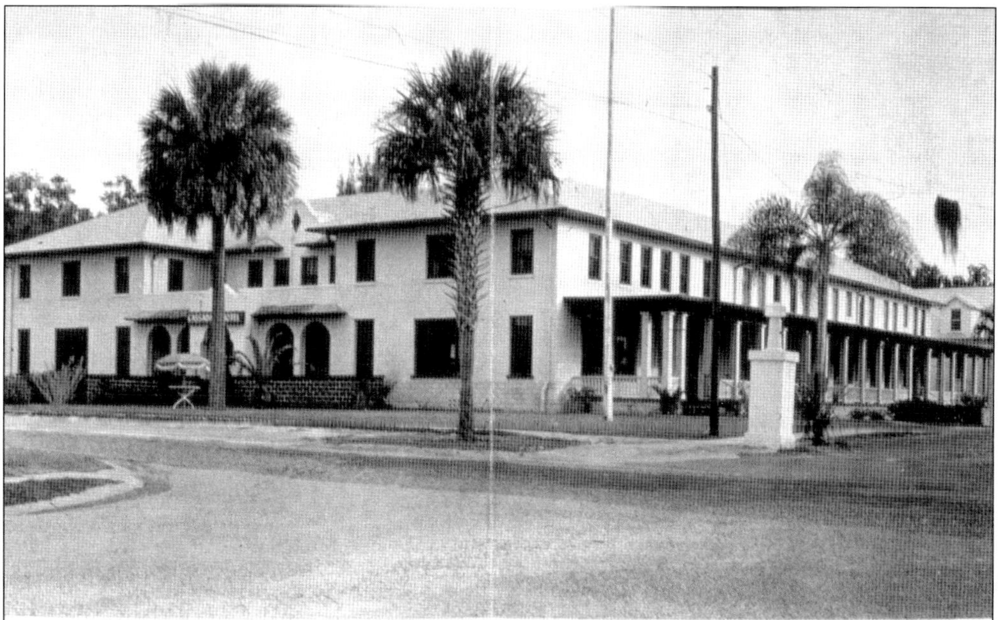

OUTSIDE VIEW OF HOTEL CASSADAGA

Changes have only been made to the interior of the hotel. On the outside, the Cassadaga Hotel remains mildly altered from its original 1928 design. (Courtesy of the Bill Dreggors family.)

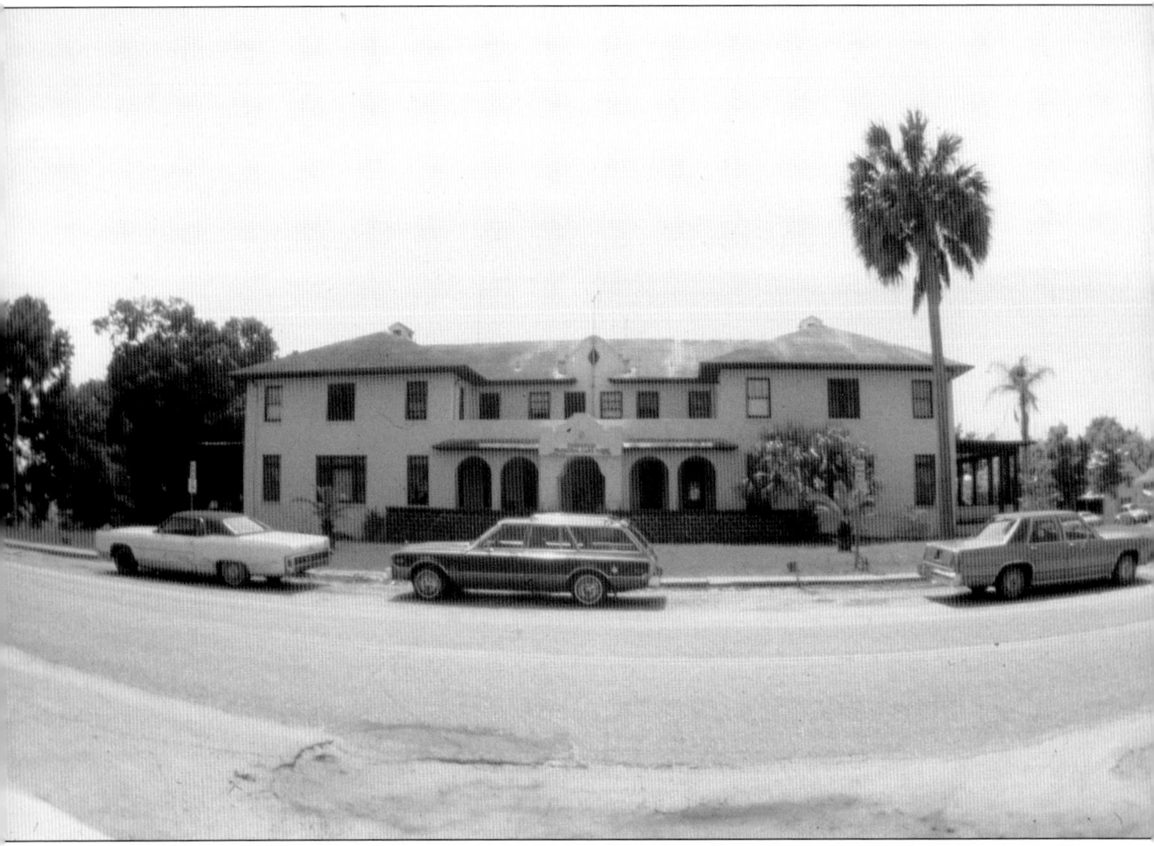

The Cassadaga Hotel today still operates as a hotel with a restaurant and coffee bar. The hotel also hosts meetings and tours of the Cassadaga Spiritualist Camp. (Courtesy of the Bill Dreggors family.)

Eight

Orange City

DeYarman Hotel

The DeYarman Hotel was first built by Hugh and Sophia DeYarman. The pair had owned a hotel in Wisconsin. They initially built a one-room cottage in 1875 with the help of seven workmen at the saw mill. The couple housed the workmen, and Sophia cooked. Construction continued, and the building later become the hotel kitchen. A second building was constructed to house employees, and by 1876, the DeYarman Hotel opened. It had an office, lobby, and public rooms on its first floor. A stairway led from the lobby and another outside to the 12 bedrooms on the second floor.

The hotel was the only one in the area for many years. DeYarman Hotel hosted the first religious services in the community, and the town's Fourth of July celebration. In 1882, it was the meeting place for discussions on the town's incorporation. In 1886, Hugh DeYarman became mayor and served for six years. He was also postmaster for Orange City from 1889 to 1893.

During the early 1900s, two more wings were added to the west and east sides of the hotel. This increased the rooms on both floors of the west wing with two rooms sharing a bathroom. The east wing gained a dining room and kitchen on the first floor and eight more rooms upstairs. Through the decades, ownership of the DeYarman changed. It was used by the Methodist Camp, catered to Daytona race car drivers, and served as a convalescent home. During that time, a center wing with a bar was added to the first floor and three more rooms upstairs. Bathrooms were added to every room, and the veranda was also extended around the building.

In 1902, it was the Orange City Hotel. At one time, it became a venue for craft stores and was called the White Elephant. By 1995, its new owner opened the hotel, renamed it the 1876 Heritage Inn, and added a postal museum. The building was sold again in 2012, and its owner attempted to further restore the hotel. Personal problems have forced the owner to place the hotel on the market for sale.

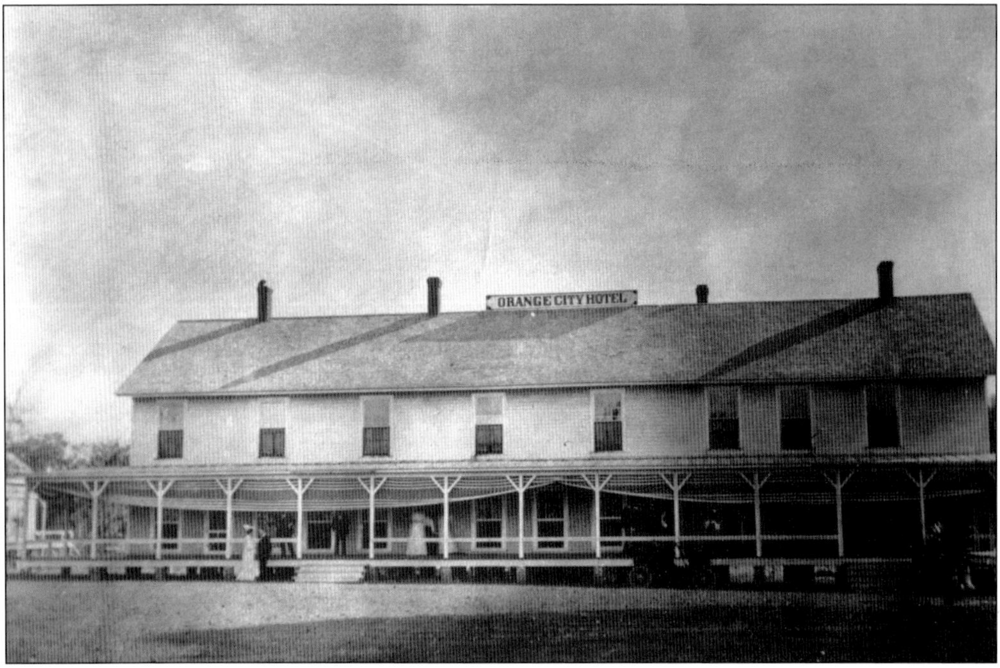

The DeYarman Hotel began small but soon expanded to meet the needs of a growing community and winter guests. This is how the hotel appeared in the 1880s, when it was referred to as the Orange City Hotel. (Courtesy of State Archives of Florida, Florida Memory.)

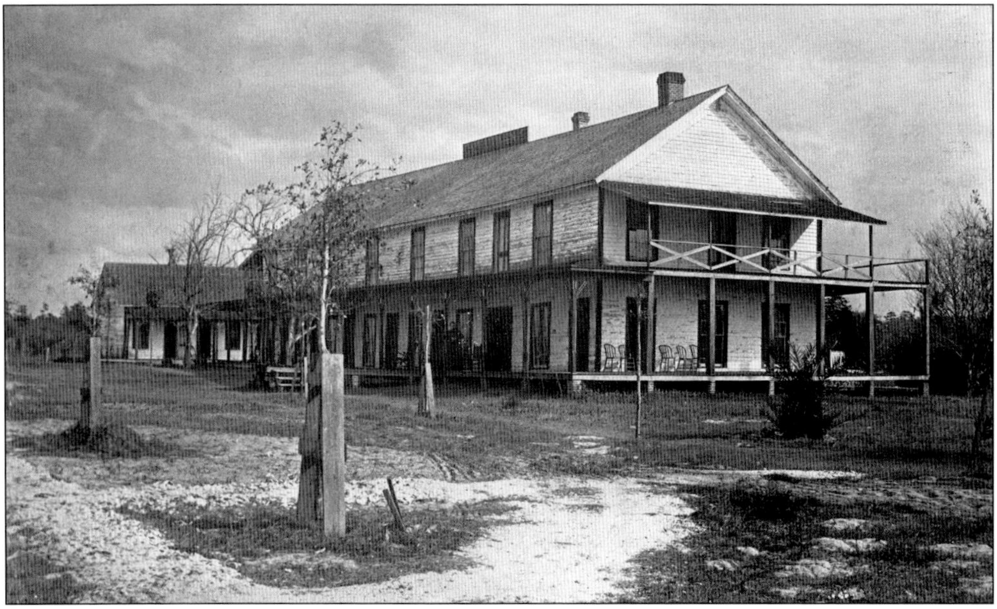

Orange City suffered the same fate as other West Volusia County communities after the winter freeze of 1894–1895. With the citrus gone, the landscape was bare, so residents were encouraged to plant trees, as seen in this photograph. (Courtesy of State Archives of Florida, Florida Memory.)

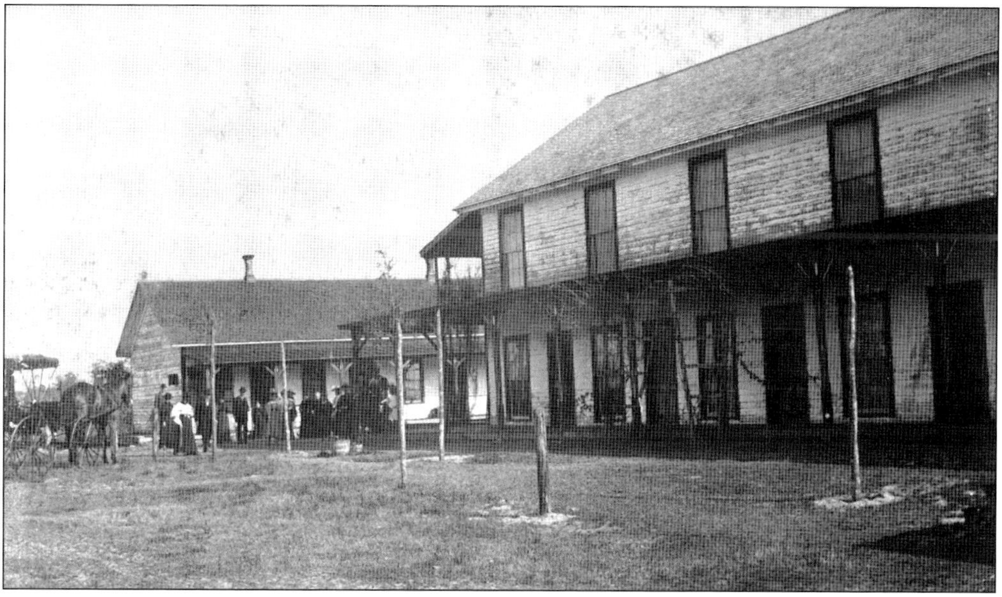

The DeYarman Hotel was one of the largest buildings in town. Before other buildings were erected, the DeYarman served as the meeting place for community gatherings as well as civic meetings. (Courtesy of State Archives of Florida, Florida Memory.)

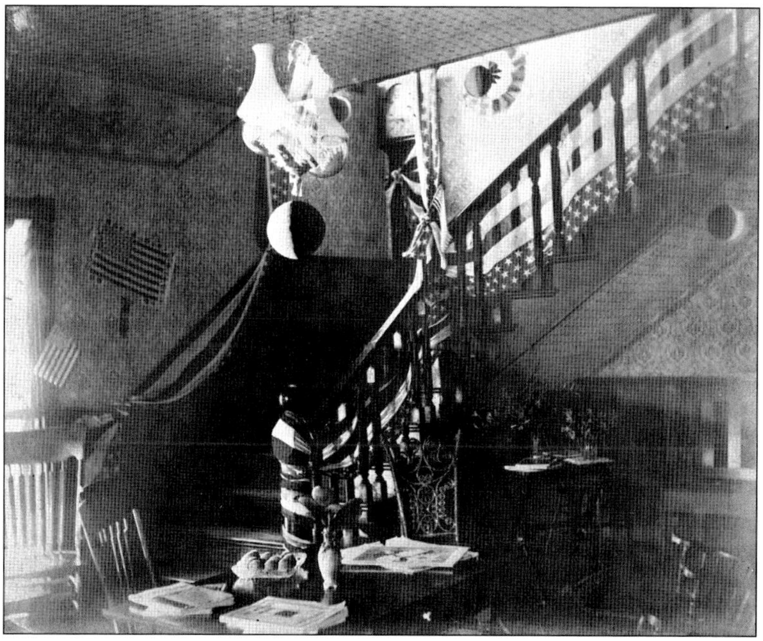

This image from 1906 shows the main interior stairway in the main lobby of the DeYarman Hotel. The room is decorated with flags and punting in preparation for a patriotic event. (Courtesy of State Archives of Florida, Florida Memory.)

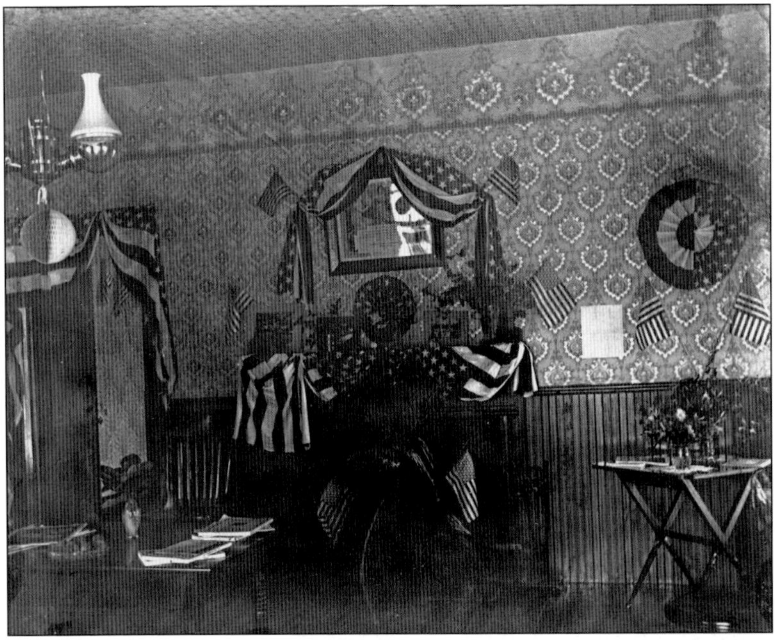

This photograph from the same time is the opposite side of the lobby viewed earlier. Note the detail of the wainscoting paneling and wallpaper in this image. (Courtesy of State Archives of Florida, Florida Memory.)

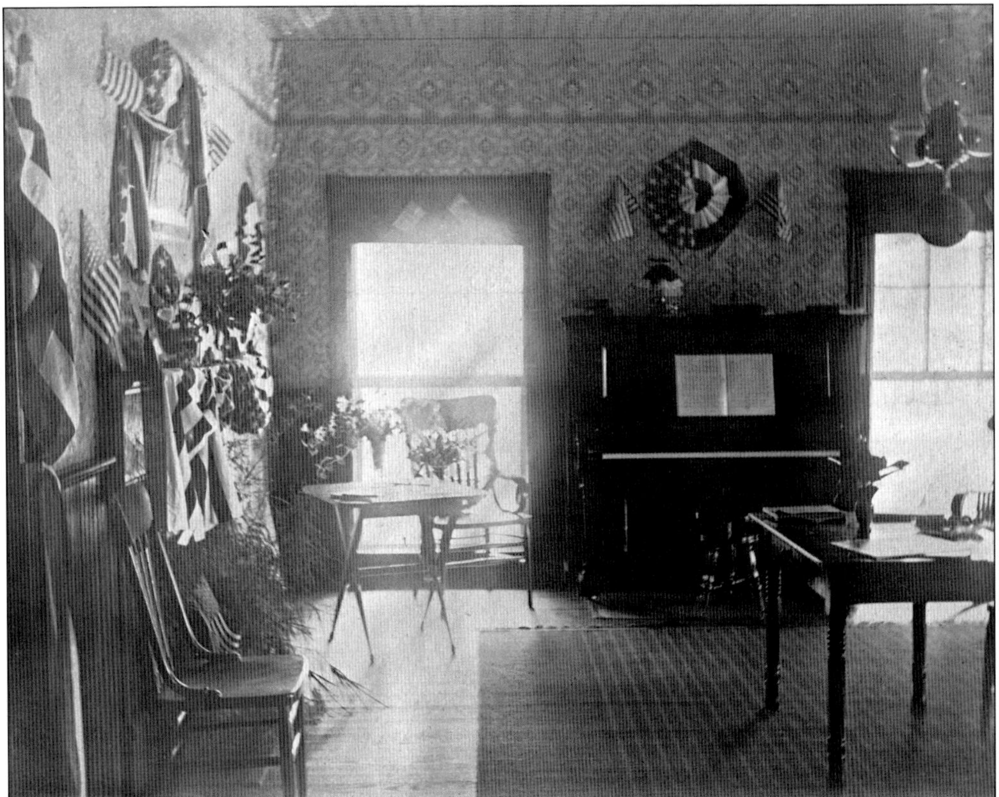

This is another photograph of the lobby with its decorations. The view is from the left of the stairway, looking across the room to the porch windows. (Courtesy of State Archives of Florida, Florida Memory.)

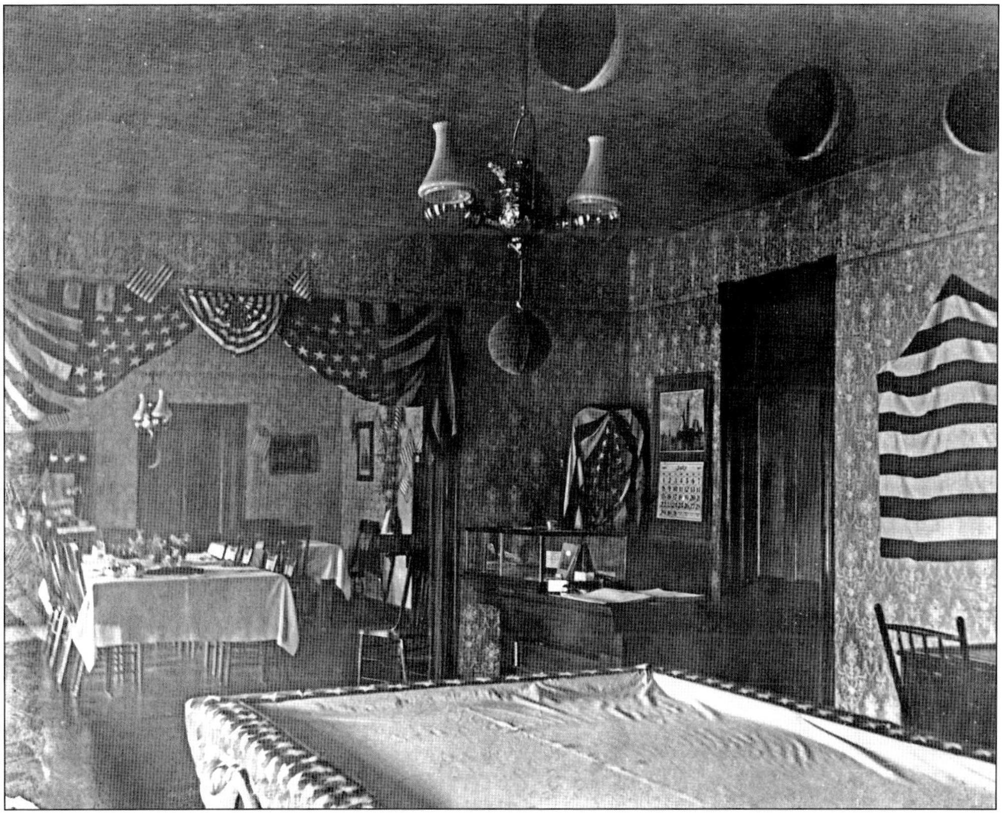

In this 1906 photograph from the DeYarman Hotel, the view looks toward the dining area. Along with all of the decorations, there appears to be what looks like a pool table covered in decorative fabric in the foreground. (Courtesy of State Archives of Florida, Florida Memory.)

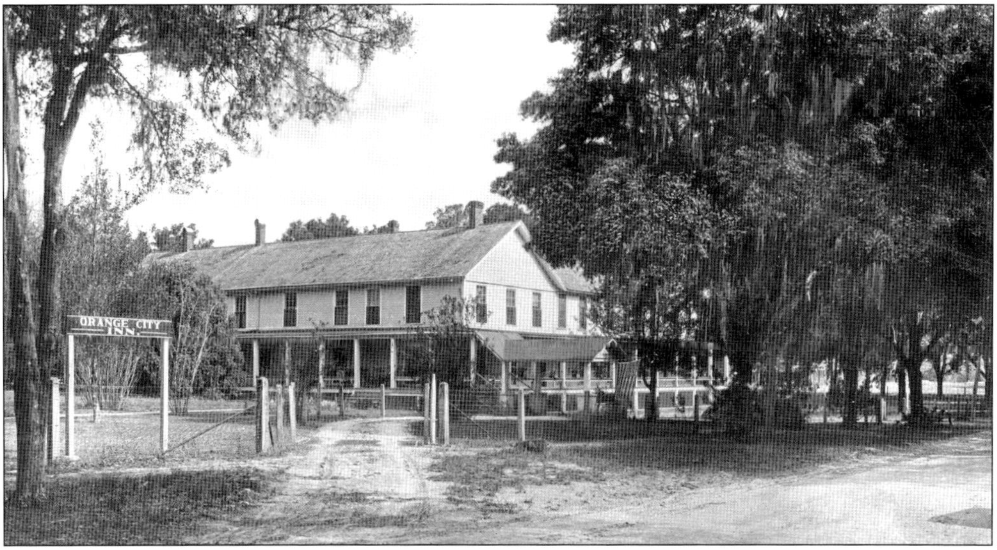

Like the other grand hotels in West Volusia County, the DeYarman suffered a loss in attendance over time. The hotel changed hands a number of times, and owners have tried to maintain it. (Courtesy of State Archives of Florida, Florida Memory.)

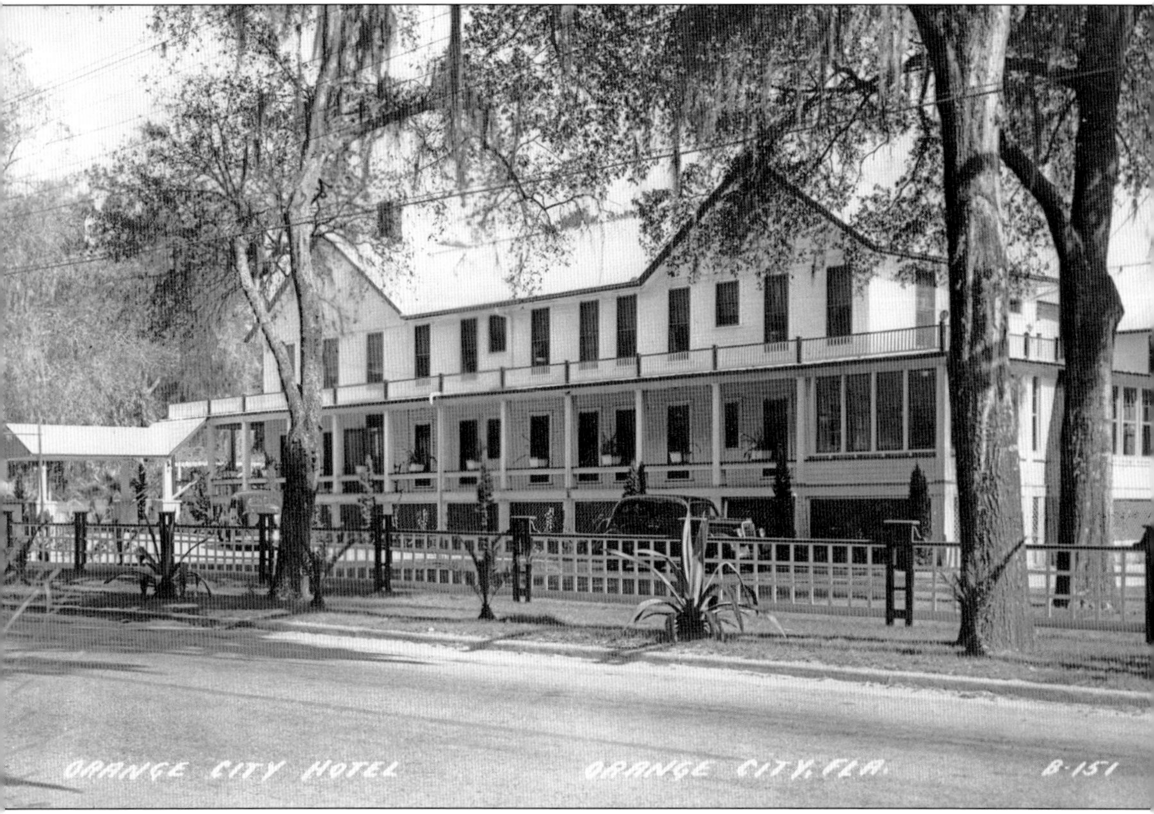

The DeYarman Hotel is now called the 1876 Heritage Inn, and its outside appearance is somewhat like that of this 1940s image. The hotel is still open for guests, but the property was currently up for sale when this book went to print, leaving the future of this surviving landmark in question. (Courtesy of State Archives of Florida, Florida Memory.)

Nine

Enterprise
Brock House

In 1855, Capt. Jacob Brock had a steamboat, a wharf on the shore of Lake Monroe in Enterprise, and Brock House. Brock was probably the first to envision the notion of "build it and they will come."

Brock House was a large three-story white wooden hotel with green shutters sitting broadside to the lake. It was built to accommodate up to 50 guests and catered to sportsmen who wanted to hunt, fish, and see the country. Word was already out about Brock House. The *Florida Republican* newspaper noted on October 25, 1855, that a "large and commodious hotel which has been (underway) from some time past at Enterprise, owned by Jacob Brock . . . is nearly completed and will be open early the coming winter." The article went on to say that Brock had hired a reputable northern hotel manager already on the scene "with cooks and waiters from the north for the purpose of fitting up the House for the reception of guests."

Brock transported tourists on a 206-mile three-day trip from Jacksonville to Brock House with an overnight stop at Palatka. Once at Brock House, guests were provided with all of the conveniences of the time to enjoy their stay. The Civil War interrupted this business plan but it resumed after the war. Brock could not compete with other entrepreneurs and had to sell Brock House in 1876. His hotel was renovated and became famous, attracting both notables and celebrities of the era. Among the guests to Brock House were Grover Cleveland, Ulysses S. Grant, Jay Gould, Rutherford B. Hayes, the Vanderbilts, James Rockefeller, Gen. William T. Sherman, and even Henry Addison DeLand.

The name of the hotel was changed to Benson Springs Inn and, later, the Epworth Inn. When the Methodist Church began seeking a home for orphans, the old hotel was used for a time. In 1937, the hotel was torn down, and its lumber used for the construction of other buildings in Enterprise. The property was purchased by the Methodist Church, and the Methodist Children's Home was built there. Pilings from the steamboat wharf are the last reminder of the Brock House.

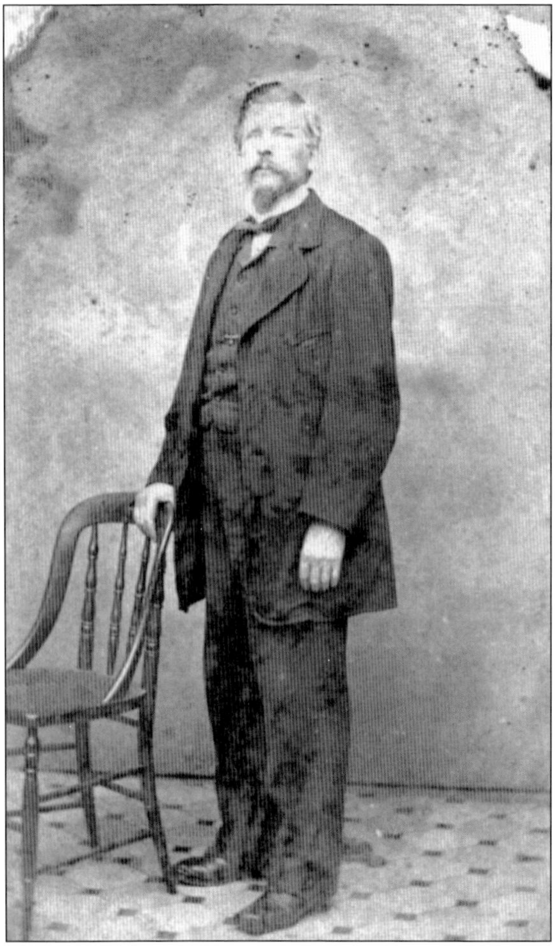

Jacob Brock was a steamboat captain and entrepreneur. In 1850, Brock realized the value of supplying commerce to settlements and transportation to visitors along the upper St. Johns River in Volusia County. (Courtesy of State Archives of Florida, Florida Memory.)

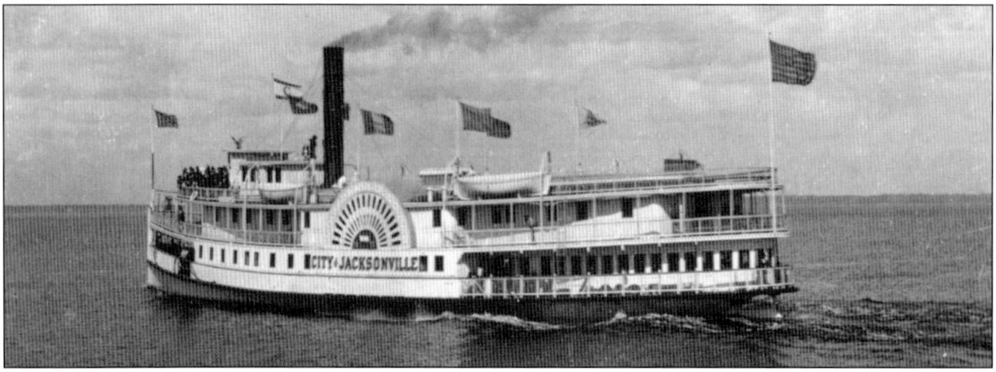

Brock had a head start in developing an enterprise off of the use of steamboats on the upper St. Johns River. He soon had competitors like Frederick de Bary, who also built a fleet of steamboats that included the elegant *City of Jacksonville*. (Courtesy of Edward A. Mueller.)

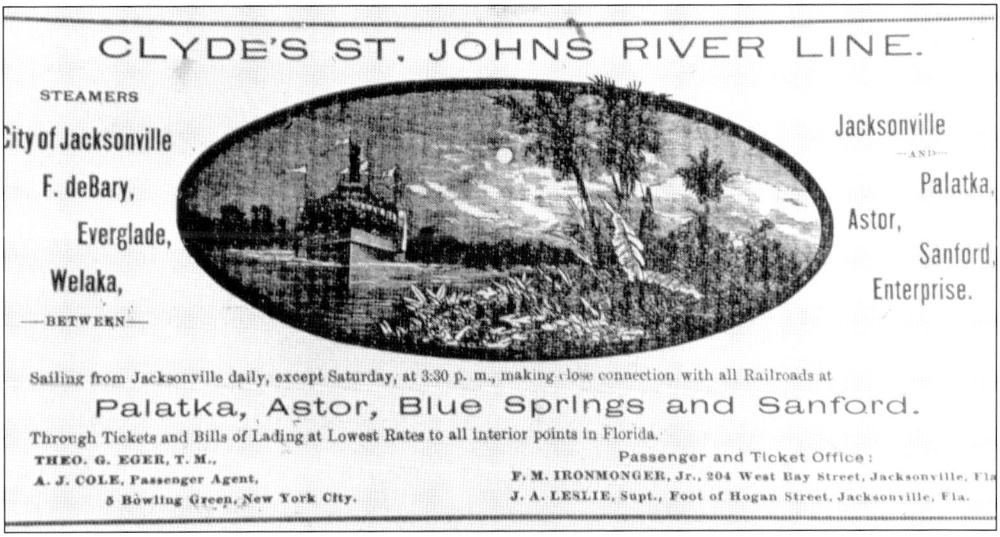

The St. Johns River was the most convenient means to enter Central Florida in the 1870s. This ad from the Clyde Line lists the various stops the steamships would make as they traveled along the river. (Courtesy of the Bill Dreggors family.)

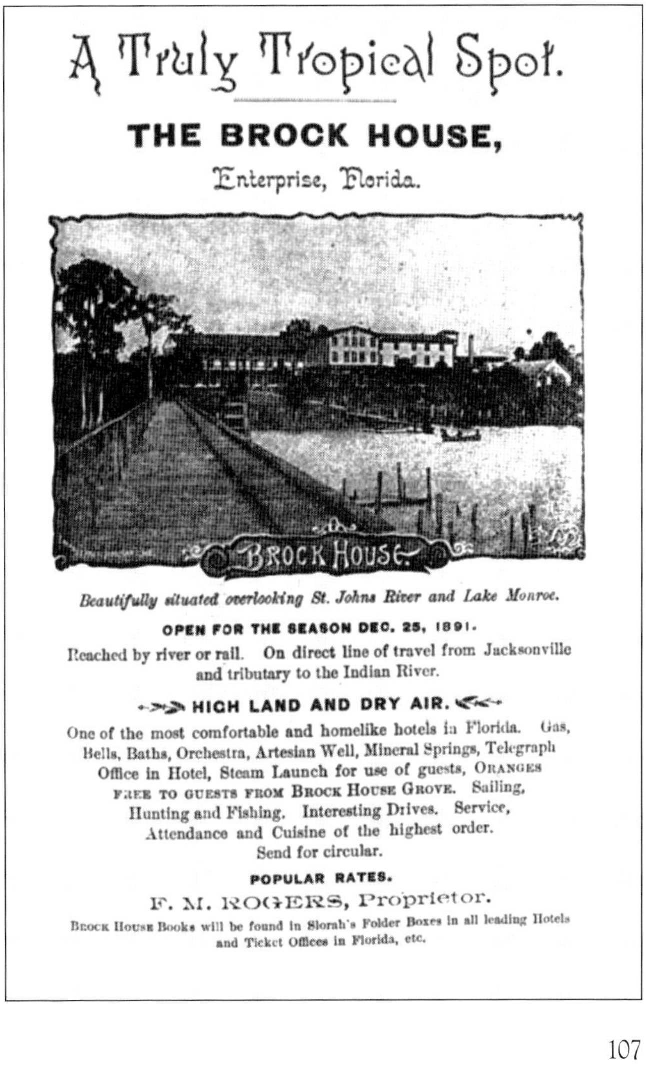

The Brock House was the premier hotel in West Volusia County, as indicated in this flyer. During its peak years, it was reached by both steamboat and rail. (Courtesy of Courtesy of Jim Cara.)

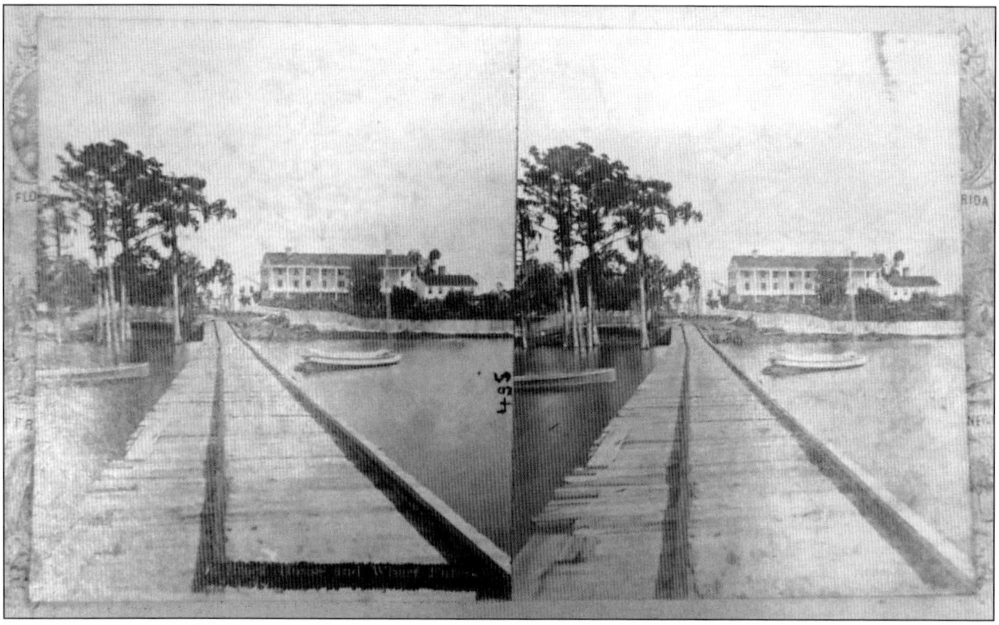

Brock understood how important it was to provide for the needs of travelers and vacationers. In 1850, he built the Brock House pictured here in stereoscopic view in Enterprise at the end of his steamboat route. (Courtesy of the Enterprise Heritage Center and Museum.)

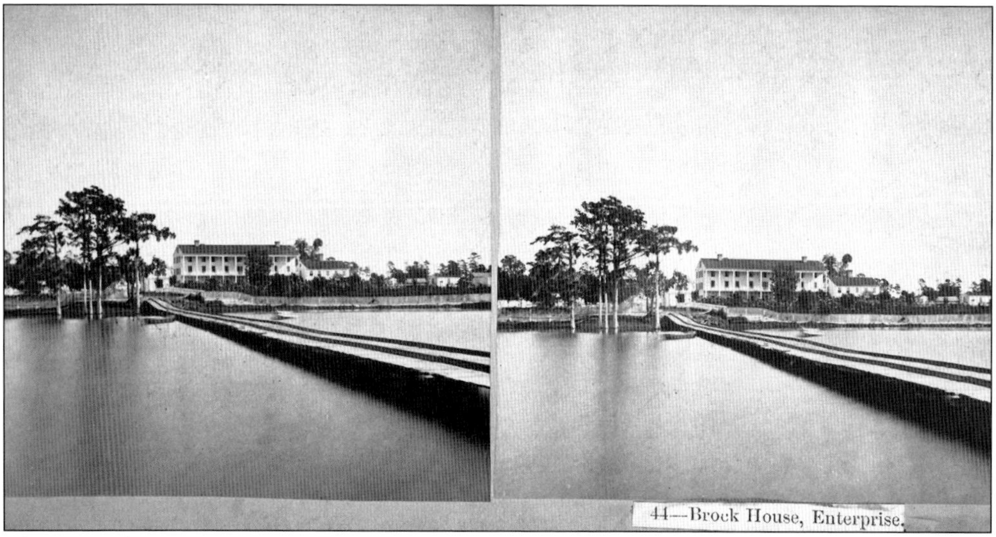

This is another stereoscopic image of Brock House with a wider view. Brock built his hotel on the high bluffs overlooking the northern shore of Lake Monroe, with a long dock that used a rail cart to move goods from arriving steamboats. (Courtesy of State Archives of Florida, Florida Memory.)

Steamboats would offload passengers and their luggage at the wharf at the end of the dock. Pictured here is a group of travelers in 1905 waiting on the wharf to be transported. (Courtesy of the Bill Dreggors family.)

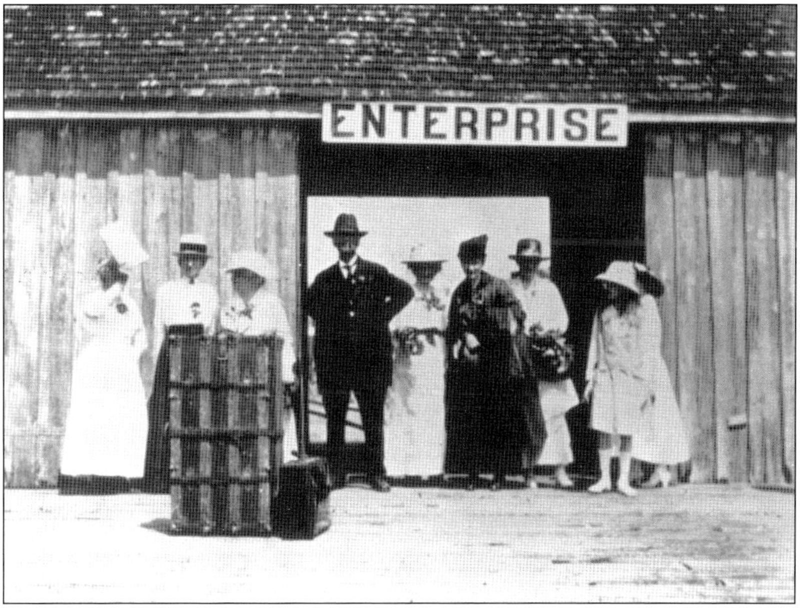

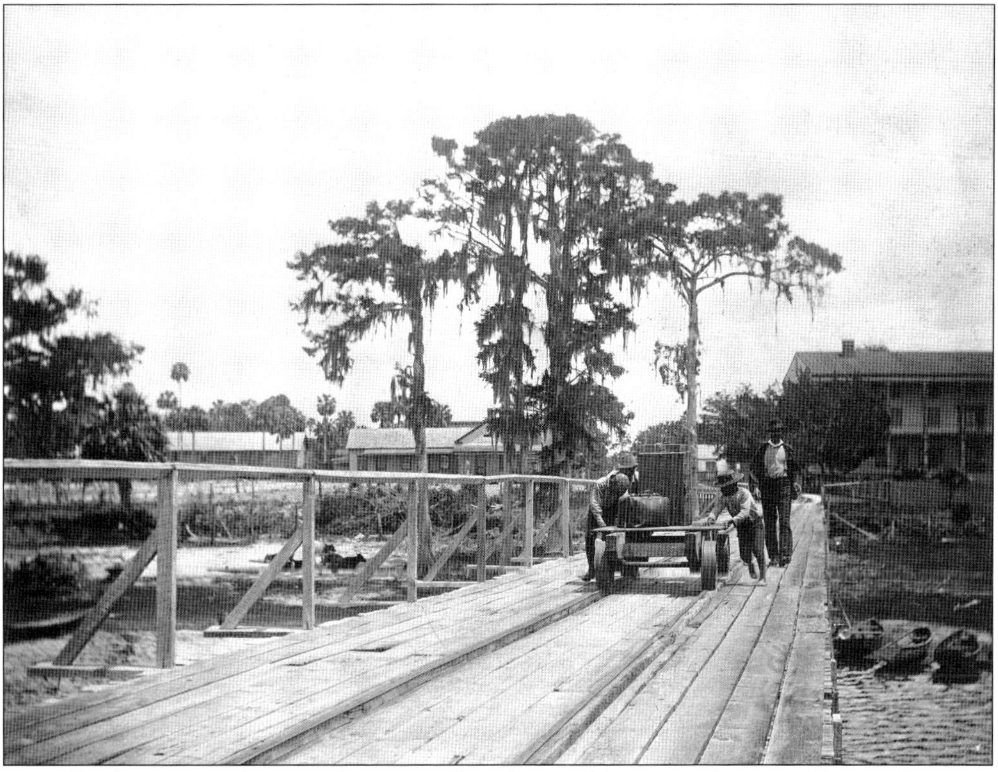

A small railcar was used to move luggage and goods to and from steamboats and the Brock House. Once loaded, the cart was either pulled or pushed along the rails to and from the hotel. (Courtesy of the Bill Dreggors family.)

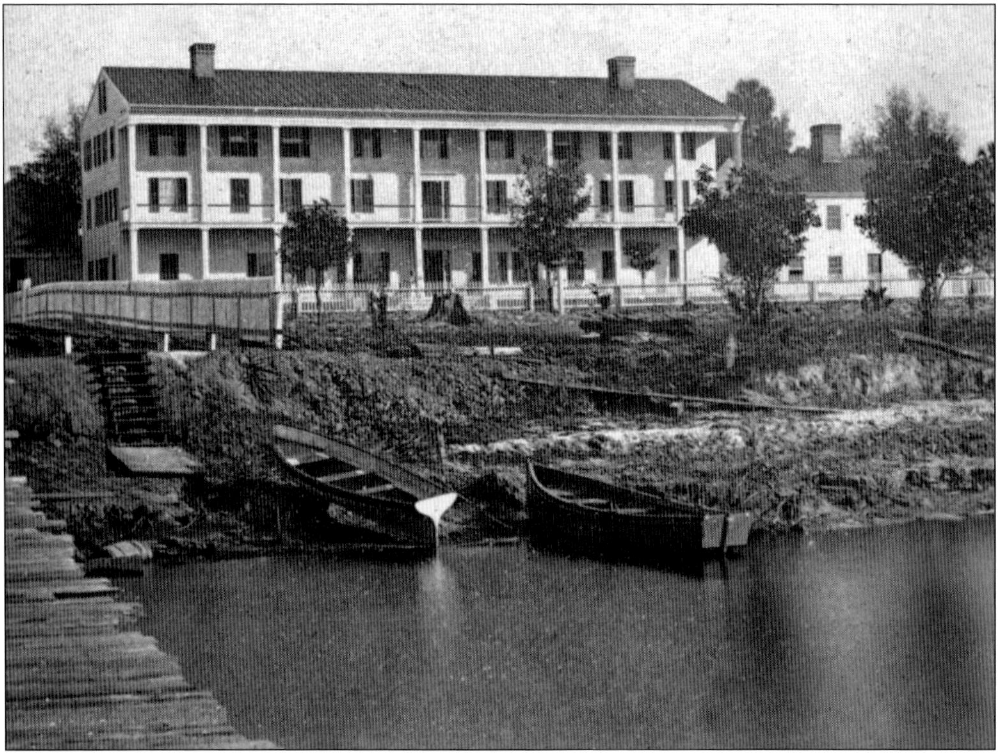

This 1875 photograph of the Brock House provides a better view of the hotel. The porches and large windows allowed for a better enjoyment of the breezes that blew off the lake. (Courtesy of the Enterprise Heritage Center and Museum.)

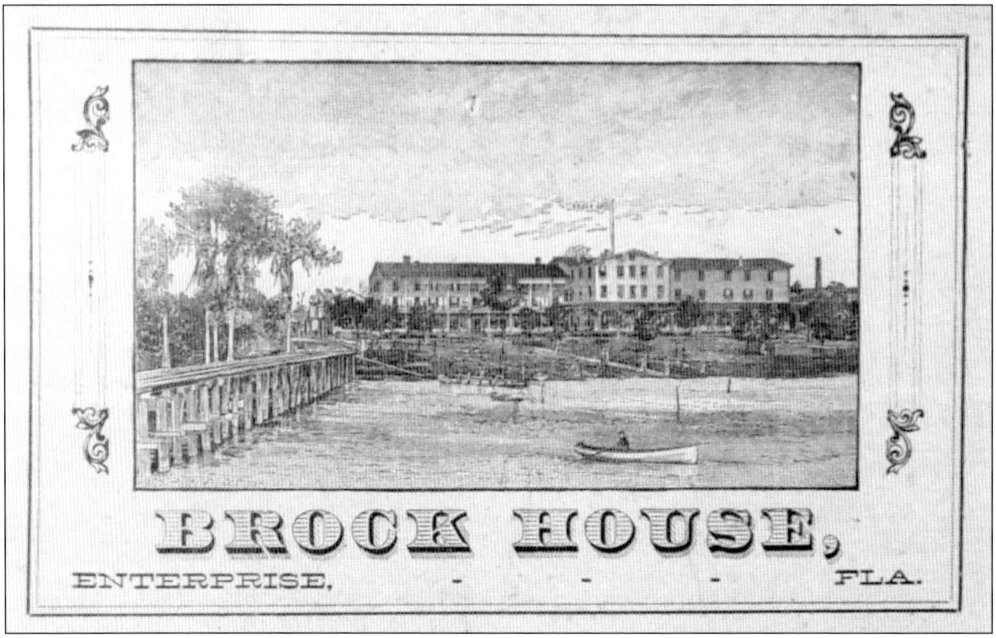

The Brock House offered its guests a number of amenities. This is one of those special touches that guests received: a boxed lunch. (Courtesy of the Enterprise Heritage Center and Museum.)

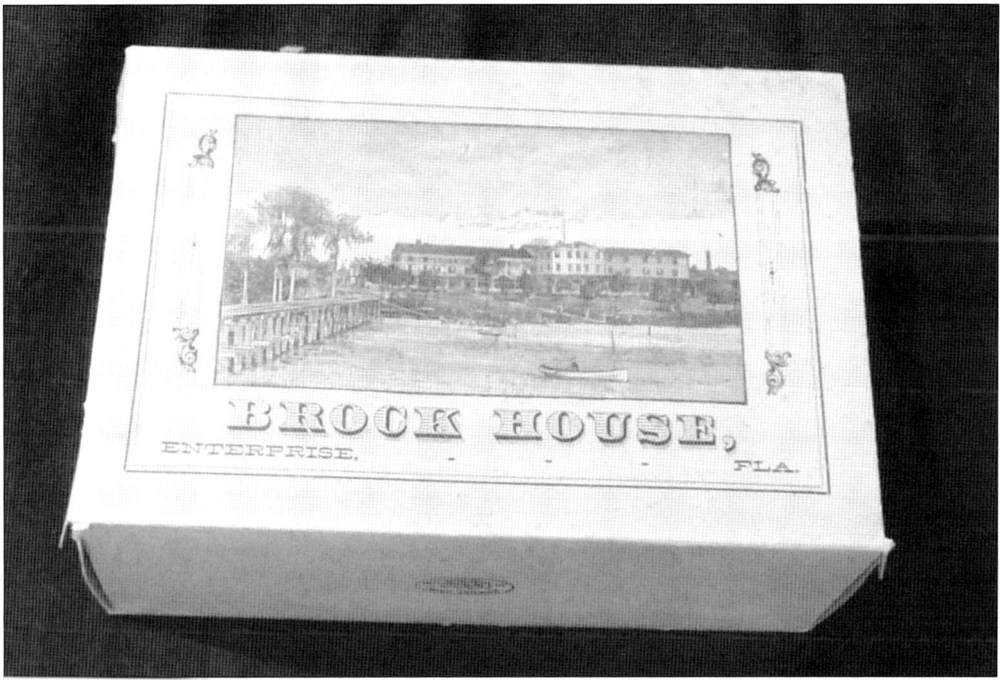

Here is another view of the same lunch box showing its folded construction. The practice of providing hotel guests with boxed lunches is still carried on at some resorts and hotels today. (Courtesy of the Enterprise Heritage Center and Museum.)

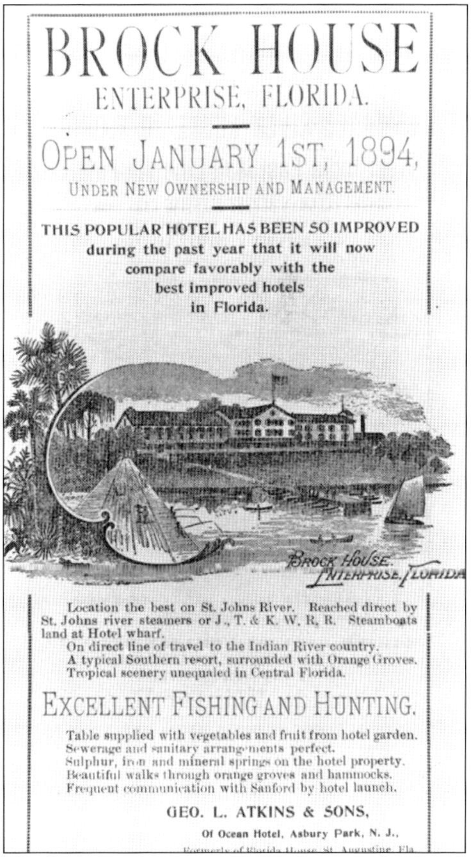

Brock eventually lost his hotel after extending himself too much financially trying to compete against the De Bary steamship line. The hotel changed hands prior to the big freeze that would impact the area's economy. (Courtesy of the Bill Dreggors family.)

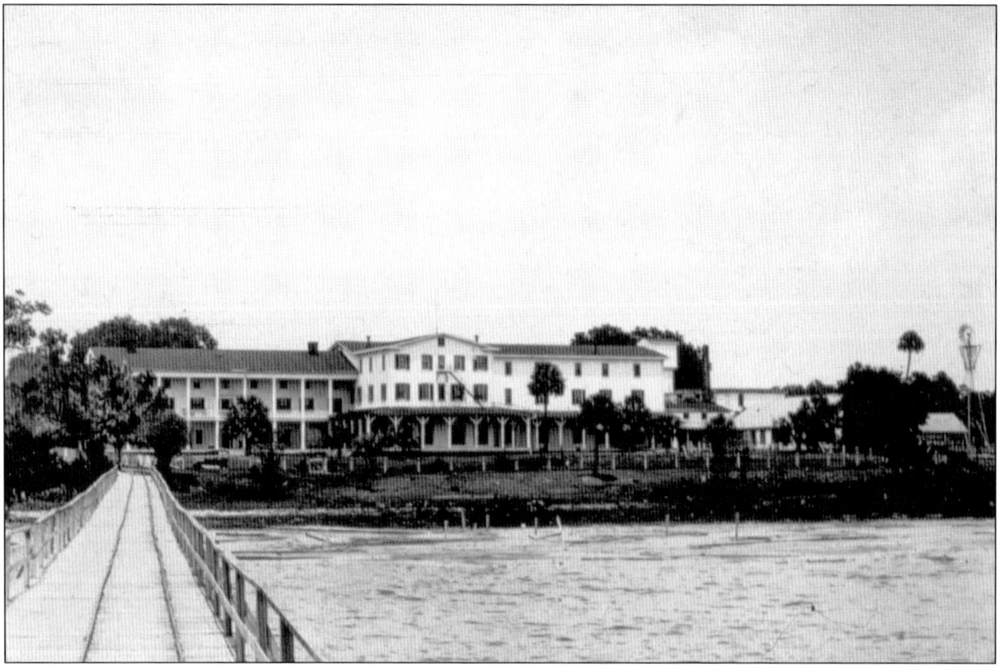

Changes were made over the years to Brock House. In this photograph, the hotel has increased in size with additions, and the dock has been improved with railings. (Courtesy of the Bill Dreggors family.)

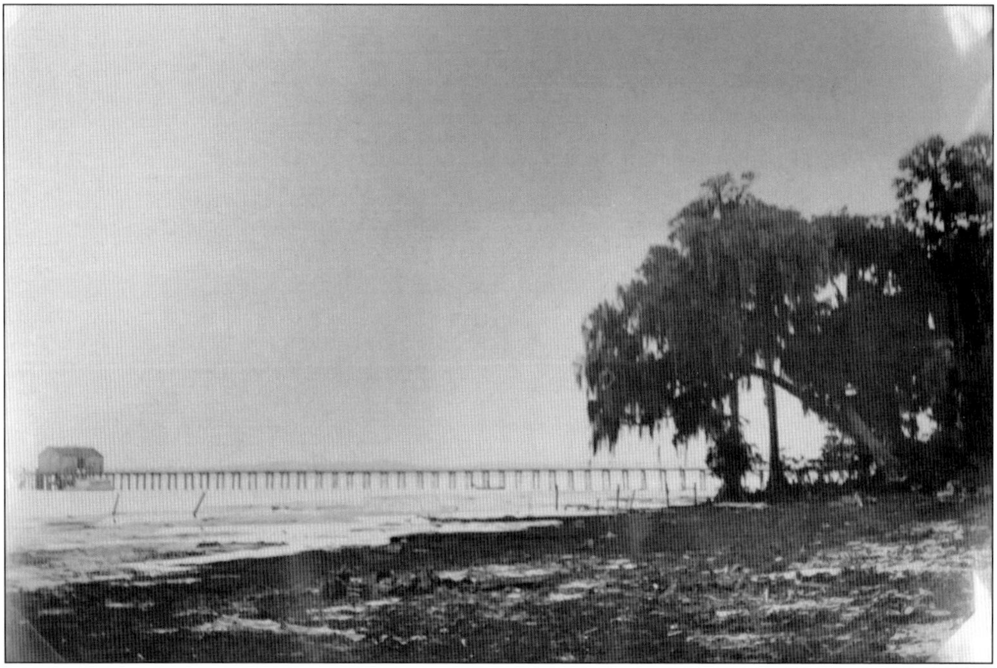

The steamboat dock had to be long to reach out beyond the shallow portion of the lakeshore to steamboats. In this image taken from shore off to the east of Brock House, one can get a good impression of just how long the dock really was. (Courtesy of the Enterprise Heritage Center and Museum.)

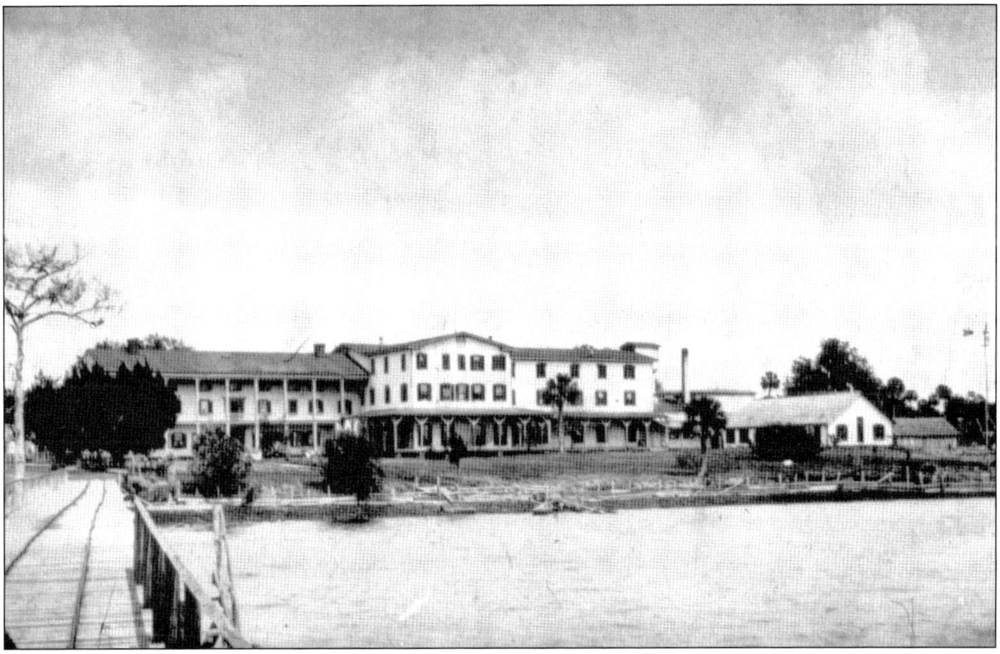

In this 1890s photograph of Brock House, there is a little closer view of some of the changes undergone to improve upon the hotel. Parts of what were once the long, open porches have been enclosed to enlarge rooms. (Courtesy of the Bill Dreggors family.)

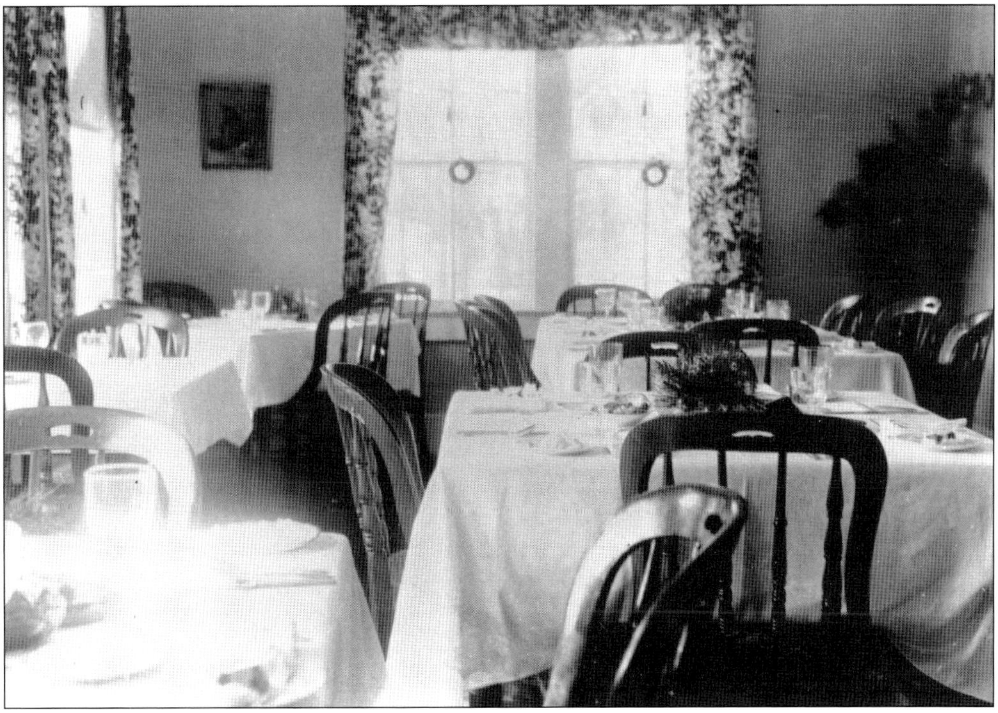

This is what the Brock House dining room looked like around 1920. Tables were fully furnished with plate ware and utensils, and the room was well ventilated with large windows. (Courtesy of the Bill Dreggors family.)

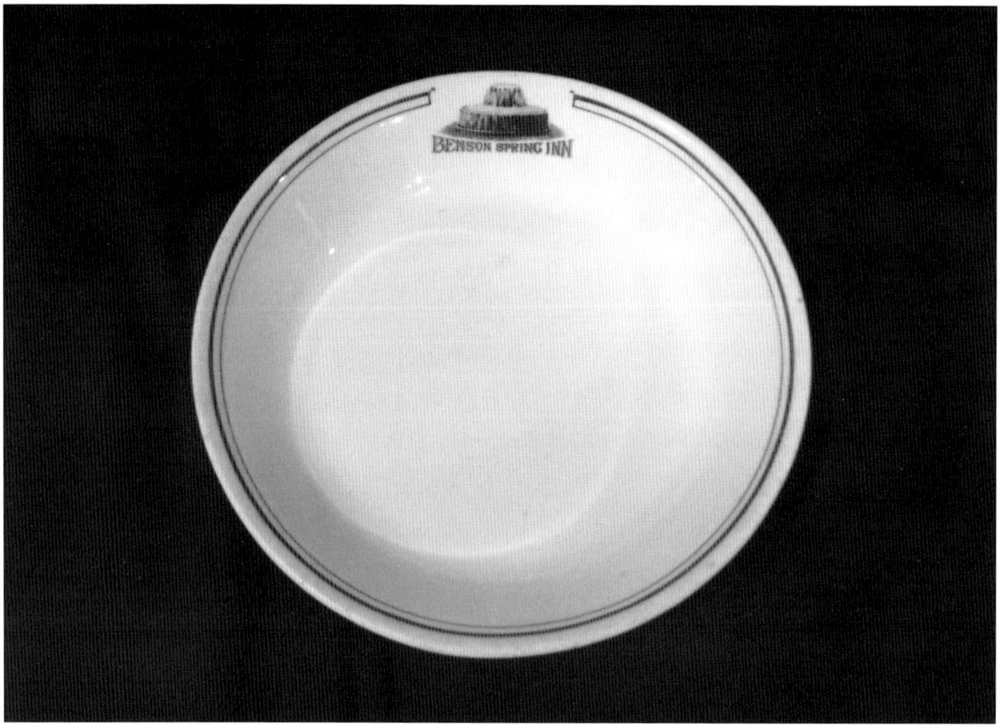

After the Brock House changed in ownership, its name became the Benson Spring Inn for a mineral spring once located to the west of the hotel. This large bowl from the dining room bears the new name. (Courtesy of the Enterprise Heritage Center and Museum.)

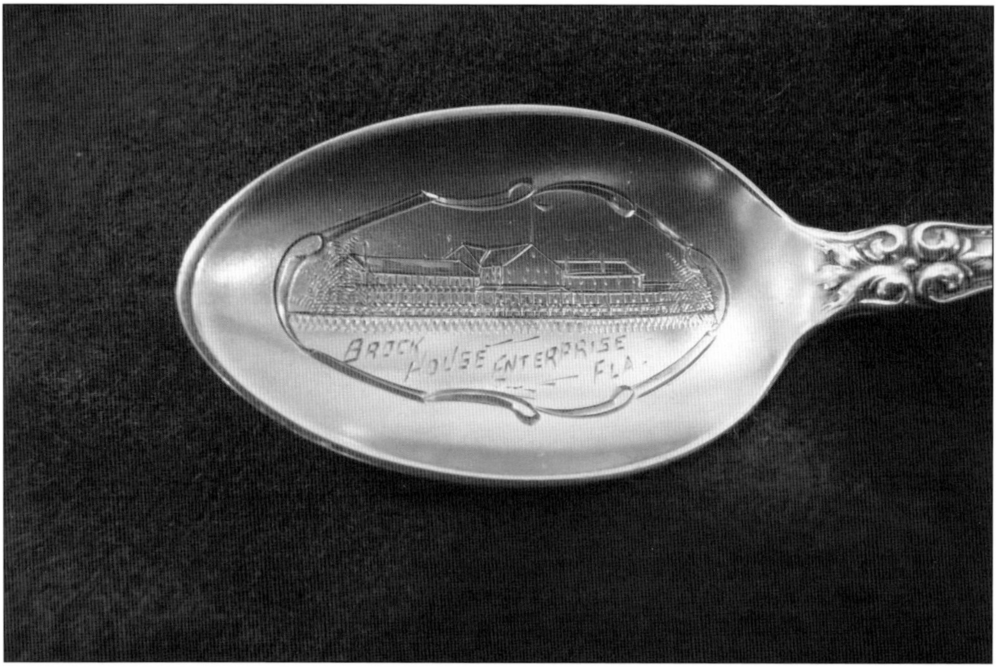

Like the other grand hotels in West Volusia County, the Brock House had crafted silverware. This silver spoon bears a detailed engraving of the hotel. (Courtesy of Jim Cara.)

This brochure for the Benson Springs Inn was made with foldout features. Someone has marked the former name of the hotel and the length of time it was in business on the cover. (Courtesy of the Enterprise Heritage Center and Museum.)

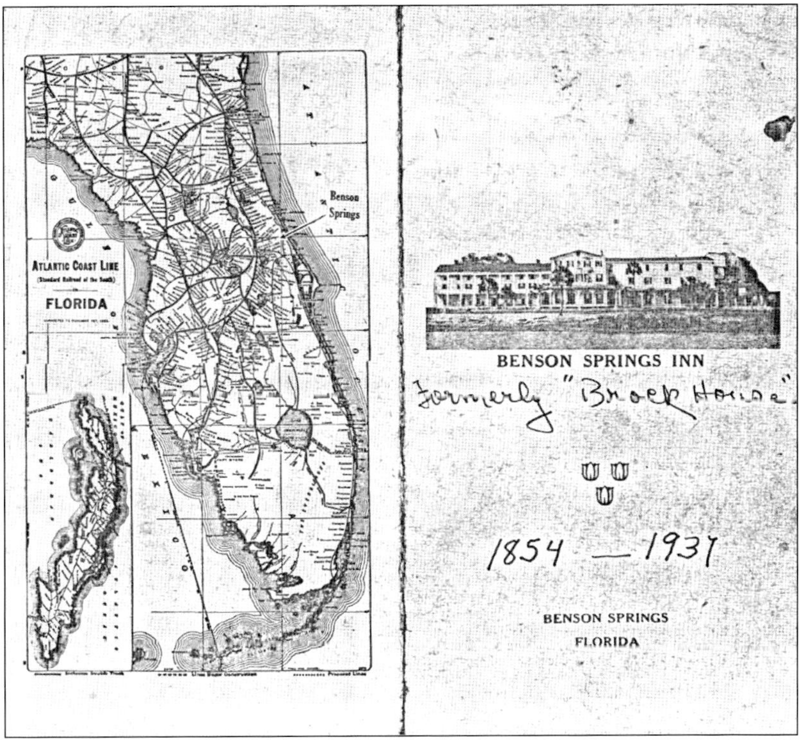

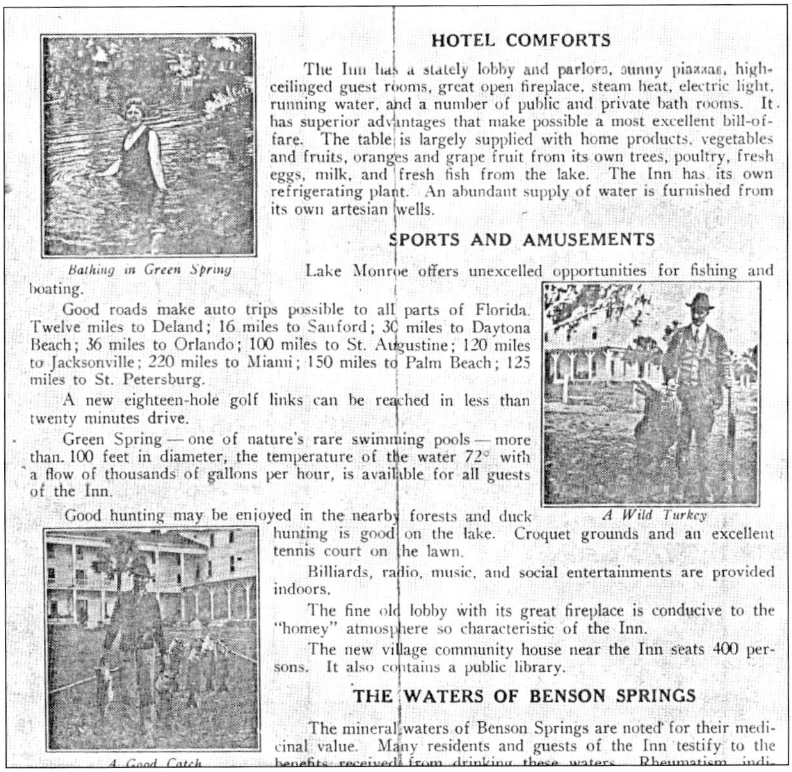

HOTEL COMFORTS

The Inn has a stately lobby and parlors, sunny piazzas, high-ceilinged guest rooms, great open fireplace, steam heat, electric light, running water, and a number of public and private bath rooms. It has superior advantages that make possible a most excellent bill-of-fare. The table is largely supplied with home products, vegetables and fruits, oranges and grape fruit from its own trees, poultry, fresh eggs, milk, and fresh fish from the lake. The Inn has its own refrigerating plant. An abundant supply of water is furnished from its own artesian wells.

Bathing in Green Spring

SPORTS AND AMUSEMENTS

Lake Monroe offers unexcelled opportunities for fishing and boating.

Good roads make auto trips possible to all parts of Florida. Twelve miles to Deland; 16 miles to Sanford; 30 miles to Daytona Beach; 36 miles to Orlando; 100 miles to St. Augustine; 120 miles to Jacksonville; 220 miles to Miami; 150 miles to Palm Beach; 125 miles to St. Petersburg.

A new eighteen-hole golf links can be reached in less than twenty minutes drive.

Green Spring — one of nature's rare swimming pools — more than 100 feet in diameter, the temperature of the water 72° with a flow of thousands of gallons per hour, is available for all guests of the Inn.

A Wild Turkey

Good hunting may be enjoyed in the nearby forests and duck hunting is good on the lake. Croquet grounds and an excellent tennis court on the lawn.

Billiards, radio, music, and social entertainments are provided indoors.

The fine old lobby with its great fireplace is conducive to the "homey" atmosphere so characteristic of the Inn.

The new village community house near the Inn seats 400 persons. It also contains a public library.

THE WATERS OF BENSON SPRINGS

The mineral waters of Benson Springs are noted for their medicinal value. Many residents and guests of the Inn testify to the benefits received from drinking these waters. Rheumatism indi-

A Good Catch

The inside of the brochure lists the comforts the hotel offered. The hotel provided such amenities as steam heat, electric lighting, running water, locally supplied foods, and a number of public and private bathrooms. (Courtesy of the Enterprise Heritage Center and Museum.)

gestion and nervous disorders are among the ailments for which the use of these mineral waters is recommended.

REST AND ENJOYMENT

Benson Springs is an ideal place for rest and enjoyment. With its many charms, there is nothing to distract. The Inn is conducted on the basis of a high-grade home. In appointment, equipment, and social atmosphere the purpose is to afford guests a resort of the highest character.

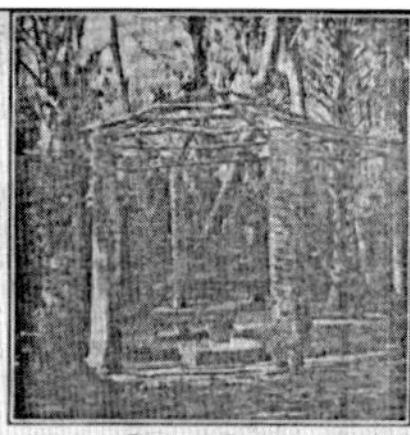

Benson Springs

RATES

The Inn is run exclusively on the American Plan and the rates maintained are exceedingly moderate. For transients the prices vary from three to seven dollars a day. Rates are given for season guests. Auto parties are accommodated. The Inn has its own garage.

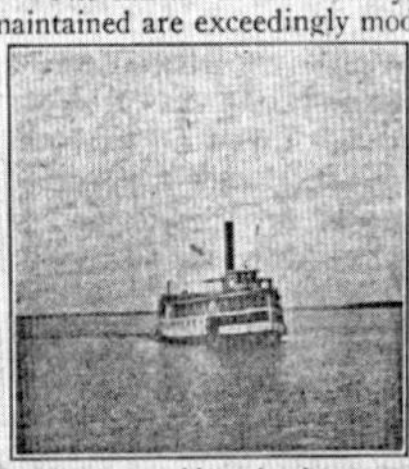

Approaching the Inn

THE WINTER SEASON

The Inn opens December first and closes April fifteenth. Correspondence should be addressed to *Benson Springs Inn, Benson Springs, Florida.*

HOW TO REACH BENSON SPRINGS
(Formerly Enterprise)

BY BOAT: Take the Clyde Line Steamer on the St. Johns River, at Jacksonville or at intermediate points for Benson Springs and you will land at the Inn dock.

BY RAIL: On the Atlantic Coast Line, take express to either Deland or Sanford, notifying the Inn by wire or letter of the time of arrival and the Inn auto will meet you. For local service use Enterprise Junction; express trains do not stop at this station. On the Florida East Coast Line, change cars at Titusville for Benson Springs (formerly Enterprise) or change at New Smyrna for Orange City, six miles from the Inn, where the Inn auto will meet you upon request.

BY BUS: Daily buses run between Daytona and Orlando, crossing the Benson Springs road three miles from the Inn. The Inn auto will meet the bus upon request.

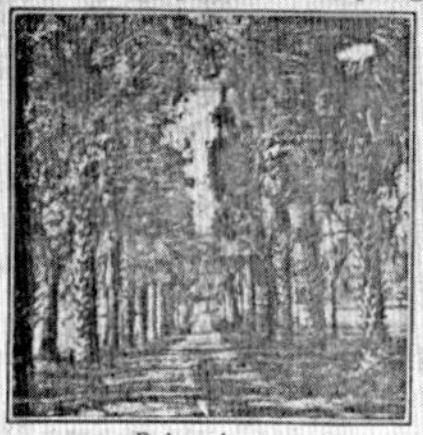

Palm Avenue

The remaining text on the inside of the brochure offers a hint as to why the name of the hotel was changed. The Benson Springs Inn at the time the brochure was printed in the 1920s was accessible by steamboat, train, and bus. (Courtesy of the Enterprise Heritage Center and Museum.)

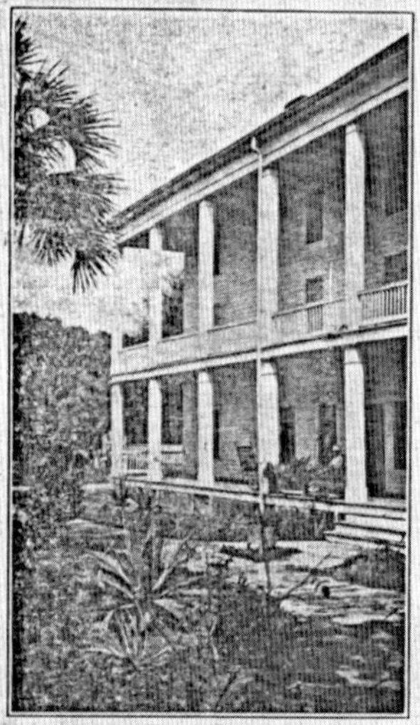

Sunny Piazzas

A WINTER IN FLORIDA

Of course you are going to Florida next winter—to escape the snow and ice and to enjoy the sunshine, the flowers and the fruits. The teasing question is "where can I find comfortable quarters, good food, healthy amusements, a fine tropical environment with congenial friends. Perhaps we can help you find a satisfactory answer.

A NOTED SOUTHERN RESORT

The "Brock House," opened over seventy years ago, was the first large winter resort south of Jacksonville, and has had as its guests General Grant, Joe Jefferson, Grover Cleveland and many other celebrities.

This old "House," with its quaint Southern charm, was made a part of the enlarged and remodeled Inn. The Inn is surrounded with ample ground, on which orange trees and shrubbery grow, and adjacent tropical woods provide many delightful shaded walks. Lake Monroe, with the Clyde Line Steamers, is at the door. The beautiful outlook over the lake has brought a number of Northern and Eastern people to build winter homes here in the Land of Sunshine and Flowers.

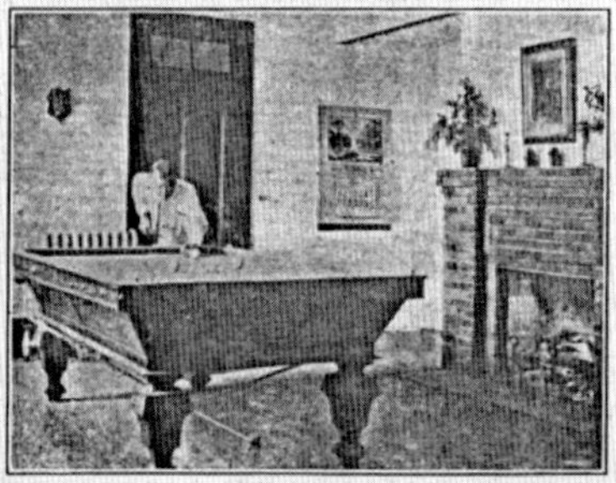

Billiard Room

The back of the Benson Springs Inn brochure tells the hotel has been a vacation stop for over 70-years. The flyer also mentions the names of some of the notables who have stayed at the hotel. (Courtesy of the Enterprise Heritage Center and Museum.)

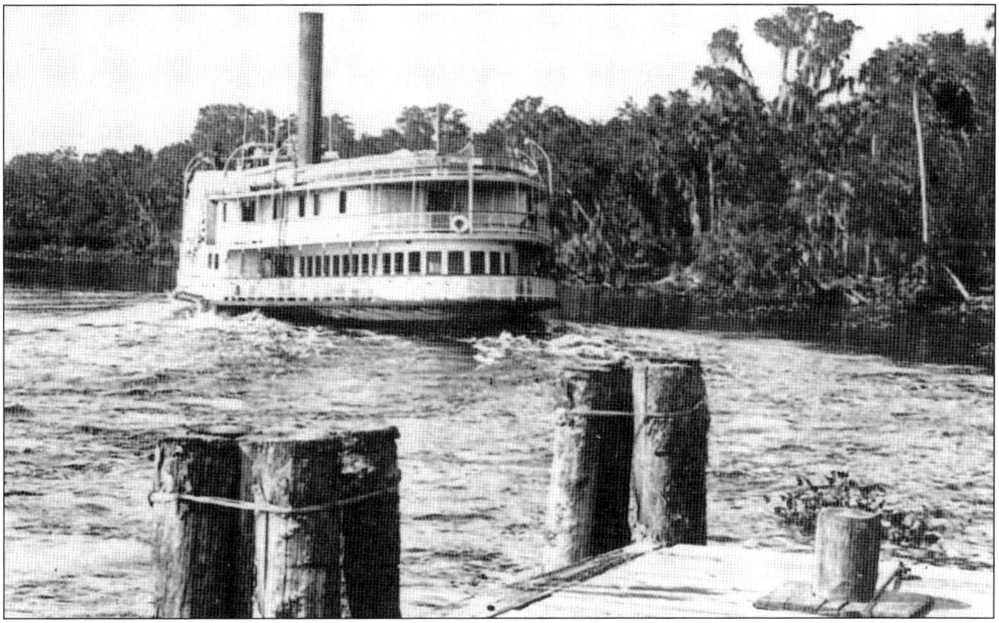

The draw that the Brock House and the surrounding area had on visitors brought all kinds of people to West Volusia County. Steamboats, like this image of Frederick de Bary's *City of Jacksonville*, and other vessels made regular trips along the river and to the hotel. (Courtesy of Edward A. Mueller.)

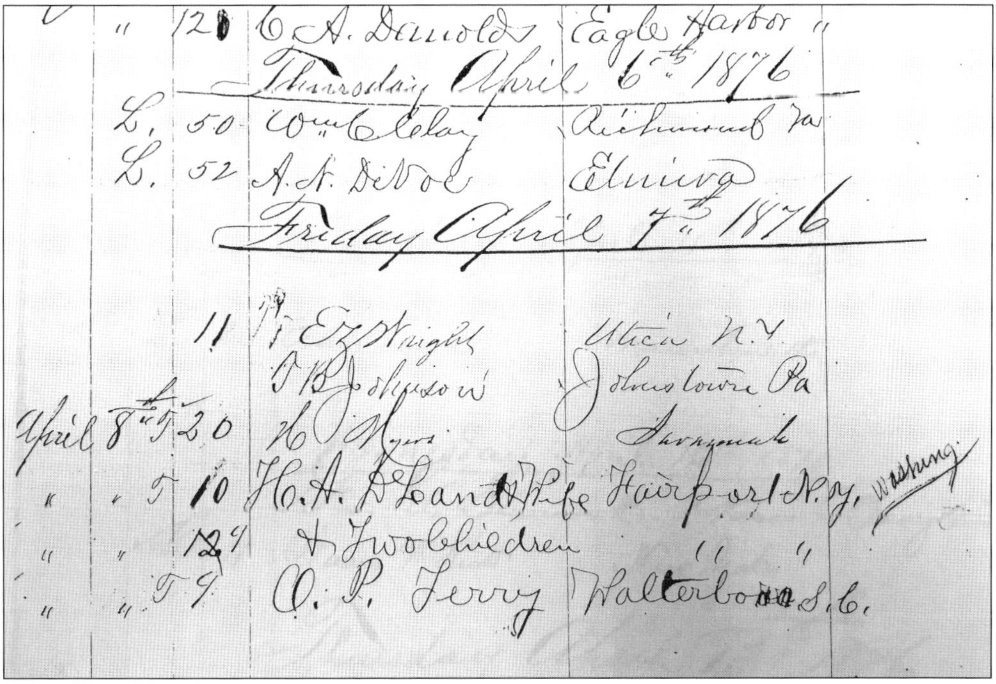

" 12 C. A. Danolds Eagle Harbor "
Thursday April 6th 1876
L. 50 Wm Clay Richmond Va
L. 52 A. N. DeVoe Elmira
Friday April 7th 1876
11 E. Z. Wright Utica N.Y.
J. B. Johnson Johnstown Pa
April 8th 20 H Myers Savannah
" 5 10 H. A. DeLand & Wife Fairport N.Y. Washing
" " 12 & Two Children " "
" " 9 O. P. Terry Walterboro S.C.

The Brock House was indeed the gateway for many important people coming to Florida. On Friday, April 7, 1876, the Brock House Register shows an H.A. DeLand (H.A. stands for Henry Addison), his wife, two children, and O.P. Terry signed in as guests. (Courtesy of the Enterprise Heritage Center and Museum.)

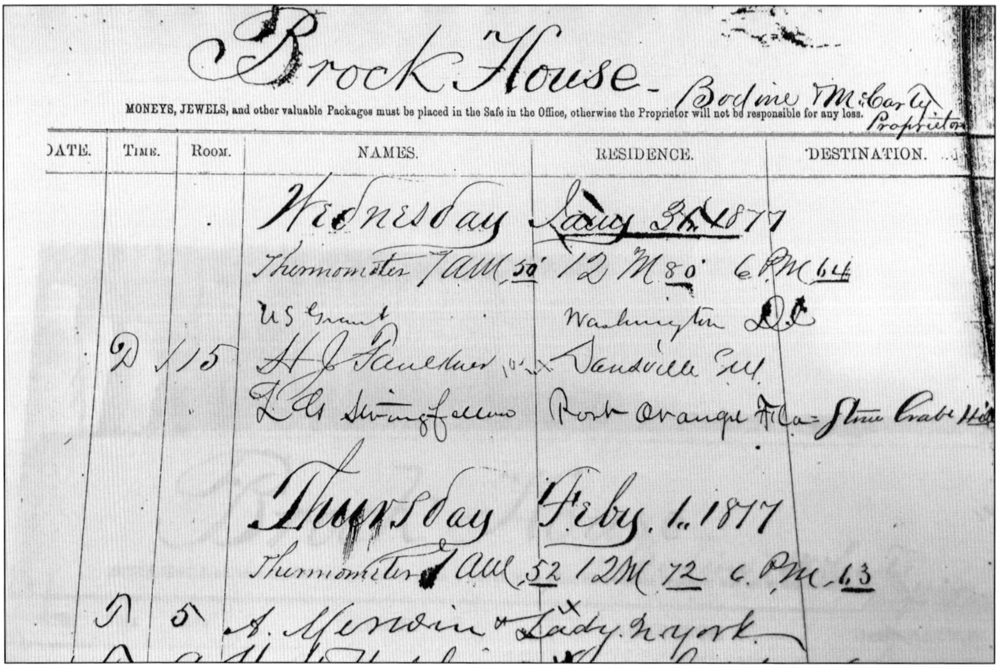

Brock House - Bodine & McCarty Proprietors

MONEYS, JEWELS, and other valuable Packages must be placed in the Safe in the Office, otherwise the Proprietor will not be responsible for any loss.

DATE.	TIME.	ROOM.	NAMES.	RESIDENCE.	DESTINATION.
			Wednesday Jany 31st 1877		
			Thermometer 7 AM 50° 12 M 80° 6 PM 64		
			U S Grant	Washington DC	
			Thursday Feby 1st 1877		
			Thermometer 7 AM 52 12 M 72 6 PM 63		

A year later, on Wednesday, January 31, 1877, an outgoing president of the United States came to Brock House to get away from it all. The Brock House register shows on that date that U.S. (Ulysses S.) Grant signed in as a guest at the hotel. (Courtesy of the Enterprise Heritage Center and Museum.)

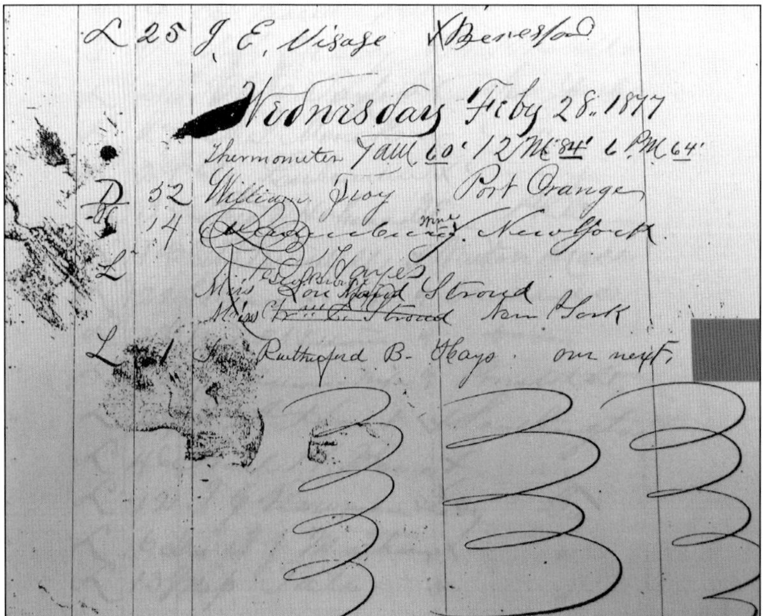

Wednesday Feby 28th 1877

Thermometer 7 AM 60° 12 M 84° 6 PM 64°

William Troy Port Orange

Rutherford B. Hayes

As one president was coming to Brock House to relax at the end of his term, another came for rest before his. On Wednesday, February 28, 1877, the Brock House register shows incoming president Rutherford B. Hayes signed in as a guest. (Courtesy of the Enterprise Heritage Center and Museum.)

On this 1880 business receipt is a glimpse of some of the commerce that took place in the operation of the Brock House. On February 11 of that year, a delivery of oranges was made and paid for. (Courtesy of Jim Cara.)

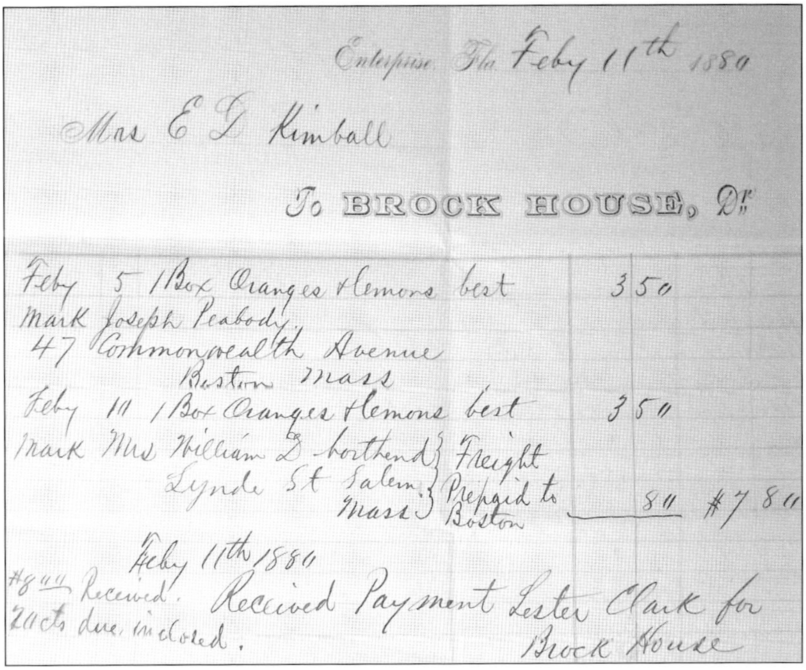

Enterprise Fla Feby 11th 1880

Mrs E. D. Kimball

To BROCK HOUSE, Dr.

Feby 5 1 Box Oranges & Lemons best 3 50
mark Joseph Peabody
47 Commonwealth Avenue
Boston Mass
Feby 11 1 Box Oranges & Lemons best 3 50
mark Mrs William D. Northend } Freight
Lynde St Salem } Prepaid to
Mass } Boston 80 $7 80

Feby 11th 1880
#8 00 Received. Received Payment Lester Clark for
20cts due, inclosed. Brock House

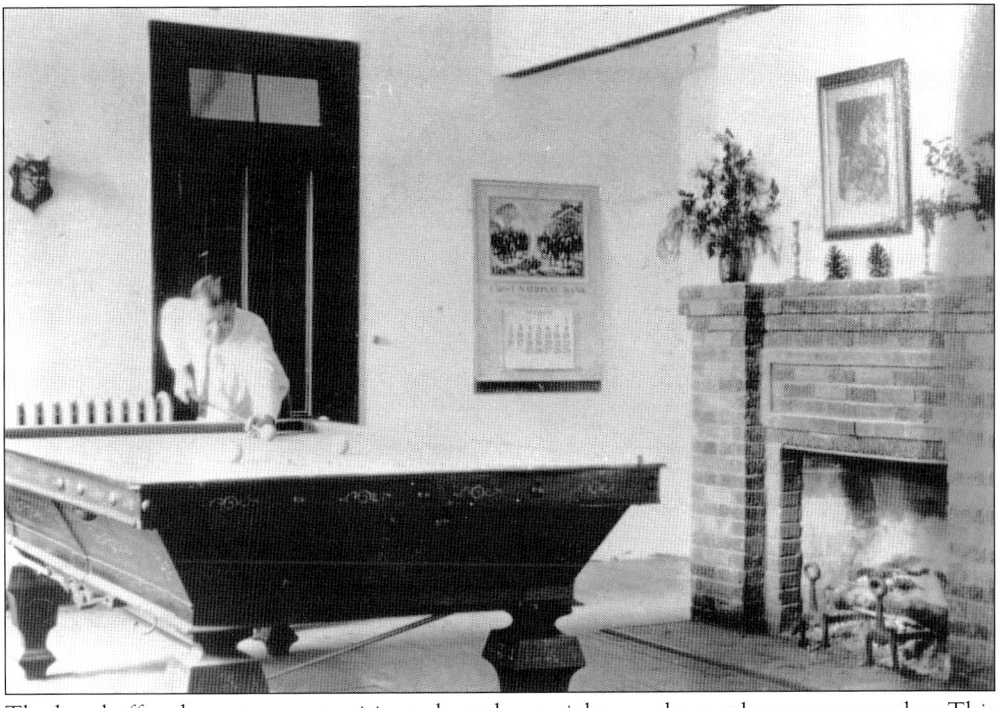

The hotel offered guests opportunities to boat, hunt, sightsee, play outdoor games or relax. This guest is playing a game of pool. (Courtesy of the Bill Dreggors family.)

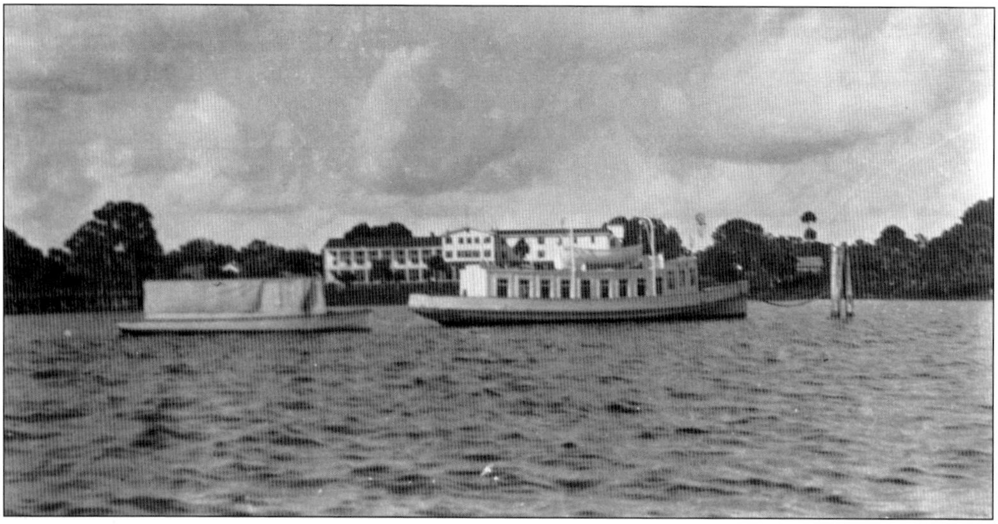

The Brock House was an impressive sight. This may have been one of the first views of the hotel steamboat passengers had as they approached the dock. (Courtesy of the Bill Dreggors family.)

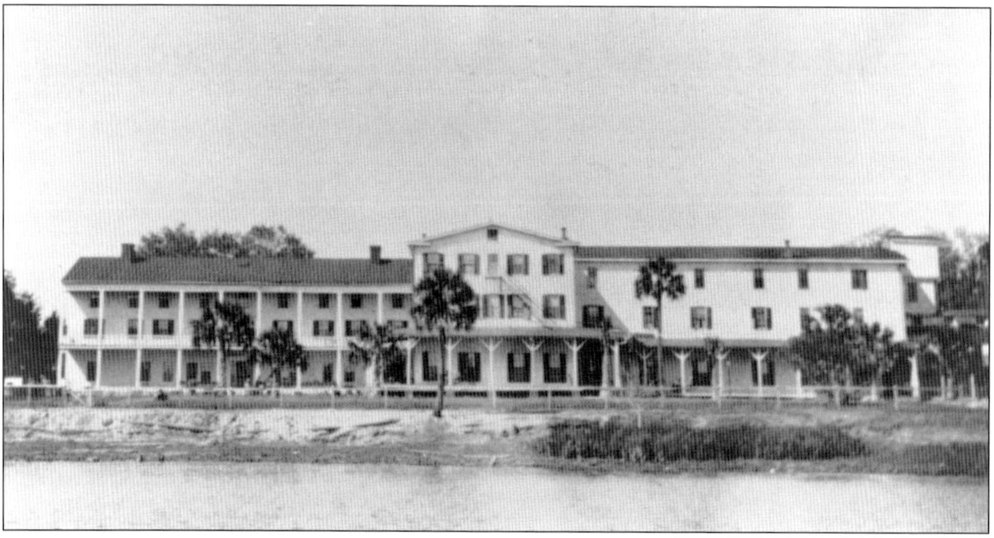

Here is another view of the Brock House from a couple of yards offshore. This 1920s picture more clearly shows the changes made to the hotel after Brock had sold it. (Courtesy of the Bill Dreggors family.)

This water pitcher had been broken and then painstakingly pieced back together. It is another of the few artifacts that remain from the Brock House. (Courtesy of the Enterprise Heritage Center and Museum.)

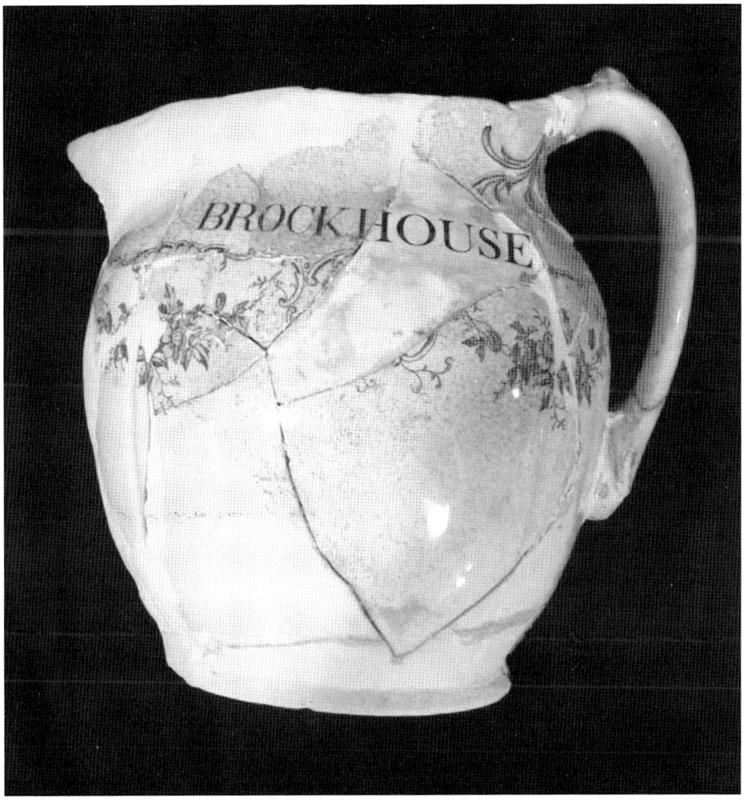

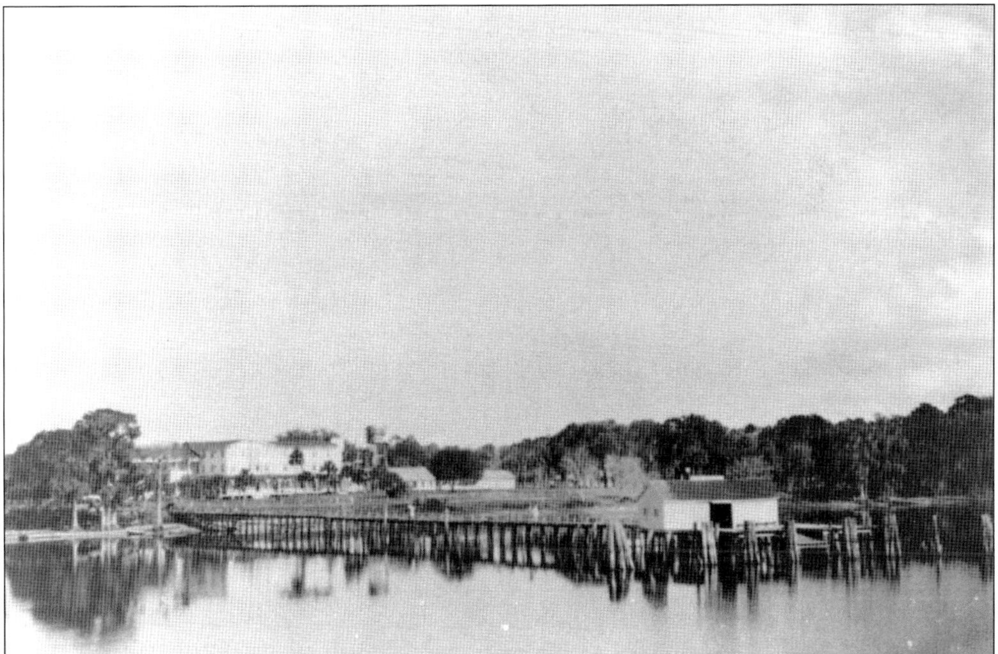

This is a 1910 view of the dock and hotel taken from out in Lake Monroe. Brock House was still a location destination, but tourism in Florida was shifting. (Courtesy of the Bill Dreggors family.)

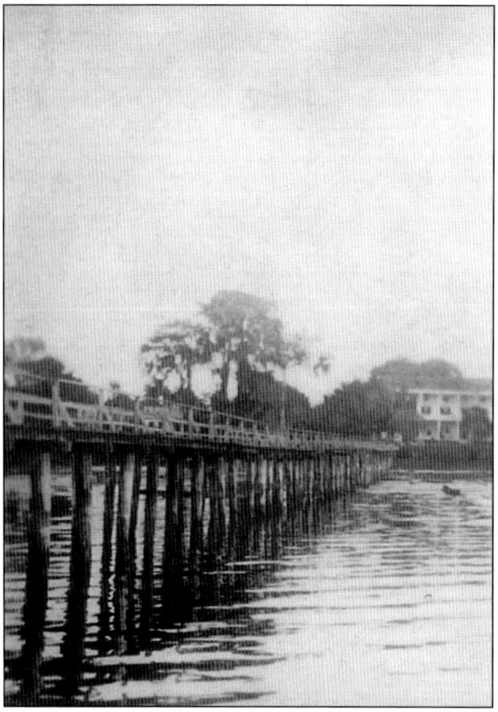

Here another image from around the same time period. Throughout the history of the Brock House, the dock was a prominent feature of the hotel. This image is from around 1910. (Courtesy of the Bill Dreggors family.)

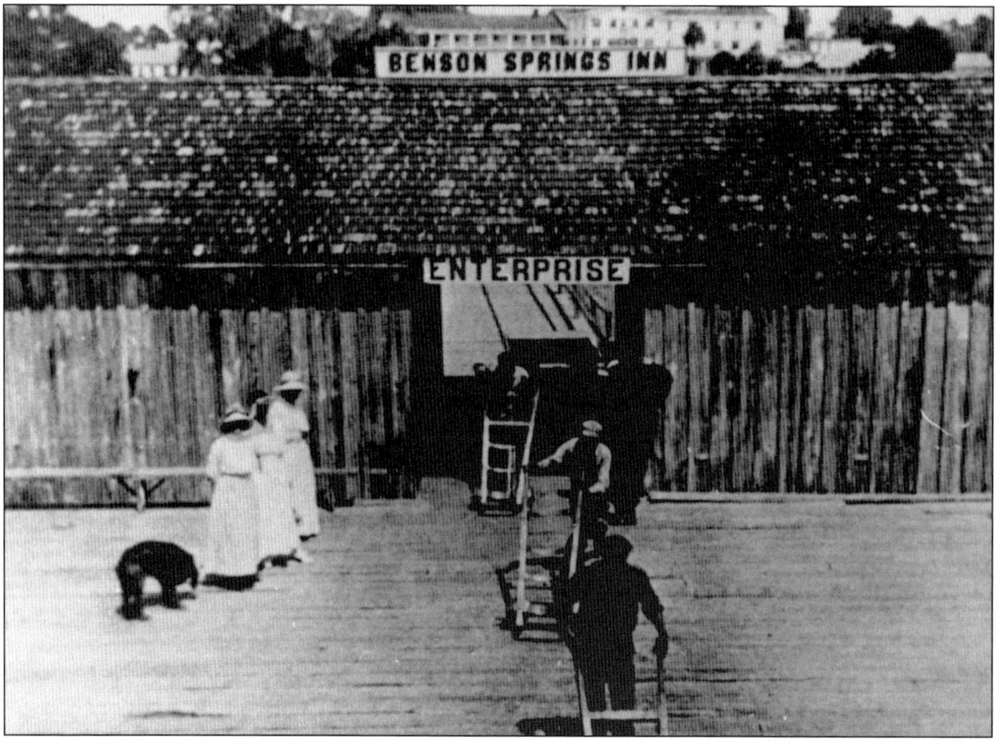

This c. 1900 picture appears to have been taking during the span when the hotel was called the Benson Springs Inn. The hotel name is mounted on the top of the dock house, but the sign indicating the town of Enterprise is still in place. (Courtesy of the Bill Dreggors family.)

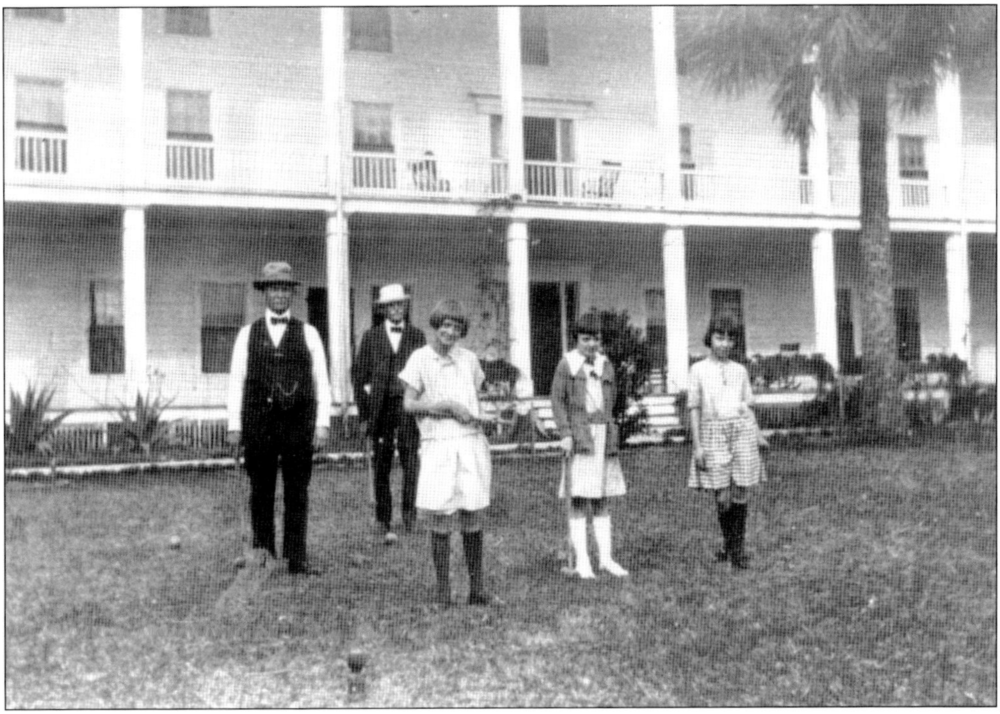

In 1920, visitors were still staying at the hotel. These guests are engaged in a game of croquet on the lawn on the lakeside front of the hotel. (Courtesy of the Bill Dreggors family.)

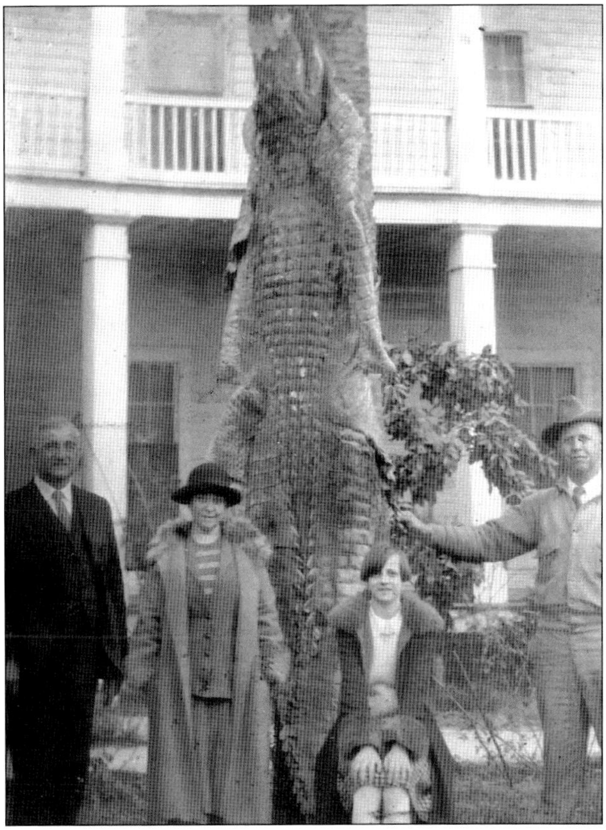

Tourism in the area may have been shifting away from Brock House to the coast, but there were still sights to be seen. Here, guests pose in front of an alligator on display. (Courtesy of the Enterprise Heritage Center and Museum.)

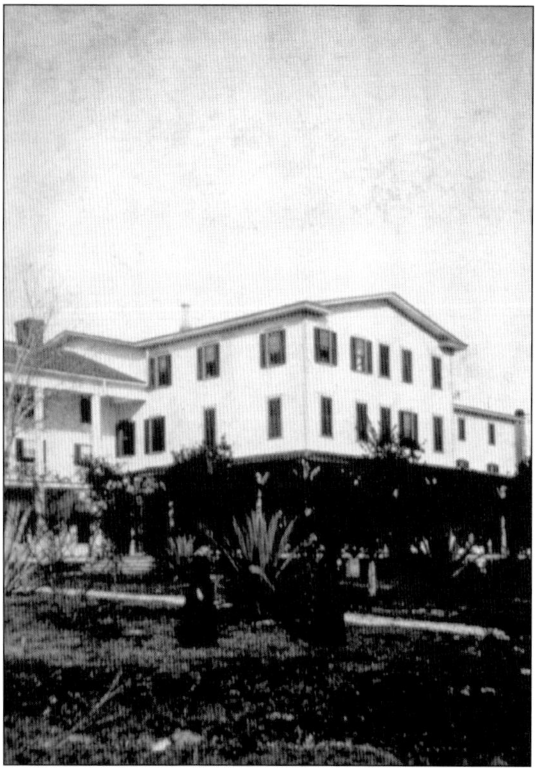

In this 1920s photograph taken of the front of the hotel on the lakeside, two darkly dressed women stand on either side of a huge cycad plant in the lawn. At this time, guests at the hotel were dwindling. (Courtesy of the Bill Dreggors family.)

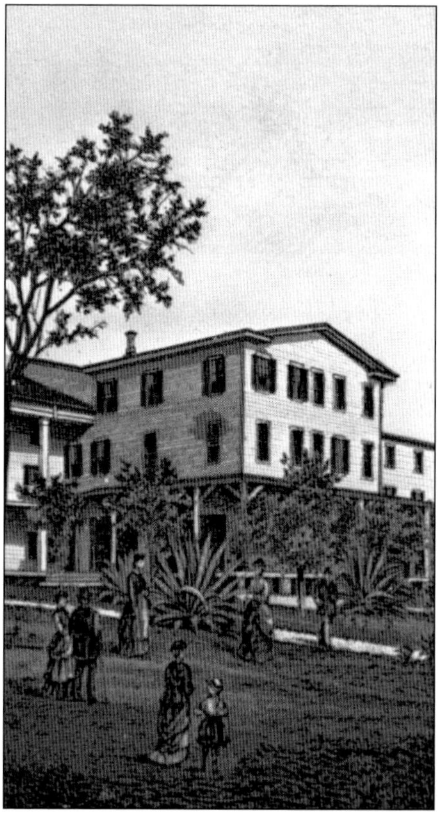

This is one of the few postcards found for this printing of the Brock House. The imagery on the card is very similar in some respects to the photograph above. (Courtesy of State Archives of Florida, Florida Memory.)

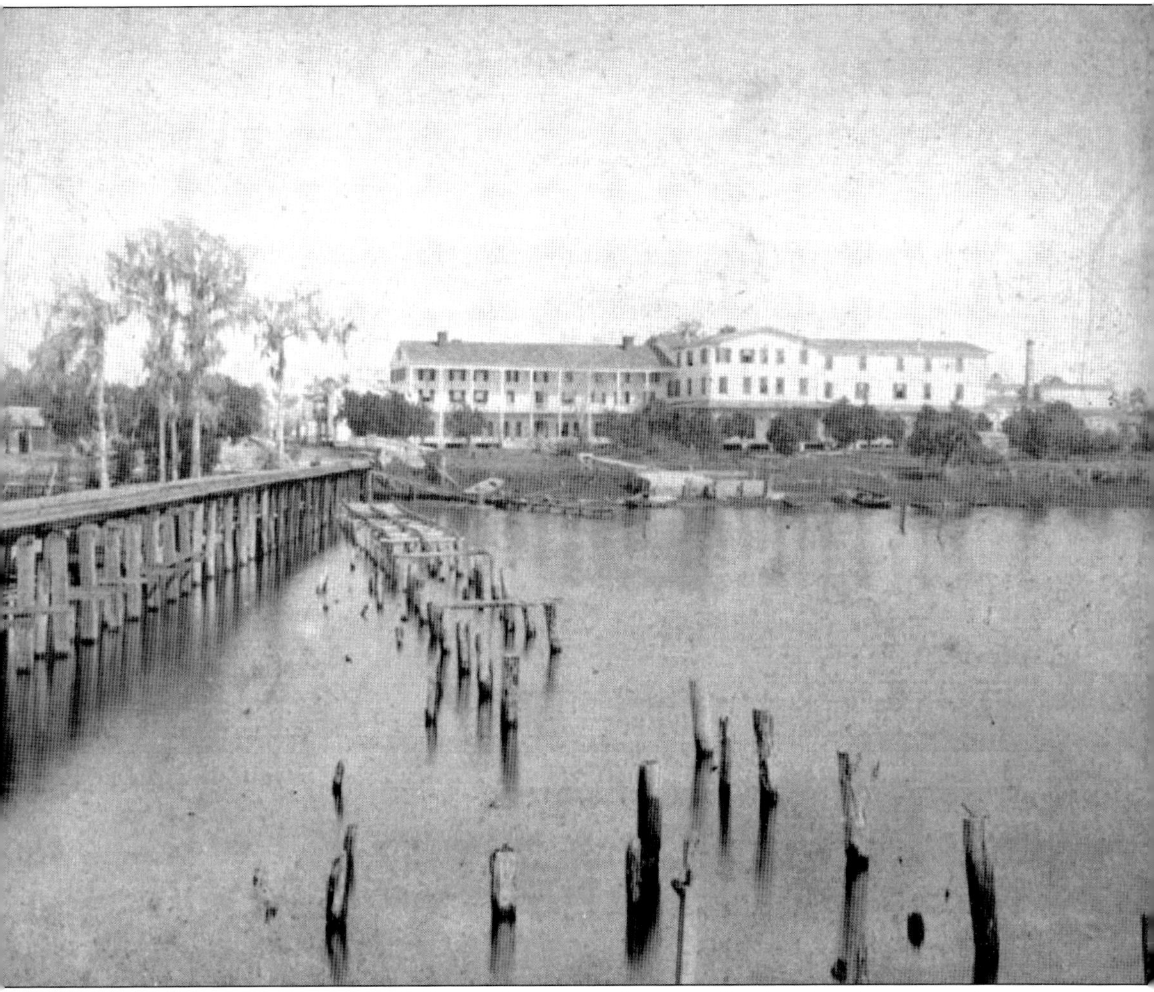

As the decades passed, the hotel fell into disrepair and eventually closed and was torn down in 1932. The property was bought by the Methodist Church, and an orphanage was built on the site where the hotel had been, leaving only the old pilings from the dock as evidence that the grand hotel had existed. (Courtesy of the Enterprise Heritage Center and Museum.)

Bibliography

aarf.com/festem95.htm

Into Tropical Florida: A Trip Upon the St. Johns River. Clyde Steamship Co., The South Publishing Co., Artistic Engravers and Printers, New York, 1890.

jackncb.wordpress.com/architecture/deland-area/putnam-hotel-deland

Mueller, Edward A. *First Coast Steamboat Days. A history of travel by steamboat from Georgia and South Carolina to Northeast Florida.* Jacksonville Historical Society, Inc., Jacksonville, FL, 2005.

myfloridahistory.org/frontiers/article/11

www.abandonedfl.com/hotel-putnam

www.geocities.ws/krdvry/hikeplans/deland/plandeland.html

www.jackjollygolf.com/t-about.aspx

www.lakehelen.com/History.html

www.news-journalonline.com/news/20160922/delands-historic-hotel-putnam-up-for-sale-again

www.news-journalonline.com/news/20170501/deland-hospitable-to-hotel-putnam-proposal

www.oldenterprise.org/history0.aspx#history08

www.planetflorida.net/deland-hist/

www.planetdeland.com/delandhistory/road17.htm

www.volusia.org/residents/history/volusia-stories/enterprise-on-the-st-johns-river/

www.volusia.org/residents/history/volusia-stories/enterprise-on-the-st-johns-river/brock-hotel.stml

INDEX

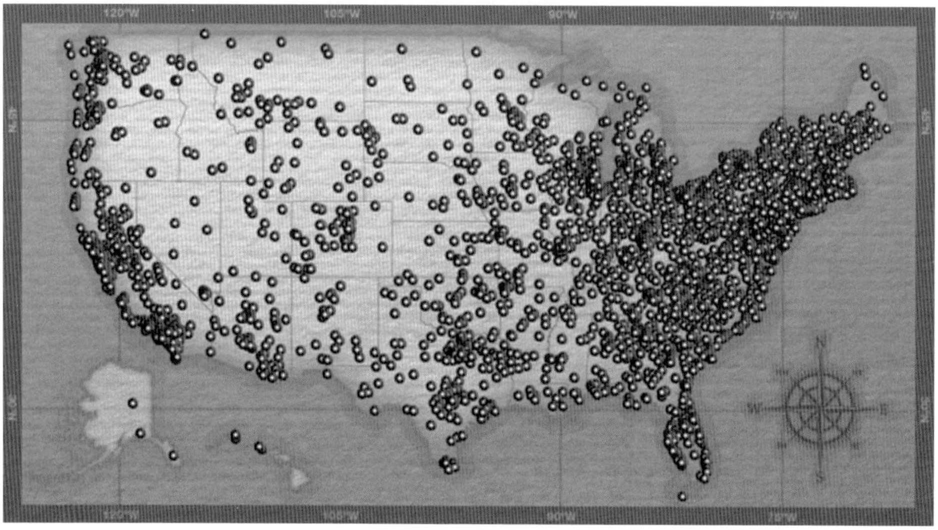

Consistent with our mission to preserve history on a local level, this book was printed in South Carolina on American-made paper and manufactured entirely in the United States. Products carrying the accredited Forest Stewardship Council (FSC) label are printed on 100 percent FSC-certified paper.

MADE IN THE USA